AFGHAN NOMADS IN TRANSITION

AFGHAN NOMADS IN TRANSITION

First published in Great Britain in 1994
by Thames and Hudson Ltd, London

First published in the United States of America in 1994
by Thames and Hudson Inc., 500 Fifth Avenue, New York, New York 10110

This edition first published in Scandinavia in 1994
by Rhodos International Science and Art Publishers A/S, Copenhagen

EDITORIAL COMMITTEE: Ida Nicolaisen and Per Øhrgaard
COPY EDITOR: Niels Peder Jørgensen
TRANSLATOR: Geoffrey Bibby

British Library Cataloguing-in-Publication Data
A catalogue record for this book is available from the British Library

ISBN 0-500-01639-9

Library of Congress Catalog Card Number: 94-61394

Lay out : Sunna & Ruben Blædel
Production Rhodos
Printed and bound in Denmark

Gorm Pedersen

AFGHAN NOMADS IN TRANSITION

A CENTURY OF CHANGE AMONG THE ZALA KHĀN KHĒL

Ida Nicolaisen
Editor-in-Chief

THE CARLSBERG FOUNDATION'S NOMAD RESEARCH PROJECT

THAMES AND HUDSON

RHODOS INTERNATIONAL SCIENCE AND ART PUBLISHERS

CONTENTS

EDITOR'S PREFACE 7

ACKNOWLEDGMENTS 15

GLOSSARY 17

INTRODUCTION I 21

DANISH NOMAD RESEARCH IN AFGHANISTAN · 21

The historical background for the research · 24

The Danish Scientific Mission to Afghanistan 1975-76 · 31

INTRODUCTION II 49

THE TERM NOMAD - A CLARIFICATION · 49

PRESENTATION · 54

I. THE LAND OF THE NOMADS 57

NOMADISM · 76

II. ZALA KHĀN KHĒL 87

STUDYING ZALA KHĀN KHĒL · 87

ZALA KHĀN KHĒL AT A GLANCE · 92

GENEALOGY AND IDENTITY · 98

III. EXPANSION AND CONSTRAINTS: 105

PASTORAL ECONOMY AND NOMAD TRADE UP TO THE 1960s · 105

THE COMPLEX SOCIETY · 105

The ecological basis of nomadism · 106

The aggregated economy · 121

ZALA KHĀN KHĒL'S NOMADISM AND TRADING I · 25

Pastures and economic potentials · 126

Organisation · 127

CHANGING CIRCUMSTANCES · 129

Political changes · 129

Changes in the summer areas · 129

Changes in the winter areas · 135

Frontier problems · 137

Infrastructural development · 138

IV. A TURNING POINT: THE 1950s AND 1960s 141

TRADING COMES TO AN END · 141

SOCIO-ECONOMIC DIFFERENTIATION · 145

Land purchase · 146

Frontier closing, geographical dispersal, and economic reorganisation · 148

V. ECONOMIC DEVELOPMENT AND DECLINE: ZALA KHĀN KHĒL IN THE 1970s 150

THE SETTLED LORRY-OWNERS · 150

Lorry transport · 151

Kote Sangi · 154

Qala-i Niazbeg · 160

THE MIGRANT LANDOWNERS · 162

Agriculture in Dahana-i Ghori ·173

Mechanisation and new trends · 177

A new migration pattern · 178

THE POOR MAN'S LOT ·179

New annual economic pattern · 179

The winter camps · 192

An unstable situation · 204

BAZAAR-I OMAID · 208

VI. A WAY OF LIFE COMES TO AN END 212

SETTLEMENT AND NEW MIGRATION PATTERNS · 212

GENEALOGICAL DIVISION · 216

CHANGES IN THE ROLE OF LEADERSHIP · 218

IDENTITY AND TRANSFORMATION · 219

VII. ZALA KHĀN KHĒL IN EXILE 223

WAR AND INSTABILITY

EXILE ·227

THE REVIVAL OF NOMADISM? · 238

A REFLECTION 245

BIBLIOGRAPHY 247

INDEX 259

INDEX OF AUTHORS 265

PHOTO CREDITS 267

EDITOR'S PREFACE

DANISH NOMAD RESEARCH - AN OVERVIEW

Pastoral nomads have always fascinated the more earthbound peoples among whom they live. Forever on the move with tents and belongings, and with their flocks of goats, sheep, cattle, yaks, camels, horses, or reindeer, these elusive folk have captured our imagination. They call into question the very way of life that we peasant or urban people live by defying our idea of a stable and secure homestead. They stir our emotions by questioning values that we take for granted, and by offering a vision of an alternative and, as we tend to believe, carefree existence.

Awe and respect for the Scythians, Huns, Old-Turks, Mongols, and the Arab Bedouins, all of whom carved out for themselves a prominent place in the history of the Old World, lie deep in the Western mind. Images of Tibetan nomads and their yaks, existing at altitudes where agriculture is impossible because there are too few frost-free days, of Tuareg mounted on the camels with which they held sway over the Sahara desert for centuries, controlling trade between the Atlas and the West African states, or of the Masai wandering with their cattle through the tall grasses of the East African savannah are part of our perception of the world. Some of these images are out of date, but still they persist for these are people who arouse our curiosity. Although far away in space and time they yet manage to enrich our lives.

Pastoral nomadism is a way of life confined to the Old World. Until the first decades of the 20th century, pastoral nomads pursued their way of life over a broad belt in the arid and semi-arid zone which stretches from North Africa through the Middle East, and into the heart of Central Asia. Other pastoralists wandered with their cattle on the East African plains and in South Africa, while a range of nomadic groups whose lives were based on reindeer herding lived in Northern Scandinavia and out across the tundras and forests of European and Asian Russia. The living conditions of all these peoples have now changed, but some still keep livestock and continue their migratory way of life.

Each of these pastoral societies represents or represented a unique adaptation to the environment, understood in the widest sense of the word, i.e. as the natural, social, and cultural surroundings which influence their way of life. Pastoral nomadism and the cultures of pastoral peoples are fascinating fields of research in themselves. Scholars have long been intrigued by the environmental understanding and detailed botanical knowledge of nomads, by their sophisticated techniques for handling domesticated animals, and the subtle strategies which they utilize to survive under conditions which are unforseeable and often very harsh. Pastoral nomadism is a highly specialized occupation but, through economic exchanges with agriculturalists and urban communities, the nomads are or have been an important part of the wider society.

In Denmark serious scholarly interest in the cultures and societies of pastoral nomads, including the nature, history, and transformation of nomadism, dates back almost a century. During this period explorers, photographers, and scientists - geographers, archaeologists, linguists, botanists, zoologists, and not least anthropologists - have made a substantial contribution to the documentation and understanding of a range of pastoral societies and of pastoral nomadism in general.

Geographically, Danish research efforts have centered on three areas: Central Asia, South West Asia, and North Africa. From these regions scholars and explorers have brought back rich collections of artefacts to Danish museums which, together with field notes, photographs, films, and music recordings, have formed part of the documentation of a range of nomadic cultures and their ingenious technical, esthetical, and symbolic expressions. Others turned their energies to lengthy in-depth studies of the ecology, culture, and social organization of pastoral groups.

A substantial part of these studies and unique collections have not been published to date. To remedy this the Carlsberg Foundation's Nomad Research Project was formed to arrange a series of publications of which this is the fifth. The project deals with the cultures of nomads as different as the Mongols, Tibetans, Kirghiz and Turkmen of Central Asia, Pashtun nomads of Afghanistan, the Lurs of Iran, the Bedouin of Qatar, the Tuareg of the Sahara, and the Kreda and Haddad of Chad.

Just as the lives of nomadic peoples have changed over time, so the theoretical interests of the Danish anthropologists who endeavoured to record, understand, and describe such peoples have also changed. The problems which interested these investigators and the questions they asked were long influenced by the kind of culture-historical ethnology which dominated Danish anthropology until the early 1950s and the emphasis on subsistence systems and material culture studies which was an essential part of this academic tradition.

Anthropology was established as a university discipline in Denmark only in 1945. Prior to that time it was pursued by scholars who had been trained as geographers. These were either attached to the Department of Geography at the University of Copenhagen or were curators in the Department of Ethnography at the National Museum of Denmark. Among the former were Professor H. P. Steensby (1875-1920) and Professor Gudmund Hatt (1884-1960), while most notably among the latter were Dr Carl Gunnar Feilberg (1894-1972), who later became Professor of Human Geography, and Dr Kaj Birket-Smith (1893-1977), who became Copenhagen University's first Lecturer in Ethnography.

The historical roots and development of anthropology in Denmark had a marked influence on the theoretical perspectives which scholars brought to the study of pastoral societies. It characterized their concept of nomadism and defined the scientific problems which occupied them. Their focus was on the typology, origin, and historical transformation of pastoral nomadism.

Arising from his expedition to North Africa in 1908 H. P. Steensby argued, as had the French scholars A. Bernard and N. Lacroix, that the various forms of pastoral nomadism in that region had developed from subsistence systems based on both agriculture and animal husbandry in adaptation to increasingly scarce resources. Gudmund Hatt, in his studies of reindeer nomadism, suggested that this had its roots in a hunting culture in which tame reindeer had been used as decoys. In later works though he discussed the origin of nomadism in more general terms, he ultimately returned to links with elements of hunting cultures. Feilberg, who carried out fieldwork among Lur pastoralists in Persia in 1935 (cf. *Les Papis.* Copenhagen 1952), dealt with the history of nomadism through an intricate analysis of the structure and distribution of the black tent (*La Tente Noire.* Copenhagen 1944).

Parallel with this theoretically oriented research on pastoral nomadism, impressive collections of ethnographic specimens from a wide range of pastoral peoples were finding their way into the National Museum of Denmark. The most important of these were those made by Ole Olufsen (1865-1929) in the Pamirs, West Turkestan, and North Africa, by Henning Haslund-Christensen (1896-1948) in Mongolia, and by C. G. Feilberg from his fieldwork among the Lur. After the Second World War the National Museum in Copenhagen and the Prehistoric Museum, Moesgaard near Aarhus received new collections. A major Tibetan one was donated by His Royal Highness Prince Peter of Greece and Denmark (1908-1980). The collections were further enriched by Lennart Edelberg (1915-1981) and Klaus Ferdinand (b.1926) who carried out research among Afghan nomads. Edelberg also made substantial field collections among the Lur, while Ferdinand did the same among the Bedouins of Qatar. Finally, Johannes Nicolaisen (1921-1980) and Ida Nicolaisen (b.1940) brought back collections from the Tuareg of the Sahara and the Sahel, and the Kreda and Haddad of Chad.

The earliest of the major Danish collections of nomad artefacts are those from Ole Olufsen's expeditions to the Pamirs and West Turkestan almost a century ago. Olufsen was a military man with a keen interest in geography and the exploration of little known regions of the earth. He was appointed Honorary Professor of Geography at Copenhagen University. In 1896-97 and 1898-99 he organized and led two expeditions to the Pamirs and West Turkestan under the auspices of the Royal Danish Geographical Society. In the course of these he gathered topographical, meteorological, hydrographical, zoological, and botanical data. Olufsen travelled widely within the Emirate of Bokhara and Russian Turkestan. He was interested in the cultures of the various ethnic groups and collected some 700 artefacts among the pastoral Kirghiz and Turkmen, the Uzbeks, and various urban ethnic groups. Later expeditions in 1908 and 1922-23 took Olufsen to North Africa where he collected botanical, mineralogical, and ethnografic specimens, including a tent and numerous other objects from among the Tuareg. Although Olufsen published accounts of his travels, his most enduring contributions lie in the opening up of new research areas for others and in the ethnographic collections which he brought back.

A unique Mongol collection of some 3,000 artefacts was put together by the Danish explorer and ethnographer Haslund-Christensen, assisted by Georg Söderbom, his Swedish colleague on the Sven Hedin expedition. Unlike most other collectors of museum specimens of the time, Haslund-Christensen understood the necessity of providing detailed information on the use, the place of origin, and the circumstances under which the artefacts were obtained. The collection includes objects of everyday life such as tools, costumes, jewellery, and household utensils from most of the twenty or so Mongol groups, but mainly from the Chahar Mongols. The exquisite garments of this magnificent collection, a total of more than 400 pieces, are analysed and described by Henny Harald Hansen in *Mongol Costumes*, published in this series in 1993.

Haslund-Christensen had come to Mongolia in 1923 with five other adventurous young Danes on the initiative of the physician Carl I. Krebs (1889-1971) to establish a farm South-West of Lake Baikal in Uriankhai. During the three years he spent there, Haslund-Christensen came to know and like the Mongols. He learned the language and much about their culture. In 1926 he left the farm, went to Ulan Bator and later to Peking, where he was engaged between 1927 and 1930 by the Swedish geographer and explorer Sven Hedin as a caravaneer for the Sino-Swedish Expedition. In the years 1927-35 this expedition went from Kalgan through the Gobi Desert to Xinjiang and to the Torgut Mongols in the Tien Shan Mountains. Haslund-Christensen made a unique collection of sixty folk songs, which he recorded on wax cylinders, and a fine ethnographic collection for the Riksmuseet in Stockholm.

While Sven Hedin was mainly occupied with the mapping and exploration of Central Asia, Haslund-Christensen had developed a genuine and deep interest in the cultures of the peoples he met on his travels and he felt obliged to collect as much information on Mongol traditions as possible before the impact of the outside world penetrated any further and changed them forever.

In 1936-37 Haslund-Christensen was back in Mongolia, this time on his own, to collect artefacts for the National Museum of Denmark, which was planning to open in a new building with greatly enlarged exhibition space in 1938. Despite the difficulties caused by the Japanese occupation of Manchuria and Inner Mongolia, Haslund-Christensen succeeded in spending several months with the Eastern Mongols. In 1938-39 he was occupied with a second expedition to Central Asia, this time under the auspices of the Royal Danish Geographical Society, together with the linguist Kaare Grønbech (1901-1957) and the archaeologist Werner Jacobsen (1914-1979). In the course of this expedition the Southern part of Inner Mongolia was surveyed and this resulted in additional ethnographic collections for the National Museum. Thanks to Georg Söderbom a large collection of artefacts representing materials and objects used in everyday life was obtained from Mongol nomads.

In the years 1947-56 the Third Danish Expedition to Central Asia, organized and led by Haslund-Christensen, carried out ethnographical, botanical, zoological, geographical, physical-anthropological, and linguistic research in Afghanistan, Chitral, Kashmir, Ladakh, Sikkim, and Assam. It was in the course of this expedition, in 1948, that Haslund-Christensen died in Kabul. Of the dozen scholars who over the years participated in the expedition, only two carried out ethnographic research on nomadic peoples. They were HRH Prince Peter, and the botanist Lennart Edelberg. Prince Peter, who had studied social anthropology with Bronislaw Malinowski in London, worked mainly among Tibetans from his base in Kalimpong (see *A Study of Polyandry*. The Hague 1963). Among other things he made an outstanding collection of clothing, tools, implements, and household belongings among Tibetan nomads. In Afghanistan Lennart Edelberg carried out botanical research in the course of which he developed a keen interest in the cultures of the transhumant peoples of Nuristan and Afghan nomads. As a result of these experiences Lennart Edelberg came to argue the need for long-term studies of these peoples and it was for the purpose of satisfying these needs that the next Danish Expedition to Afghanistan devoted itself. His work from 1947 to 1949 resulted in important ethnographic collections being sent back to the museum in Denmark.

Lennart Edelberg was later, in 1964, a member of the Danish Archaeological Expedition to Luristan. Again he took the opportunity to make ethnographic collections, this time among the Lur nomads whom Feilberg had studied thirty years earlier. It is the studies and collections of these very scholars which provide the ethnographic data on which *Nomads of Luristan*, the second volume in this series, is based

In the early 1950s Danish research among pastoral peoples changed its theoretical and methodological scope. A new generation of trained anthropologists was emerging, spearheaded by Johannes Nicolaisen who was to become the first Professor of Anthropology at Copenhagen University, and Klaus Ferdinand who established the discipline at Aarhus University and directed the Ethnographic Department at the Prehistoric Museum at Moesgaard. With them began the kind of prolonged field research and empirical in-depth studies of pastoral peoples considered indispensable today if an understanding of another culture is to be achieved. Although both Nicolaisen and Ferdinand maintained an interest in historical analysis and the study of material culture, their emphasis was different and problems of social organization, economy and the cultural understandings of the nomads came into the foreground, as did the changes that these nomadic societies were undergoing.

Johannes Nicolaisen began his studies of North African nomads in 1947 as a student of anthropology with fieldwork among Berber and Arabic speaking pastoral groups in and just South of the Atlas mountains in Algeria, an area he revisited in 1950. It was the Tuareg, however, who captured his fascination and whose society and culture became the main subject of his research when he had earned his university degree. Nicolaisen spent more than three years among these people between 1951 and 1964, living and travelling with them on camelback. All in all he visited the Tuareg nine times, studying the changes which in particular the Ahaggar and Ayr groups were experiencing.

Nicolaisen had familiarized himself with British social anthropology at University College, London between 1952 and 1954, and the theoretical issues discussed there had a profound impact on his analysis of Tuareg society. Although maintaining a culture-historical perspective, the social organization of the Tuareg became a key area of his data collecting. His works examine in detail the intricate kinship systems, socio-political organization, slavery, and the religion of these nomads, as well as the ecological adaptations and socio-economic transformations of various Tuareg groups. Despite his substantial contributions to nomad studies Nicolaisen left a considerable part of his works unpublished. It is intended to remedy this in the present series. In 1963 he and Ida Nicolaisen, his wife and fellow anthropologist, took up the study in Chad of a hunting and gathering people, the Haddad, who lived among the pastoral Kreda on terms similar to slavery.

This work is also to be published in the present series.

For Klaus Ferdinand Afghan nomadism, in particular the form practised by Pashtun and Aimaq groups, became the main focus of his research interests. In 1953-55 he was in Afghanistan as a member of the Henning Haslund-Christensen Memorial Mission. This was led by HRH Prince Peter and had as its other members Lennart Edelberg and the photographer Peter Rasmussen (1918-1992). On this expedition Ferdinand worked with culture-historical studies of various forms of pastoral nomadism: semi-nomadism, trading nomadism, and "true" pastoral nomadism. A particular interest in the course of this research concerned an investigation of tent types. Prince Peter and Ferdinand were the first to document the existence of special summer trading bazaars set up and managed by the nomads in Central Afghanistan.

Klaus Ferdinand continued his ethnographic studies and museum collecting activities in 1960, 1965-66, and 1974, partly together with his wife Marianne, among nomads in East and Central Afghanistan. Little was known at that time of the social organization, economic life, and culture of these people despite the fact that pastoral nomads had played an integrative economic role in the history of modern Afghanistan. Over time Ferdinand's investigations turned increasingly to trade and trading systems of the nomads and the socio-cultural conditions within which these unfold.

In 1975 Klaus Ferdinand returned to Afghanistan to pursue the study of nomadic traders and the now rapidly changing economies and cultures of the nomads. This time he was accompanied by three of his students: Birthe Frederiksen (b.1949), Asta Olesen (b.1952), and Gorm Pedersen (b.1949), each of whom was to conduct separate fieldwork among the Afghan nomads. Birthe Frederiksen carried out her work among the Hazarbuz of the Mohmand tribe, Gorm Pedersen among the Zala Khan Khel of the Ahmadzai tribe, both groups which relied on or had been heavily involved in trading in the past. The data of the latter are presented in this volume. Asta Olesen took up the study of non-pastoral nomads, the highly specialized itinerant craftsmen and peddlers who practice so-called peripatetic nomadism. Her work, *Afghan Craftsmen* was published in 1994 also in this series. Ferdinand devoted his own time to the collecting of information on the history of nomad bazaars and traditional caravan activities and trade routes. All of these studies will be published in this series.

In 1959 Ferdinand took part in the Danish Archaeological Expedition to Qatar, which was part of a programme of extensive Danish archaeological investigations in the Gulf States, initiated by Professor P. V. Glob. Together with the photographer Jette Bang (1914-1964) he studied both Northern and Southern groups of Bedouin and collected ethnographic specimens. His study of these little known and nowadays sedentarized nomads appeared under the title *Bedouins of Qatar* as the first volume of the series in 1993.

Taken as a whole, these Danish studies of nomadic cultures and societies are widely different in kind, reflecting the educational background, interests, and theoretical orientation of the explorer or scholar who carried them out, the length of time spent in the field, and the period in which the expedition or fieldwork took place. As ethnographic data they must be appreciated and analysed against this background. Museum collections cannot be fully understood by viewing them simply and uncritically as adequate and objective representations of the cultures which produced them. Invariably, each collection is a result of selection by the fieldworker who has made choices on the basis of implicit or explicit criteria of representation, and as such what is brought back represents to some degree Western cultural principles, scientific ideas, and esthetic values over time. Removed from their original context the objects are then rearranged in exhibitions where they may give the impression of replicating such abstract wholes as, for example, Mongol culture. The interpretations and evaluations of the ethnographic collections and other ethnographic data which are to be presented in this series of publications take such issues into consideration.

After 1979 it became apparent that Danish research among pastoral peoples had reached a new phase. Afghanistan, a country where no less than eight Danish anthropologists had been working during the 1970s was closed to further fieldwork for the forseeable future. Afghan refugees, including pastoral nomads, poured by the millions into neighbouring Pakistan and Iran following the communist takeover in 1978, the Soviet invasion, and the ensuing war. Luristan, another core area of Danish research interest, was likewise barred to foreign researchers due to the political changes which followed the coming to power of Ayatollah Khomeni and his government. At the same time, the situation of pastoral nomads all over the world had been radically transformed due to changed ecological, demographic, economic, social, and not least political conditions. In the Sahel region severe droughts brought starvation to man and beast both in the 1970s and the 1980s and several pastoral groups were at the brink of extinction. Demographic pressure and the ensuing competition over land and pastures between nomads and peasants put severe strain on many a pastoral economy. Trade and transport, a significant economic aspect of pastoral economies in many regions, had run into difficulties. Camels and horses lost out in competition with lorries, trade routes were closed by political intervention, and traditional items of local manufacture and trade were replaced by new industrially produced goods. In the Gulf the oil adventure put an end to the traditional way of life of the Bedouins. The Bedouins of Qatar among whom Klaus Ferdinand had carried out research in 1959, gave up their nomadic migrations in the 1960s when the men obtained employment at the refineries and in other petroleum related fields. A main obstacle to the continuous existence of pastoral nomads in most cases was and is nevertheless the development of modern bureaucratic administrations in areas where pastoral nomads have had virtual autonomy, and the interests of governments in getting the nomads settled and under control.

Against this background it is evident that anthropological research is today faced with an entirely new situation and must address itself accordingly. New problems of inquiry and analysis force themselves upon the researcher, not only in the wake of insights already gained and of issues on the current theoretical agenda, but first and foremost because of the socio-economic changes and political obstacles that pastoral nomads are facing all over the world, and the radical transformations that their cultures have already undergone within living memory. It is also clear that ethnographic collections and the unpublished data on the lives and traditions of these various pastoral peoples, which in some cases are already of the past, attain a new significance in this situation. Each of these cultures represents a singular social and cultural experiment in the history of mankind. As such each of them carries evidence that is significant to the overall effort to explore the common denominators of cultural and social formation and the factors which limit the variability of these, which is the ultimate goal of anthropology.

The greatest value of the collections and studies, however, lies perhaps in the fact that they serve to document unique cultural histories which are not only of significance to the descendants of these intriguing nomadic peoples, but are important as both symbols and records of ethnic identity.

In 1985 the Carlsberg Foundation received an application for funds for the preparation and publication of this fine and varied Danish research on nomad cultures. The initiative for this came from Klaus Ferdinand. In the past, the Carlsberg Foundation had funded a considerable part of the field research among pastoral nomads. In 1986 the Board of Directors of the Carlsberg Foundation decided to grant funds to support the study and writing up of unpublished materials from the Danish ethnographic collections and the cultural and social data from anthropological field research among pastoral nomads of Central and South West Asia, Qatar, and North Africa. Accordingly, a substantial grant was given to THE CARLSBERG FOUNDATION'S NOMAD RESEARCH PROJECT for a five year period.

The work was supervised by a committee chaired initially by Professor Henrik Glahn, and later by Professor Poul Christian Matthiessen, both of the Carlsberg Foundation. The other members were the late Professor Tove Birkelund of the Carlsberg Foundation, Associate Professor Klaus Ferdinand, Curator of the Ethnographic Department of the Prehistoric Museum, Moesgaard, Curator Rolf Gilberg of the Danish National Museum, and Associate Professor Ida Nicolaisen of Copenhagen University. Niels Petri of the Carlsberg Foundation carried the secretarial burden, assisted by Sven Dindler.

In 1990 an editorial committee was formed with Poul Christian Matthiessen and Ida Nicolaisen as members. In 1993 Per Øhrgaard took over from Matthiessen and Gunver Kyhn from Petri. Ida Nicolaisen was appointed Editor-in-Chief of the series.

I would like to take this opportunity to thank the National Museum of Denmark, the Prehistoric Museum at Moesgaard, the Institute of Anthropology, Copenhagen University, the University of Aarhus, and Danish and foreign colleagues for help and interest in the work presented here. I wish moreover to express my gratitude to the Carlsberg Foundation for the generous support it has given to the Danish Nomad Research Project and the series of publications which will fulfill the aims of that project. Over the past century the Carlsberg Foundation has enabled the National Museum of Denmark and the Prehistoric Museum, Moesgaard to acquire the collections which are now the jewels in their ethnographic crowns. It has offered Danish scientists unique opportunities to record the way of life of a range of pastoral peoples in the Pamirs, in Mongolia, Afghanistan, Iran, Qatar, and North Africa. Last but not least, it has provided scholars with the opportunity to analyse their field data and/or the associated museum collections for publication in this series.

Ida Nicolaisen
Editor-in-Chief
Copenhagen, September 1994

ACKNOWLEDGEMENTS

Many persons and institutions have contributed to the carrying out of this work. First and foremost I owe a debt of gratitude to Zala Khān Khēl, with whom I lived in Afghanistan in 1975-76 and in Pakistan in 1986. The fieldwork in Afghanistan was supported by The Research Foundation of Aarhus University, and was carried out in collaboration with Kabul University. For varying lengths of time I worked with interpreters and colleagues from Kabul University. These Afghans - Azim Safi, Sher Agha, Abdul Wahed, and Shah Mahmood - were not merely co-workers; they also became good friends and travel comrades. Shah Mahmood's fate I do not know, but the three others accompanied the Zala Khān Khēl and over five million other Afghans into exile, after the Afghan revolution of 1978 and the Soviet invasion of 1979 brought war to Afghanistan. Azim Safi came to Denmark and later Canada, Sher Agha to Australia, and Abdul Wahed to England. I owe a debt of gratitude to all of them.

A grant under The Carlsberg Foundation's Nomad Research Project coupled with my fortunate position as guest researcher at the Ethnographic Department of the National Museum, Copenhagen made it possible for me to write up my field data. The Carlsberg Foundation also financed my field visit to Pakistan in 1986. During field-visits to Pakistan in 1986, 1988, and 1992 I received assistance from the staff of The Danish Committee for Aid to Afghan Refugees (DACAAR) which facilitated the follow-up research in a most valuable way.

I owe a particular debt of gratitude to Klaus Ferdinand, who as my teacher at the Department of Ethnography and social Anthropology of Aarhus University introduced me to Afghanistan and who has since been a constant source of inspiration to my work through advice and fruitful discussion.

Many friends and colleagues have throughout the years been of importance to my work. Among these I should single out Asta Olesen and Birthe Frederiksen - travelling companions, friends, and fellow anthropologists - who for years have shared my interest in Afghanistan and who, together with Klaus Ferdinand, have constituted a steadfast forum for the development of ideas, for criticism, and for debate. I also wish to thank Azim Safi for providing linguistic information and clarification, and Geoffrey Bibby and Peter Crawford for translation work. Finally, I am most greatful to Ida Nicolaisen, Editor-in-Chief of this series and Niels Peder Jørgensen, Copy Editor, for valuable assistance in the final stages of preparing this book.

Gorm Pedersen

GLOSSARY

Names and words known in a standard anglicised version are retained in this book. Other local words are printed in italics and they are explained when fist used. Below are listed local terms and less common words, including measures of weight, area, and currency, frequently used in the text. The languages spoken in Afghanistan have influenced each other with many loanwords. The list gives the origin of each word by the indications Pe. = Persian, Pa. = Pashto, Ar. = Arabic, Hi. = Hindi, and Tu. = Turkish.

afs. Abbreviation of *afghānī*, the Afghan currency. In 1975-76 1 US$ = about 53 afs.

'allafi (Pe.) *'allaf* = grass, forage, fodder, food; *'allafi* = dealing in grain.

biswā (Hi.) Land measure, 1/20 of a *jarīb* (see below).

chapān (Tu.) An outer garment of caftan-type, normally worn cloak-like hanging loose over the shoulders. In Afghanistan it is traditionally associated with ethnic groups in the northern part of the country but it is today also widely used in other parts.

dihqān (Pe.) Tenant farmer.

dihqān-karī (Pe.) The work of a *dihqān*.

farmān (Pe.) A mandate, command, or decree; here used about the royal allocations of grazing grounds in Hazarajat to, among others, the Pashtun nomads. A *farmān*-letter is a document showing the title to the land.

General Transport
The common translation of *Riasat-i Omumī Transport-i Dawlatī* Pe., the Afghan government agency for transport.

gharībī (Pe.) Poor-man's work; the work of unskilled labourers for example in harvest and house construction.

hajjī (Ar.) Title given to a Muslim who has been on pilgrimage, *hajj*, to Mecca.

hamsāya (Pe.) Literally "common shadow". The term is used for neighbour, but is most commonly used for a person or family which is attached to another person or family in a way that involves a servant relationship and subservience in return for security and protection. Well-off households both in town and country often have a *hamsāya* family living within their compound walls. It is in this latter sense that the term is used in this book.

hawā-khūrī (Pe.) Literally "eating air" (*hawā* = air, *khūrī* = eating); used to designate that something is done for pleasure, holiday.

jarīb (Pe.) Land measure, 1 *jarīb* = 20 *biswās* = about 0.2 hectares = about 0.5 acres.

jihād (Ar.) Strife for the Muslim faith. Popularly used about religiously sanctioned war.

jirgah (Pa.) Traditional council of the Pashtuns, where decisions are reached by unanimous agreement. A *jirgah* can be held at many levels from sub-lineage to tribe. The Afghan National Assembly is called *Wolasi Jirgah* and the *Loya Jirgah* is the Grand Assembly or the Constituent Assembly.

khān (Pe.) Unofficial title used for "big men" and men of influence. The term is also widely used simply as part of a person's name (i.a. Abdul Khān) without any reference to its value as a title.

khēl (Ar.) Kin-group. When used as an affix to a person's name it designates a specific descent-group, especially among the Pashtun, i.a. Suleman *Khēl* are the descendents of Suleman (See also *zai*).

kīlīnar or *clīndar* probably comes from the English "cleaner". The *kilinar* is a person who is in a sort of apprenticeship with a lorry or bus driver working as his assistant.

kūchey (Pa.) from Pe. *kūch* = move, set off, migrate; and *kūchi* which designates wandering people. In the East Afghan context used about tent-dwelling pastoral nomads and usually not about other itinerant groups of people.

lukh (Pe.) Bulrush (Lat.: typha anguatata), a marsh plant, reed, with long stiff leaves; in the East Afghan lowlands used for the building of seasonal huts.

madrasa (Ar.) Literally a place where you take lessons, but in practical terms only designating a school of religious teaching or a *mullah*-school.

malik (Ar.) Official title given to an appointed or elected leader at village or countryside level.

mir-āb (Ar.) *Mir* = leader, Pe. *āb* = water; a man appointed by the farmers in a certain area to look after the maintenance of the irrigation system and the correct distribution of water. He usually collects a fee from the farmers proportional to the size of irrigated land and the use of water.

mujāhedin (Ar.) Plural of *mujāhed* = one who does *jihād*, strife for the Muslim faith; the Afghan resistance movement (and members of that movement) who took up armed fight against the communist regime in Kabul and the Soviet occupation forces.

mullah — From Ar. *mawlā*, a Muslim learned in theology. In Afghan context a Muslim priest.

Partition — The partition of British India after British withdrawal in 1947. The former colony was divided into two independent states: India, which is predominantly Hindu, and Pakistan, which is predominantly Muslim. (In 1971 Pakistan was further divided when East Pakistan became independent Bangladesh.)

PDPA — People's Democratic Party of Afghanistan, *Hizb-i Demokratiqi Khalq-i Afghanistan*, founded in 1965. Splits in 1967 into two factions, *Khalq* (The People) and *Parcham* (The Flag) - named after the newspapers which they published. In 1977 the two factions reunite to plan and successfully carry out the coup in 1978.

powindah — (Pa.) From *pewal* = to graze. Used in the southern parts af Afghanistan for pastoral nomads. In British India/Pakistan the term is broadly used for Afghan nomads but has especially come to designate the trading nomads who cross into Indian/Pakistani territory.

purdah — (Pe.) Literally "curtain". System of keeping women out of public view, practiced by many Muslim people.

qal'a — (Ar.) A type of large farmhouse constructed with high defence walls surrounding a rectangular courtyard.

qurūt — Pe. from Tu. Dried buttermilk; a common milk preserve shaped into small balls which are later grated and mixed with water to be consumed.

sēr — (Pe.) A unit of weight which varies from one part of Afghanistan to another. 1 *Kabul-sēr* = 16 *pow* = about 7.0 kg, 1 *Kandahar-sēr* = 10 *pow* = about 4.4 kg, and 1 *Herat-sēr* = 8 *pow* = about 3.5 kg. An attempt at standardisation by introduction of the metric system has been made, but the old system with its local variations is still in normal use.

serāy — (Pe.) A closed yard usually with four building-wings and one main entrance. Along the old caravan routes caravan-*serāy*s were placed at regular intervals as places of commerce but first of all as protected rest houses for the travelling trader and his caravan of loaded camels.

serāydār — (Pe.) The caretaker or manager of a *serāy*.

tālib — (Ar.) A religious student.

zai — (Pa.) Literally 'son'. Designates a kin-group when used as affix to a person's name, i.a. Ahmad*zai* is a descendant of Ahmad.

zamīn-dārī — (Pe.) *Zamīn* = land, *dārī* = ownership of. In restricted use it indicates land-owning or living of land without actually oneself being the tiller.

INTRODUCTION

DANISH NOMAD RESEARCH IN AFGHANISTAN

Four anthropological field studies were carried out by *The Danish Scientific Mission to Afghanistan 1975-76*. Three of these were developed under the common working title *Nomad Caravaneering and nomad bazaars in Central Afghanistan and related nomad developments in Afghanistan from the end of the 19th century to the present day*. The objectives were to follow up and complete earlier studies within these fields, carried out in 1953-55 and in 1960, subsequently published by HRH Prince Peter of Greece and Denmark (1954) and Ferdinand (1959a, 1959b, and 1962). No intermediate studies had been carried out. The fourth study concerned gypsy-like groups of specialists, craftsmen, and petty traders engaged in seasonal migrations in East Afghanistan. The project emanated from the Department of Ethnography and Social Anthropology, Aarhus University and was headed by Klaus Ferdinand. Together with Birthe Frederiksen and Gorm Pedersen he studied trade nomadism, whilst Asta Olesen concentrated her work on the gypsy-like groups later described as peripatetic nomads. In an Afghan context this was, at the time, a new and unexplored field which shortly after was also studied by the Indian scholar Aparna Rao (see Rao 1982 and Rao (ed.) 1987). The Danish research was followed up by shorter field trips to Afghanistan in 1977-78 and, in conjunction with the publishing of results under the auspices of *The Carlsberg Foundation's Nomad Research Project*, was supplemented with visits amongst Afghan trading nomads, by then refugees in Pakistan, in 1986 and 1987. The results of this research, parts of which had previously been published as occasional papers or articles (see the bibliography), are now presented in monograph form. They are Klaus Ferdinand's *Caravaneering and nomad bazaars in East and Central Afghanistan* (forthcoming), Birthe Frederiksen's *Nomads and bazaar merchants* (forthcoming), Asta Olesen's *Afghan Craftsmen* (1994), and the present volume on *Afghan Nomads in Transition* by Gorm Pedersen.

Other examples of Danish anthropological fieldwork in Afghanistan, carried out amongst villagers, are provided by the work of Inger W. Boesen and Asger Christensen among the Pashtun, and by Jan Ovesen among the Pashai. Both studies were carried out in the Kunar Province, 1977-78.[1]

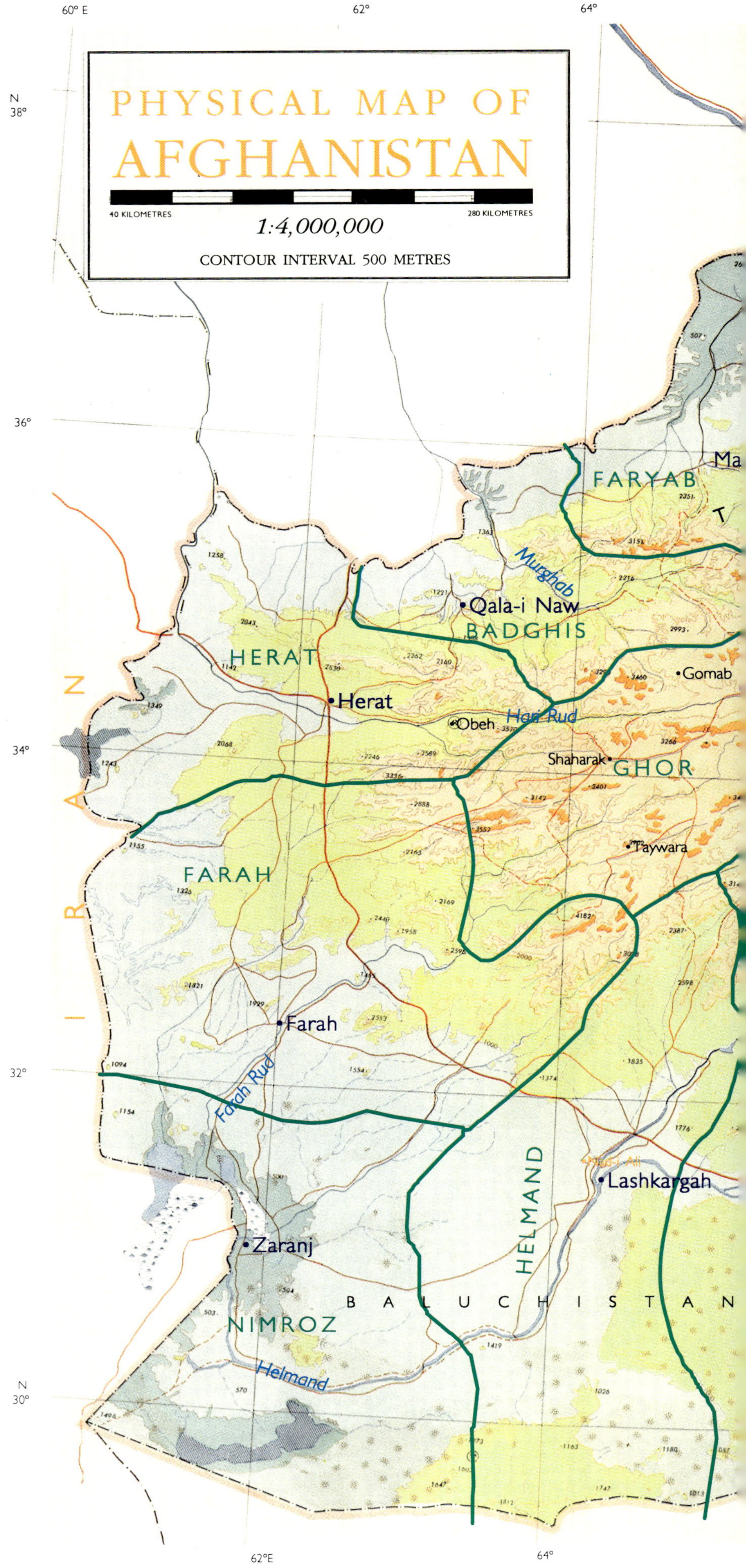

21 Physical Map of Afghanistan (Source Cartographic & Cadastral Survey Institute, Kabul, 1975-6)

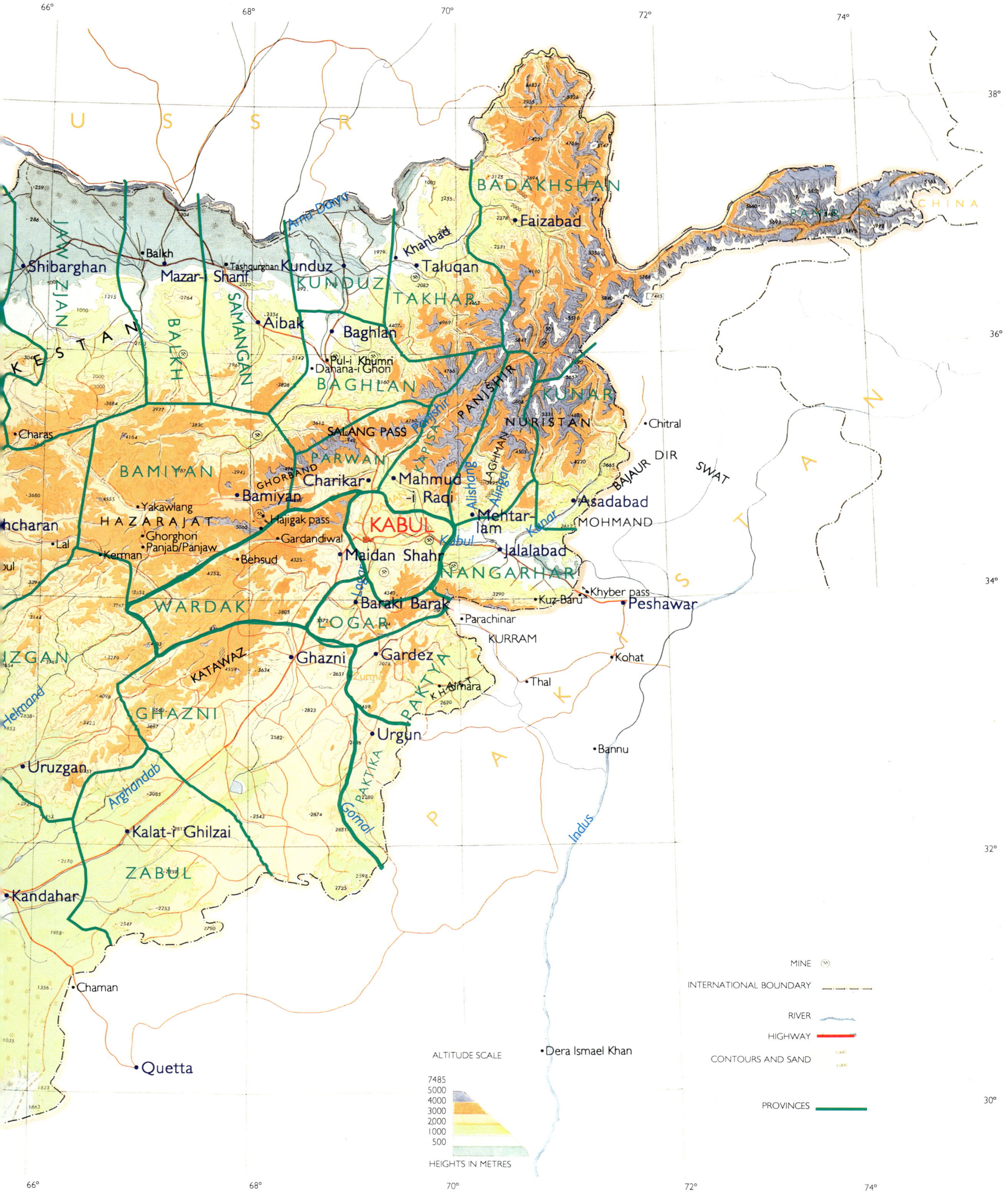

U S S R
CHINA
PAKISTAN
BADAKHSHAN
Faizabad
Khanbad
Taluqan
TAKHAR
KUNDUZ
Kunduz
Tashqurghan
Mazar-i Sharif
Balkh
Shibarghan
JAWZJAN
BALKH
SAMANGAN
Aibak
Baghlan
Pul-i Khumri
Danana-i Ghori
BAGHLAN
SALANG PASS
PARWAN
Panjshir
PANJSHIR
KAPISA
LAGHMAN
NURISTAN
KUNAR
Chitral
DIR
BAJAUR
SWAT
Asadabad
MOHMAND
Mehtar-lam
Alishang
Alingar
Kunar
Kabul
KABUL
Charikar
Mahmud-i Raqi
GHORBAND
Bamiyan
BAMIYAN
Yakawlang
HAZARAJAT
Hajigak pass
Gardandiwal
Ghorghori
Panjab/Panjaw
Kerman
Behsud
Lal
Charas
Maidan Shahr
Jalalabad
NANGARHAR
Khyber pass
Kuz Baru
Peshawar
Parachinar
KURRAM
Kohat
Thal
Logar
Baraki Barak
LOGAR
WARDAK
Ghazni
Gardez
KATAWAZ
GHAZNI
PAKTYA
KHOST
Zurmat
Urgun
Bannu
PAKTIKA
Gomal
Uruzgan
Helmand
Arghandab
Kalat-i Ghilzai
ZABUL
Kandahar
Chaman
Quetta
Indus
Dera Ismael Khan
MINE
INTERNATIONAL BOUNDARY
RIVER
HIGHWAY
CONTOURS AND SAND
PROVINCES
ALTITUDE SCALE
7485
5000
4000
3000
2000
1000
500
HEIGHTS IN METRES

The historical background for the nomad research

The history of Danish research in Afghanistan begins with the travels and investigations carried out by the explorer and ethnographer Henning Haslund-Christensen in Mongolia in the 1930s (see Editor's Preface). It was in fact he who started the work in Afghanistan during *The 3rd Danish Expedition to Central Asia 1947-56*. A brief outline of the multi-faceted results of these expeditions and the ensuing ethnographic work of *The Danish Scientific Mission to Afghanistan 1953-55 (The Henning Haslund-Christensen Memorial Mission)* is provided by Edelberg and Ferdinand (1958).

The inclusion of Afghanistan in the geographical scope of *The 3rd Danish Expedition to Central Asia* formed part of an ambitious research project in which current research would be linked with that of previous studies by C. G. Feilberg in Iran (in 1935), Ole Olufsen in West Turkestan and Pamir (in 1896-97 and 1898-99), by Henning Haslund-Christensen (in 1936-37), and by Henning Haslund-Christensen, Kaare Grønbech, and Werner Jacobsen in Mongolia (in 1938-39). The general objective of the project was to fill gaps in our knowledge about Central Asia through work in the fields of ethnography, cultural geography, the history of religion, and the natural sciences. The original plan envisaged that three teams of scientists starting in Afghanistan, Sikkim, and northwestern China would work their way to a common meeting-place and during their travels study the areas they passed through. However, the ambitious research project was abandoned due to the political difficulties of the time in Asia. The main focus of the work was therefore on Afghanistan where a number of research projects were carried out between 1947 and 1949.[2]

Afghan nomadism as such did not form part of the research programme of *The 3rd Expedition,* but Haslund-Christensen intended to record folk music and carry out investigations among the semi-nomadic Aimaq and the settled Hazara in Central Afghanistan in order to trace their origin, especially their possible link to Central Asian Mongols. Unfortunately, Haslund-Christensen died in Kabul on 13 September 1948 before any of these plans were carried out. He was buried the following day next to another Asia scholar, Sir Aurel Stein, in the Christian cemetery.

Haslund-Christensen had arrived in Afghanistan in December 1947 together with the four first members of the expedition. He immediately started collecting ethnographic artifacts in Kabul, an activity in which he was very competent following his previous work in Mongolia. He collected household objects and utensils, toys, and a precious collection of amulets. This work was later to be continued by Lennart Edelberg and Halfdan Siiger. Apart from carrying out his own collecting activities, Haslund-Christensen also encouraged the natural scientists to collect ethnographic artifacts during their trips to various locations in the country. As a result the National Museum in Copenhagen today houses one of the early large Afghan collections outside the country itself, including a small collection of items from Pashtun nomads. Lennart Edelberg, the botanist and geographer, put particular effort into this work, primarily in Nuristan, the region in which he carried out most of his research, but also in other parts of the country. In general, Edelberg considered it to be an obligation to continue the ethnographic work which had been initiated by Haslund-Christensen. He collected ethnographic artifacts among the Aimaq, the Hazara, and in other places.[3]

01,2 Haslund-Christensen's camp in Afghanistan during the Third Danish Expedition to Central Asia (M.K., 1948).

On his return to Denmark Edelberg joined the Department of Ethnography at the National Museum, 1949-50, in order to catalogue the ethnographic items collected in Afghanistan. His ideas and plans concerning future ethnographic research in Afghanistan were formed then and were later on elaborated in collaboration with the ethnologist and social anthropologist Klaus Ferdinand. The fact that very little ethnographic research had been carried out in Afghanistan and especially on its nomadism, which Edelberg (1950) had described as a significant and particular element of Afghan culture in general, served as a special incentive for future work.[4] He later wrote a programmatic article on Afghanistan as a field for future ethnographic research in the journal *Naturens Verden* (1952). He there refers to a number of cases of historical and ethnographic interest, cases which had been discovered by *The 3rd Danish Expedition to Central Asia* and which he felt were obvious areas into which scientific

01,3 Based on his experiences of the Third Danish Expedition to Central Asia Edelberg (right) outlined the possibilities of future ethnographic research in Afghanistan. Edelberg concentrated continued research on the cultures of Nuristan (M.K., 1948).

activities should move. He also mentioned the limited knowledge of Afghan nomadism and the fact that two different types of the black tent existed in the region and that the Pashtun were both semi-nomads and full nomads (Edelberg 1952).

Using Edelberg's outline as a point of departure several new research projects were initiated in Afghanistan in 1953. The study of Afghan nomadism formed an important part of the new expedition, *The Danish Scientific Mission to Afghanistan 1953-55*, which was led by Prince Peter and as members had Lennart Edelberg, the cinematographer Peter Rasmussen, and Klaus Ferdinand, whose specific responsibility was nomad research.[5] The mission's first work was carried out during a trip through Central Afghanistan, which included a visit to the nomad summer bazaar at Abul. The mission provided the very first documentation of this particular nomad phenomenon (Prince Peter 1954; Ferdinand 1956b). It became the start of a Danish tradition for nomad research in Afghanistan which has continued till today.

The first step was to acquire an overview of the area of distribution of nomadism and its cultural-geographical forms. In conjunction with this general aim a registration and mapping of dominant tent types was carried out, work which supplemented Feilberg's cultural-historical analysis of the development and distribution of the black tent from an area where almost no information was available (see Feilberg 1945: 97-8; Ferdinand 1956b, 1959a, and 1959b). These studies were innovative and the members of the expedition regarded themselves as part of something new. It later turned out that there did exist a general overview of the various categories and types of Pashtun nomads and migrational workers who during the winter travelled from Afghanistan into British India. This information could be found in, for example, *Census of India Publications* and was thoroughly described e.g. by Latimer (*Census of the N.-W. F. P.* 1911: 45 ff.). A few monographic descriptions also existed, such as Jamiat Rai's *Rough Notes on the Nasar, Kharot, and other Afghan Pawindahs* (1922). J. A. Robinson's encyclopedic book *Notes on the Nomad Tribes of Eastern Afghanistan* (1935), written by the former *Powindah* (i.e. nomad) Officer, was the most important governmental publication. Ferdinand encountered this book for the first time during the winter of 1954 in Peshawar unable, however, to open it since its contents were still regarded as confidential. At the time it was lying on the top of the desk of the *Powindah* Officer in Peshawar. In 1957 Ferdinand saw a copy from the Secret and Political Department at the India Office Library in London which he was permitted to consult under the condition that he did not quote from the work! *Census Reports*, *Gazetteers*, and similar publications were publicly available in special libraries at an early stage and many are now reprinted or available on microfilm. Archival material concerning Afghanistan and Afghan relations to British India is now available to the public in London, New Delhi, and Peshawar. This material is extremely valuable but primarily deals with the relationship between Afghan nomads and the British colonial administration and only covers the internal situation in Afghanistan indirectly. The material may be used as an important historical supplement to first-hand records from Afghanistan and will be referred to in Ferdinand's monograph in particular.

Klaus Ferdinand further developed his studies of nomads during later trips to Afghanistan. During the summer of 1960 (April to October) on his own and together with his wife, Marianne Ferdinand, during the winter of 1965-66 (November to May), he carried out more elaborate studies among two groups of Pashtun, with short and long migration routes respectively, in East Afghanistan. In 1960 Ferdinand in addition studied Pashtun nomads' trade with the resident Hazara and their caravan trading in Central Afghanistan in general. In that context he also visited the nomad summer bazaars in Abul and Gomab (Gomao). This work resulted in the first detailed description and analysis of nomad trading activities and their social and economic context (Ferdinand 1962). The groups studied were the short-range migrating Tara Khēl, who migrated between Laghman and the Kabul area, and the long-range migrating Jani Khēl, Musa Khēl of the Ahmadzai, who migrated between the areas of the Mohmand and the province of Nangarhar to Hazarajat. This research focused on current social change in Hazarajat. The different forms of nomadism were no longer regarded as

01,4 The Abul nomad summer bazaar in the central highland of Afghanistan (K.F., July 1953).

independent forms, as they were in Ferdinand's previous work, but rather as consequences of a continuous adaptation to social and political changes triggered by the natural and cultural environment. The initial emphasis was on pastoral nomadism and the seasonal migrations between the eastern lowland areas, situated between 300 and 1,100 metres above sea-level, and the plateaus and mountainous regions towards west situated between 1,900 and 3,800 metres above sea-level. These migrations created an extremely advantageous position for the East Afghan Pashtun nomads. They were able to exploit a number of different niches in the surrounding socio-economic landscape. If finances were low it was normally possible to find work, so-called 'poor man's work', as a day labourer for settled people during the harvest or to engage in work within local transport. It was actually possible to develop an annual cycle which was related to the differing harvest seasons caused by differences in altitudes such as, for example, between the areas of Nangarhar and Kabul. For those who were better off economically there was the potential of further expansion. When it comes to nomads involved in long-range migrations, caravaneering and the caravan trade, as it is known from Hazarajat and the Aimaq region of Central Afghanistan, were feasible options. This often led to the nomads becoming settled as for example merchants in the bazaars, landowners, or both (see Ferdinand 1969a and 1969b; see accompanying diagram, *Fig. 01,5*).

The developmental potential of East Afghan nomadism was closely related to the character of the territory through which the migrations took place. The seasonal migrations took place between and within areas with well-established settled communities and furthermore through areas with some of Asia's most important ancient trade routes, the trade routes that connected India with Western and Central Asia. The caravan routes were obvious sources of income for the Pashtun nomads involved in transport work and often served as an incentive to become traders themselves. These conditions determined the development of the particular form of trade nomadism among the pastoral nomads we deal with here.

Afghan society has undergone radical changes with modernisations penetrating all areas, including a vast development of the infrastructure, during the period in which Ferdinand has studied the various forms of Afghan nomadism. The changes have directly affected the options open to the nomads and their caravan trading. The so-called 'trade nomadism' is an old phenomenon in Afghanistan, which went through a particular boom, due to political changes, during the first half of this century. This was the case in Central Afghanistan following the Pashtun nomads' arrival in Hazarajat after the 1890s and also in the Afghan part of Turkestan when the area was cut off from trade with Bokhara and other areas north of Amu Darya following the closure of the frontier to Soviet Central Asia in the 1920s. In 1960 trade nomadism was obviously declining for political and economic reasons underlined by national and international developments. In 1961 the Afghan government ordered the nomad bazaars of Abul and Gomab to move in order to enhance political control of the nomads' trading activities. Pakistan closed its frontiers to the nomads in the same year, forcing them to redirect their migration routes and changing the basis of the nomad trade. It was becoming increasingly apparent that Afghan nomadism in general was a disappearing way of life. It was therefore a matter of providing substantial documentation before these ways of life and the connected economic activities became extinct and impossible to study in the field.

As early as in the 1930s Haslund-Christensen had called attention to the drastic changes, brought about by modern development, which were affecting the lives of Asia's nomads, especially the Mongols. It was one of his primary reasons for initiating a major Danish research effort in Central Asia. Time was scarce and instant action was demanded to procure the information needed in order to elucidate the traditional ways of life in the region and its cultural history. The informants would soon vanish and take the information with them. The background to the work in Afghanistan was similar.

As to the East Afghan nomads it was evident that they had played a particular role in the recent economic and political development of the country such as the integration and consolidation of the Afghan state through their trading activities in marginal areas. From a comparative perspective it was obviously of great interest to cover these activities through detailed studies.

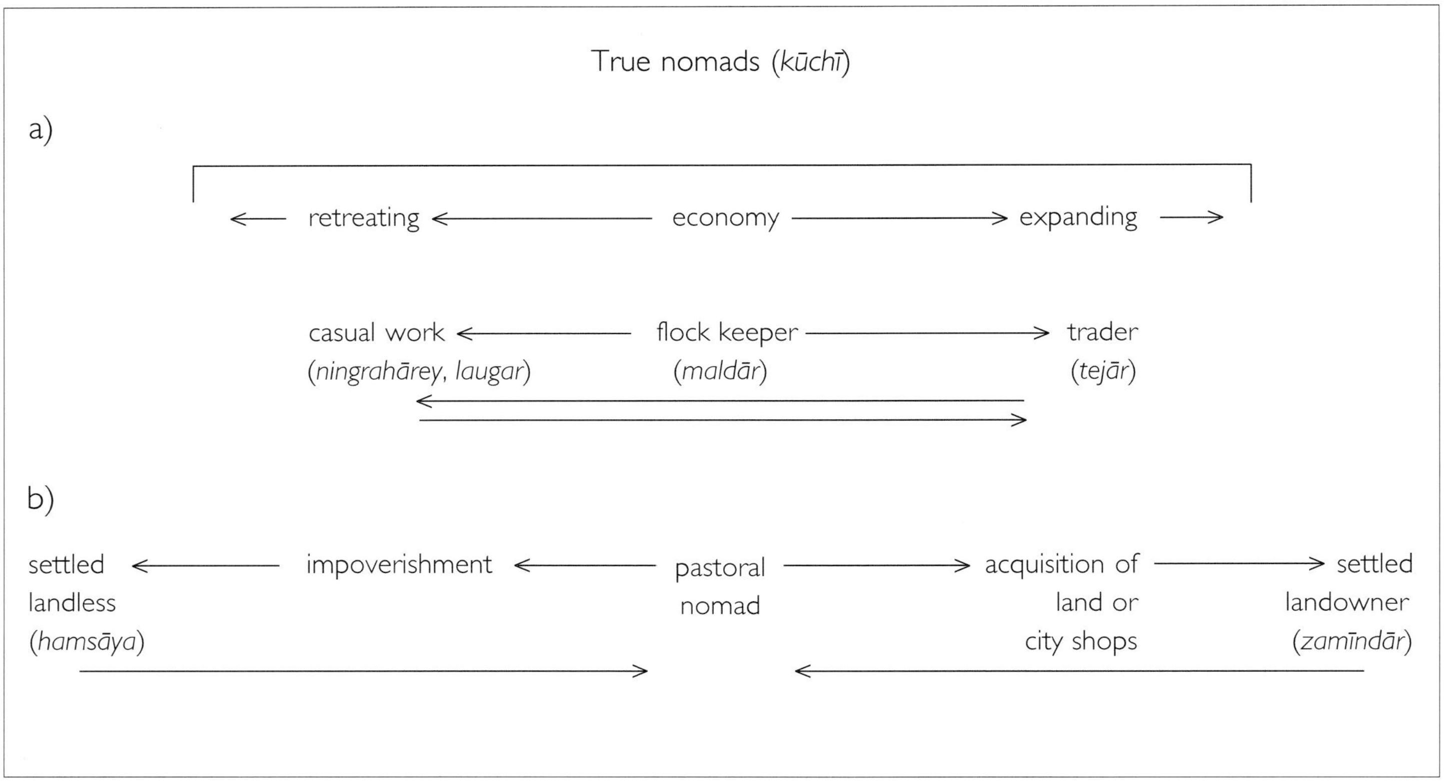

01,5 Diagram depicting occupational differentiation within Pashtun nomadism in East Afghanistan in response to economic adaptation to available possibilities. The diagram might continue on both wings with settled life as depicted in (b).
b) Diagram of the general sedentarisation process among pastoral nomads (upper part) where the process towards the right is commonly met with in our East Afghan material. The process of nomadisation (lower part) could also be met with (see e.g. Glatzer 1982) (After Ferdinand 1968a: 249 and 1969b: 114).

This was combined with a general hope of reaching a more profound historical knowledge of the Pashtun nomadic societies of East Afghanistan and a more conclusive insight into their contemporary cultural complexity.

The processes of change the Pashtun nomads were going through could obviously only be understood in the context of the general development of Afghan society and of their old winter areas in British India, later Pakistan. This conveyed a new dimension to the study of these processes of change and emphasised the need for analyses at both micro and macro levels.

It appears to be a general feature that nomads, following "modernisation" and the ensuing bureaucratisation of national governments, found it difficult to acquire sufficient space and tolerance within the framework set by the nation-states to continue their way of life. Nomads were, and often are, perceived as primitive and "savage" (*wāshī*), a characterisation we recurrently overheard in Afghanistan, thus allegedly constituting a developmental problem. In many countries this has led to an abolition of nomadism by force. In Afghanistan official policy has been more moderate. As indicated below government policy has imposed certain restrictions on nomadism, leading to its abolition, but in recent years measures have not been drastic to an extent where they have included forced settlement. They have, however, included the government offering cheap land in North Afghanistan. In this context it is worth recalling that the nomads to which we refer belong to the dominant and leading ethnic group in Afghanistan! The official government policy may thus be seen as a deliberate attempt to promote Pashtun ethnic identity and political control measures.

Danish Scientific Mission to Afghanistan 1975-76

In 1975-76 the Danish nomad studies in Afghanistan were resumed. The background was the experiences described above, a brief, preparatory field trip carried out by Ferdinand in the autumn of 1974, and the fact that there had been no further studies of nomad trade and bazaar activities since Ferdinand's early work from 1953 and 1960, despite the fact that a number of scholars had worked with Pashtun nomads in Central Afghanistan in the 1960s and 1970s, e.g. in the Aimaq area (see Bourgeois 1972, Jentsch 1973, Glatzer 1977, R. Tapper 1974) and in East Afghanistan (see Janata 1972).

Trade in Central Afghanistan, as in other parts of the country, was in the hands of both settled people and nomads, but we wished to focus on the trade in which pastoral nomads were involved. Ferdinand's early work was concentrated on Pashtun nomads travelling to Hazarajat and entering Afghanistan by way of the southern routes via Gomal and Kurram. These routes went through the former provinces of Junubi, currently the provinces of Paktika and Paktya, and Ghazni. We intended to include the nomads who used the northern routes such as Khyber and through the old province of Mashriqi, now Nangarhar. Our main interest was in the processes of change of nomadic society as a socio-economic and historical phenomenon and its interplay with the surrounding society. Fredrik Barth's model of transformation of nomad societies provided us with a major source of inspiration (Barth 1961). In general, however, we were motivated by the fact that the development of Central Afghanistan appeared to be unique and that Central Afghanistan was, presumably, one of the few places in the world where one could study and analyse nomadic caravaneering in its traditional context. In accordance with this, the general objectives were to:

a) document in detail the contemporary structure and function of the caravan trade and the nomad bazaars in Central Afghanistan and the historical development and change of these activities, with an emphasis on the period after 1960 when Ferdinand had visited the summer bazaars at Abul and Gomab. In addition we intended to elucidate the commercialisation of the Pashtun. The way we intended to accomplish this was by

b) carrying out a case study of a small group of nomads involved in caravaneering and nomad bazaars in Central Afghanistan, a task to which Gorm Pedersen was assigned, and

c) to carry out a similar case study of a group of former nomads previously engaged in caravan trade in North Afghanistan, who were by then involved in trade in the urban bazaars. This was to be the responsibility of Birthe Frederiksen.

01,6 The modern bazaar of Chaghcharan is typical of the new pattern of trade which has developed in Central Afghanistan after the advent of the lorry (G.P., Chaghcharan, July 1975).

Asta Olesen planned a complementary, independent study on the economic position of the itinerant specialist groups of artisan sieve-makers, grain-cleaners, and petty traders in the East Afghan society.

The members of the mission met in Kabul in June 1975 to set out, on the last day of the month, on a joint reconnaissance expedition through the central highlands of Afghanistan, the Hazarajat, and the Aimaq region further west (see the general map of Afghanistan, *Fig. 01,1*, and map, *Fig. 01,8*). The trip first brought us across the pass of Hajigak, via Bamiyan, Yakawlang, Panjab, Kerman, and Lal to Chaghcharan, the provincial capital of Ghor and the site where the old nomad bazaars of Abul and Gomab, as mentioned above, had been compelled to move to in 1961. We expected to get in contact with various groups of trading nomads immediately and select certain groups for further studies.

01,7 Only few and small groups of nomad traders were met in the central highland in 1975. This group of Khwazak brothers, whose main trading article is second-hand clothing, may well be on their last trading tour to the highland (G.P., Chaghcharan, July 1975).

The closer we approached Chaghcharan, the more we became aware that the conditions in the central highlands were very different from what we had expected. Our observations and the information we managed to compile *en route* conveyed to us an impression of trade nomadism undergoing rapid decline. When we finally reached Chaghcharan on 3 July there was no camp of tent stalls and no buzzing nomad trade. We learned that there had been no actual nomad bazaar since 1973. Only the animal mart remained as one of the old activities. Held at the end of June and the beginning of July on an open plain south of town, it had been given legal status and was controlled by the authorities.

The obvious demise of nomad trading stood in sharp contrast to the blossoming trade of the permanent bazaar. In a matter of a few years Chaghcharan had developed into a modern, urban provincial bazaar with frequent connections by lorry to the large cities of Kabul, Herat, and occasionally Kandahar.

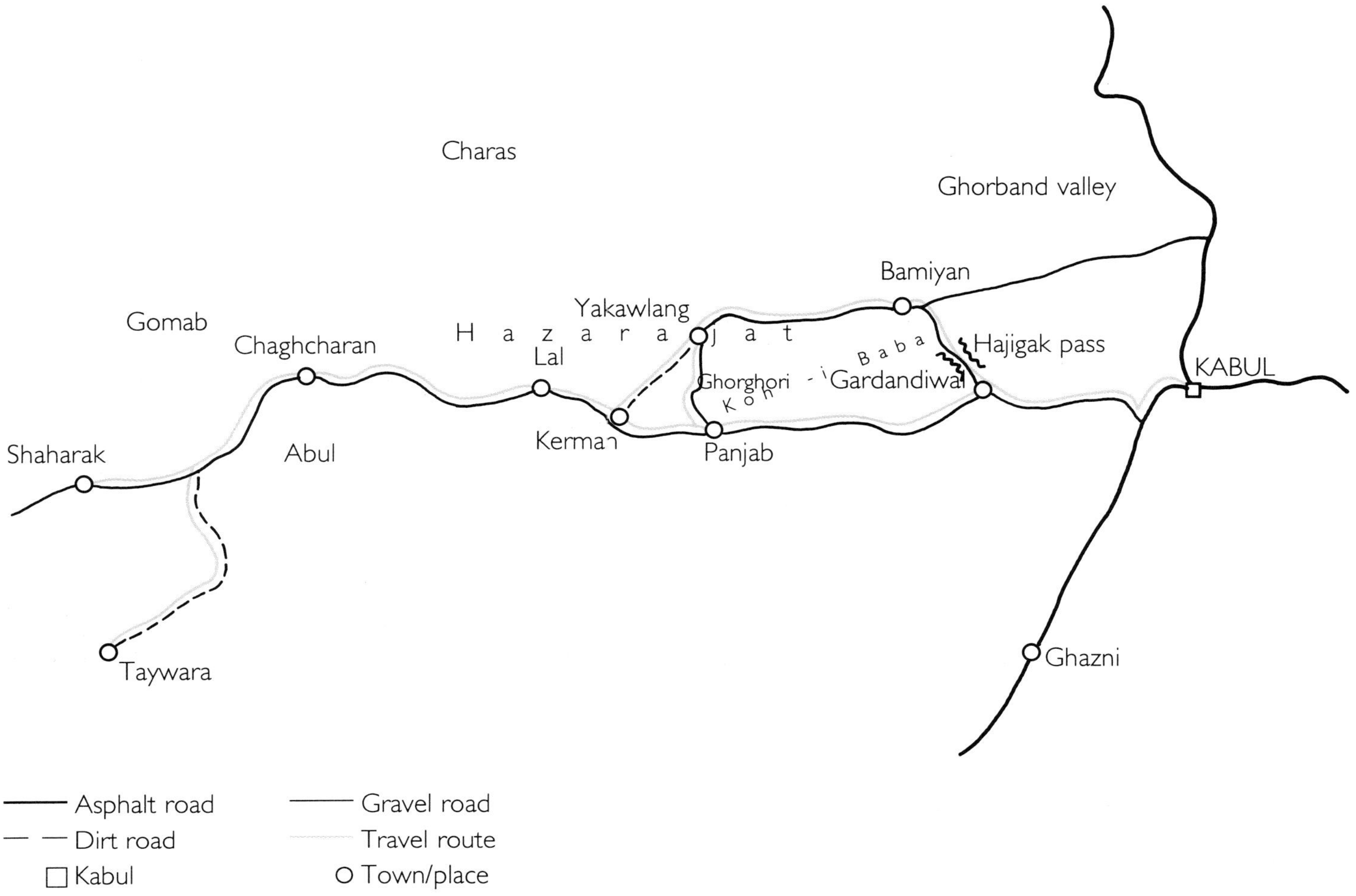

01,8. Travel route of the research tour in July 1975.

To spread out efforts and cover several aspects at the same time the group members were given different tasks. Birthe Frederiksen recorded the structure and functions of the new permanent bazaar, for future comparison with the nomad bazaars, while Asta Olesen, Gorm Pedersen, and Klaus Ferdinand visited the limited number of trading nomads that had reached Chaghcharan and the surrounding areas. Some of the trading nomads had rented shops in the urban bazaar for the summer period while others had erected their tents, or merely spread out blankets on the ground, for a few days on the outskirts of the bazaar, offering secondhand clothes and a modest selection of traditional petty trade objects.

During the first week of July a fairly large illegal camel caravan, mainly loaded with Pakistani textiles, attempted to reach Chaghcharan from East Afghanistan. The authorities intervened and the army stopped the caravan under dramatic circumstances on a mountain pass east of the town. Most of the caravan managed to get away but three arrested trading nomads and 18-19 confiscated camels, loaded with Pakistani textiles, were brought to the police station of Chaghcharan on 7 July. With this incident and our other observations we felt that we were evidently witnessing the collapse of the ancient caravaneering.

Having finished our work in Chaghcharan, Frederiksen and Olesen returned to Kabul by air, while Ferdinand and Pedersen independently travelled west to the urban bazaars of Shaharak and Taywara, in the Aimaq region, both old nomad trading posts. In the remote parts of the province of Chaghcharan and at a distance from the control of the authorities, they were supposed to study what possibly remained of nomad trade, which, indeed, was not much! Via different routes they then moved east through Hazarajat. Ferdinand, among other places, visited Ghorghori, north of Panjab in Day Zangi, where he met some of the Zala Khān Khēl nomads, with whom Pedersen were to take up fieldwork at a later stage. By the end of July the whole group had rejoined in Kabul.

A clear picture emerged from the experience built up during this initial study. The summer trade of the nomads had almost stopped in the central highlands. The very limited number of trading nomads we had met all confessed that they had merely come to the highland to try to recover old debts from former trade activities and they had only brought a number of goods out of habit. The purchasing power and ability to repay debts among the local peasants, following the disastrous economic effects of the failed harvest during the drought of 1971-72, was almost non-existent and competition was high from the new permanent bazaars, which had mushroomed adjacent to the local governmental centres of the central highlands. Finally, lorries had broken the transport monopoly of the nomads, rendering nomad trade in Central Afghanistan non-profitable.

01,9 These Niazi nomad traders have rented a shop in the permanent bazaar of Chaghcharan, thus trying to get a share of the market which no longer favours the traditional nomad trading (K.F., July 1975).

Our initial experience, although providing us with important data for our study, revealed changes so substantial that the original work plans of Ferdinand and Pedersen had to be revised. It no longer seemed pertinent to use an almost non-existent nomad trade as our point of departure. Other obvious questions arose. What had actually happened in Central Afghanistan in recent years? Had the trading adventure of the nomads ceased for good or did it merely reflect a temporary decline? What had happened to nomads who until recently had made a profit out of the trade in Central Afghanistan? What role did the nomads' pastoral economy play? And how did all these matters relate to the general development of Afghan society in a local, regional, and international perspective?

Ferdinand chose to concentrate on documenting caravaneering and the historical development of the nomad trade in Central Afghanistan, including, given the conditions, their demise and disappearance. Due to the fact that it was a fairly recent phenomenon there were still plenty of informants available, mainly elders and leading nomads who had personally been involved in the trade. Ferdinand knew several of these people from previous visits while others were contacted for the first time. Some of them still migrated while others had become settled. A few leaders among the semi-nomadic Aimaq and the sedentary Hazara were consulted. Ferdinand's fieldwork led to a considerably increased and more precise knowledge of the summer bazaars in Central Afghanistan and the circumstances under which caravaneering took place, the latter activity extending as far as the ring road in West and Northwest Afghanistan. The new work revealed, for example, that nomad bazaars were a later phenomenon than what had previously been assumed (Ferdinand 1962: 140). The Kerman bazaar in Hazarajat thus turned out to be from approximately 1919 and not from the turn of the century, while the Gomab and Abul bazaars, which replaced the Kerman bazaar, were from about 1930 as noted earlier. Oral history made it possible to study the structure and function of trade from a wider developmental perspective and to uncover the decisive impact of the policy of the Afghan national government. The trade activities of the nomads had at times been encouraged through reductions in customs duties and at other times delimited by political control and the imposition of taxes, until, as we saw in 1975, they were finally made illegal. Using the important work *Saraj ul-Tawarikh*, written by Faiz Mohammad early in this century upon Amir Habibullah Khān's request, verbal accounts of the arrival and participation of the nomads in the conquest of Hazarajat were supplemented with contemporary sources which, although confirming the role played by the nomads, appointed them a more secondary role (see Mohammad AHQ 1333 (1915); Kakar 1971 and 1979). The historical perspective of Ferdinand's work was pursued in British archives and through studies of publications from British India. It turned out that the British, after having conquered the Punjab in 1849, directly encouraged the trade activities of the Pashtun nomads by exempting them from paying customs when using the Gomal route, which was also an important migration route for pastoral nomads. Northern India soon became an area of expansion for caravaneering Pashtuns, including nomads which had developed from carriers into caravan traders and later on cloth hawkers and money-lenders. They thus expanded the scope of their operations to include major parts of North India stretching into the most remote parts of the Bengal (see Robinson 1935: 23 ff.). This expansion and transformation may be considered a parallel to the later development in Central and North Afghanistan, exhibiting a number of similar circumstances and processes. This particular perspec-

01,10 The livestock market, held at an open stretch of land on the outskirts of Chaghcharan, is all which is left of the old nomad summer bazaars of the highland (G.P., July 1975).

tive forms a central element of Ferdinand's analysis. He looks at the relationship between the state and the nomads in the specific context of the East Afghan region. Ferdinand demonstrates that nomad trade and its expansion were determined by the existence, in both the new summer areas and the winter areas, of "law and order" ensured by state power or a strong regional authority. When it comes to the nomad bazaars it was significant that animal trade formed the backbone of their existence from the beginning to the end. The analysis accentuates the general significance of pastoral nomadism in the historical development of East Afghanistan.

Birthe Frederiksen's work was not affected by the described development of Central Afghanistan. According to the plan Frederiksen would study the changes undergone by the Pashtun group Hazarbuz of the Mohmand, especially changes brought about by their involvement in transport and trade activities. The summer pastures of this group were located in Behsud on the eastern fringes of Hazarajat, while their main trade activities were in North Afghanistan. Ferdinand had earlier characterised Hazarbuz as an age-old transport people specialised in the tea trade and as "A typical example of the modernisation of trading and of the nomad existence...", but at the time there was no detailed information available (Ferdinand 1962: 156).

In 1975 Hazarbuz consisted of approximately 1,100 households with their traditional winter camps located near the Khyber pass in the province of Nangarhar. At the turn of the century they were, apart from being pastoral nomads, involved in caravaneering using the routes from Peshawar via the Khyber pass and Kabul to North Afghanistan and, until the border was closed in the 1920s, to the emirates north of the Amu Darya river, especially Bokhara. Initially they only worked as carriers but since the 1920s they began trading themselves and gradually became one of the most important trading groups to sell tea in Kabul's bazaar. Their main market, however, was in northern Afghanistan where they, following urban development, acquired shops in several town bazaars.

With the trade followed a stratification of Hazarbuz society which for example affected the households' possible involvement in and expansion of trading activities. The major traders also became large landowners, whilst a considerable middle group of Hazarbuz people invested in vineyards north of Kabul as part of directing their activities towards trade and settled life instead of nomadism, a process which had begun in the early 1950s. When studied by Frederiksen, most of the households were settled in and around Kabul, although winter was mostly spent in the traditional Hazarbuz village, Kuz Baru, in Nangarhar. Only 120 to 130 households continued the annual migration between their winter area in Nangarhar and their summer camps on the outskirts of the central highlands entering Hazarajat. Out of these households only 10 to 15 were actual full-time pastoral nomads, the others merely raising animals during the summer period.

Despite the distinct stratification of the Hazarbuz, Frederiksen's study shows that economic ties do exist between the various strata. The purchase and distribution of goods, for example, was governed by internal kinship relations and the traditional migratory households relied on financial support and loans from their more wealthy relatives in order to raise animals. The latter aspect is interpreted as the way in which the kin-group ensured the communal rights to the grazing areas in the highlands of Hazarajat, rights which could once again become important, were they to fail economically.

Gorm Pedersen eventually chose only to work with one particular group of Pashtun nomads, the Zala Khān Khēl of the Taghar, Ahmadzai, comprising 130 households. In 1975 part of this group had become well-established in the bazaar of Kabul, but its traditional winter area was in the border region of Khost in East Afghanistan and it had been using the trade routes through the southern part of the Kurram Agency to Thal east of the border. At an earlier stage Ferdinand had been in contact with this group and was aware of its significance for nomad trade in general and the summer bazaars in Central Afghanistan in particular. A detailed study of Zala Khān Khēl's history, the group's involvement in the nomad trade, and its current socio-economic context seemed to be an obvious case with which to illustrate the general problem concerning tribal society's adaptation to the state and other related matters.

This turned out to be true, the historical development of the Zala Khān Khēl being representative for nomad trading in Central Afghanistan. From a background in pastoral nomadism most Zala Khān Khēl nomads had increasingly become involved in trading during the first half of this century. During the 1950s and 1960s the decline in trade had begun and many Zala Khān Khēl had been forced to seek a means of livelihood different from that in Central Afghanistan. Some bought agricultural land while others invested in lorries and became predominantly settled. The poorest members of the group, the majority, continued their migratory life combined with trading in animals, petty trade, and casual work. With the exception of three households no Zala Khān Khēl were able to continue a life of pastoral nomadism with fulltime animal breeding in 1975-76.

In the 1970s the Zala Khān Khēl were being divided following economic stratification and the options opened by modern Afghanistan. There were new prospects of individual careers offered to some of the young people who had chosen a modern education and a job in the public sector.

The studies and analyses of the historical development and current situation of the Zala Khān Khēl and the Hazarbuz have revealed the specific differences between the two groups and their similarities when it comes to the development and context in general. The latter aspect is partly due to their common position within the Afghan national economy and in part due to the fact that they were both traditionally organised in the patrilinear and segmentary tribal system of the Pashtun. In both cases economic stratification has to a great extent followed the branches of the lineage system. It appears, however, that there are major differences when it comes to the relationship between economic stratification and the traditional sense and norms of community related to position within the lineage relations. The 1,100 Hazarbuz households seem to have maintained a high degree of unity, whereas the social cohesion of the Zala Khān Khēl had become weak and, in spite of the modest number of 130 households, this group had split up into new smaller lineages with overtly independent identities. This problem is analyzed in further detail in the works of Frederiksen and Pedersen.

* * *

The early Danish work concerning Afghan nomads has for years been accompanied by contributions from a wide international circle of scholars although there are only few contributions regarding East Afghan Pashtun nomads. Among these contributions is the fieldwork and socio-

01,11 During the weeks of livestock market the tea house keepers of Chaghcharan move their business to the market place where they set up temporary open-air kitchens to serve the traders and buyers (G.P., July 1975).

01,12 The old town gate of Taywara. Once an important commercial centre for the nomads, today the town is visited only by few nomad traders (G.P., July 1975).

economic analysis of nomadism as part of a regional development project in the province of Paktya by the Austrian ethnologist and social anthropologist Alfred Janata (1972), and the investigations of the French geographer Daniel Balland who, to a certain extent together with the French philologist Charles M. Kieffer, studied Pashtun nomads using Dasht-i Nawur as their summer pasture. Together they published informative material on the impact the drought of 1970-71 had on nomad life (Balland and Kieffer 1979; Balland 1988a). Furthermore, Balland has studied nomads and semi-nomads, their summer and winter areas and migration routes, as well as their demographic fluctuations, in connection with The Nomad Survey from 1978. This survey was mainly designed and initiated by the Belgian UN-demographer A. de Benoist. In addition, Balland has used and analyzed demographic materials from 1880 to 1941 on the East Afghan Pashtun nomads wintering in the Indian subcontinent, material which indicates a general decline in their number. The study was based on the British-Indian *Gazetteers* and *Census Reports*

01,13 After Chaghcharan the Khwazak brothers moved their tent and stock of second-hand clothing to Taywara. Business, however, remained at a low level (G.P., July 1975).

with Balland employing a political perspective under the headings "The anti-nomad policy in British India" and "The fate of Afghan nomadism in Pakistan after Partition". The study has provided us with valuable material and analyses of great relevance to the work with trading nomads (see Balland 1982, 1988b, 1989, and 1991; de Benoist 1980 and 1981).

There are two other works pertinent to our field of enquiry. One is the informative book *Les seigneurs d'Aryana* by Jean and Danielle Bourgeois, a Belgian engineer and his wife, with excellent photographs from their stay and travels in 1968 and 1970 with a group of *contrabandiers* or "nomad smugglers", as they are called by the authors. The group studied consisted of Jalal Khēl, Musa Khēl of the Ahmadzai, migrating between the Dera Ismail Khān District in Pakistan and the western part of Hazarajat (Bourgeois 1972). The other work is the compilatory and well-illustrated book on Pashtun nomads, which includes fine photo-

01,14 Klaus Ferdinand (left), assisted by Rasul Amin from Kabul University (right), interviewing Torab Khān, a 109 years old nomad trader of Mustaf Khēl, Taghar, in his home in Abchakan, Logar (G.P., Aug. 1975).

graphs of trading nomads' tent bazaars in Hazarajat, by the Italian UNESCO expert G. C. C. Gattinara (1970).

German geographers have been very active in Afghanistan, but nomads have rarely been the object of their studies. As to the work on Pashtun nomads in East and Central Afghanistan new, but limited, information on, among other things, trade nomad bazaar camps, is available in Christoph Jentsch's first research report and in his predominantly compilatory work on the nomadism in Afghanistan (Jentsch 1967 and 1973). Erwin Grötzbach's more substantial monograph on Northeast Afghanistan contains a lucid discussion of definitions of nomadism in a classical culture-geographical sense (1972: 98 ff.), as well as basic information concerning the arrival of the nomads to the area between 1880 and 1933 (ibid.: 54 ff.), and their becoming settled there (ibid.: 130 f.). The Laken Khēl of Andar were one of the groups which arrived at an early stage. After the Ghilzai rebellion in the 1880s, they came to the Baghlan

01,15 Mir Ahmad Khān was one of the Zala Khān Khēl whom Klaus Ferdinand had met during previous field-studies in the 1950s and 1960s. Here the two are seen together in Mir Ahmad Khān's winter camp in 1975 (G.P., Jalalabad, Dec. 1975).

area and established summer pastures in the Hindukush near the Khawak pass. In the 1970s they were studied and filmed by the Canadian anthropologist Asen Balikci. This group had been involved in caravan trade between Peshawar and the bazaars along the Amu Darya river valley at an early stage, a fact noted by Balikci but not elaborated in the existing publications (Balikci 1981 and s. a.). Apart from the mentioned works, there is only little and scattered information about the eastern Pashtun nomads to be found in the literature. We should mention Fischer (1970), and Wald (1969) who notes the participation of the nomads in transport and trade of wood in the Khost area. It is finally worth mentioning Rathjens' early article on caravan routes (Rathjens 1962).

There are several anthropological studies of West Afghan Pashtun nomads. Most notable is the German social anthropologist Bernt Glatzer's work on split-up groups of Durrani or durranised nomads in Northwest Afghanistan. They migrate between Badghis and the summer camps towards southwest, north of the river Hari Rud. And Glatzer gives a first-hand account of the connections between these groups and the East Afghan trading nomads and of one of the smaller nomad bazaars with a general reference to Ferdinand's work from 1962 (1977: 65 ff.). In another study he demonstrates that nomadisation and sedentarisation are salient features in Southwest Afghanistan and points out that both processes must be seen in the context of economic expansion in an area with restricted potential for growth within the agricultural and pastoral sectors respectively, expansion therefore, as it were, always taking place in the other sector (Glatzer 1982). Other essential ecological contributions by Glatzer are published as articles (Casimir et al. 1980, Glatzer and Casimir 1983). Reference must also be given to the work of Nancy and Richard Tapper, the British social anthropologists, who have carried out profound studies in the Sar-i Pul region of the Jawzjan province among both settled and nomadic Ishaqzai Durranis with their summer pastures around Chaghcharan. The Tappers' material on East Afghanistan trading nomads has, however, not yet been included in the numerous important works they have published (see N. Tapper 1973, 1977, 1983, and 1991; Tapper and Tapper 1982 and 1988; R. Tapper 1974 and 1983). The latter book, with a well-informed introduction by R. Tapper, contains valuable articles concerning the relationship between Pashtun nomads and the Afghan state (Glatzer and N. Tapper 1983). It is also worth mentioning the work of the American Bahram Tavakolian, who has studied Durrani nomads from Sheikhanzai, Nurzai in West Afghanistan (1979, 1984a, 1984b, and 1984c).

Other recent nomad studies from Afghanistan include the Afghan anthropologist M. Nazif Mohib Shahrani's analyses of adaptive processes among the Kirghiz nomads of northeastern Pamir (1976, 1978, 1979). The Kirghiz have also been the subject of many works by the French philologist and ethnologist Rémy Dor (1975). *Die Kirghisen des Afghanischen Pamirs* he wrote together with the German zoologist Clas M. Naumann, a monograph which contains an excellent bibliography (Dor and Naumann 1978). Finally, Thomas J. Barfield's analysis of transformation processes among Arab nomads in North Afghanistan (1981) shall be mentioned together with the Swiss anthropologist the late Anneliese Stücki's to a large extent unpublished material on the Turkmens (Stucki 1978).

Apart from this regionally specialised work, there is also a number of international contributions to nomad research in general, covering West Africa, the Middle East, and Central Asia. In recent years general nomad research has, as mentioned, focused on changes and transformations brought about by regional and international developments, a trend which is reflected by the actual titles of publications, such as *The Future of Pastoral People* (Galaty et al. 1981), *Nomadismus als Entwicklungsproblem* (Kraus 1969), *The Settlement of Nomads and its Social and Economic Implications* (Naderi 1971), and *When Nomads Settle* (Salzman 1980). Barth's classical study of nomads in South Persia also belongs to this category as it was a result of his participation in 1957-58 in the *Arid Zone Major Project of UNESCO*, the subject of which was resettlement problems (see Barth 1960, 1961, 1962, and 1964 as well as UNESCO 1962).

Our contributions thus belong to a number of recent studies of Afghan nomadism but our specific perspective, commercialisation and change among the East Afghan Pashtun nomads, is only marginally studied by other scholars. In a sense our work supplemented and developed material and information about nomadic trading activities and the related processes of change in the Afghan-Indian (Pakistani) borderland and in East Afghanistan, which was collected in the administrative publications of British India and other written sources, especially Robinson's work *Notes on the Nomad Tribes of Eastern Afghanistan* (1935). However, the approach to these sources as well as the position applied in our field studies have been guided by the wish to contribute to the research tradition which looks at local processes within a larger national and international perspective. We hope that our contributions to the studies of Afghan nomads will add momentum to the ongoing debate concerning nomadism in a historical context and its future development at large.

July 1994

Klaus Ferdinand, Birthe Frederiksen
and Gorm Pedersen

NOTES

1 Inger W. Boesen's study focused on the life of Pakhtun women, while Asger Christensen's was a more general political and cultural study of Pakhtun society. Both studies were carried out in the lower Pech valley, of the Kunar Province (see Boesen 1978-79, 1979, 1980, and 1983; Christensen 1980, 1981, 1982, and 1988). Jan Ovesen's project concerning 'Social organisation, cultural identity and ethno-history among the Pashai' was carried out in Darra-i Nur, the Kunar Province (see Ovesen 1978, 1981, 1982a-b, 1983a-b, and 1984).

2 The main results of the work in Afghanistan 1947-49 are published in: J. Humlum, *La géographie de l'Afghanistan*. Copenhagen 1959; Knud Paludan, *On the Birds of Afghanistan*. Copenhagen 1959; M. Køie and K. H. Rechinger, *Symbolae Afghanicae: Enumeration and Description of the Plants collected by L. Edelberg and M. Køie on "The 3rd Danish Expedition to Central Asia" ... and others in Afghanistan*, I-VI. Copenhagen 1954-65. Furthermore papers on entomology: *The 3rd Danish Expedition to Central Asia: Zoological Results*, 1-34. Videnskabelige Meddelelser fra Dansk naturhistorisk Forening, 112-29. 1950-66.

Other anthropological activities of the 3rd Danish Expedition to Central Asia include the works of the scholar of the History of Religions, Halfdan Siiger, who carried out the following ethnological field studies: among the Kalasha in Chitral, Pakistan in 1948 (see Siiger 1951, 1956, 1974, 1976; Siiger, Castenfeldt, and Fentz 1991 and forthcoming); among the Lepcha in Sikkim, India in 1949-50, a study which resulted in the monograph *The Lepchas*, I-II (Siiger 1967a-b) and other publications (1976 and 1978); among the Boro of Assam, India in 1949-50. A comprehensive outline of these three field studies and the collections made for the National Museum of Denmark is compiled in Siiger 1956.

The cultural and social anthropologist Prince Peter worked during the 3rd Danish Expedition to Central Asia among the Tibetans in Sikkim, India in 1950-56. His collected material from this study is kept at the National Museum of Denmark and is being published under The Carlsberg Foundation's Nomad Research Project by Schuyler Jones (forthcoming).

The physical anthropological investigations of the expedition are published in a single volume, HRH Prince Peter of Greece and Denmark, L. Edelberg, J. Balslev Jørgensen, K. Paludan, and H. Siiger: *Anthropological Researches from The 3rd Danish Expedition to Central Asia*. Copenhagen 1966.

3 The ethnographic collections are categorised using E-numbers, signifying West Asia, at the Department of Ethnography, the National Museum of Denmark. Most of the items are currently deposited at the Department of Ethnography, Moesgaard Museum, Aarhus:

Henning Haslund-Christensen and his assistant M. Karim Nushin: The Kabul bazaar and the Kabul, Kandahar, and Panjab (Hazarajat) regions: E 1378-1473, 1543-1685. Ethnographic Purchases for The 3rd Danish Central Asia Expedition, nos. 1-262, 5 Feb.-3 Sept. 1948, collated by

Henning Haslund-Christensen. Ethnographic Purchases List for The 3rd Danish Central Asia Expedition, Legit: Mohammad Karim, nos. 1-49.

Lennart Edelberg: Nuristan and neighbouring areas: E 768-1059, 2095-9. West Afghanistan, Sistan, Bamiyan, etc.: E 1296-1377. The Kabul area, Hazara, Aimaq, Turkestan: E 1296-1377, 1476-1542 (Nomadic saddle equipment: E 1530-42).

Halfdan Siiger, Kalasha and Chitral: E 1083-1234, 1235-69, 1294-5. The Kabul area: E 1270-93, 2109-32.

Knud Paludan and Hans Madsen: Pashtun camel equipment, Paktya 1959: E 2133-40; and miscellaneous registered under Edelberg et al.

Johannes Humlum: Kandahar area (Pirzada) (12 agricultural implements) for The Geographic Study Collection, Aarhus University (abolished), now at the Department of Ethnography, Aarhus University/Moesgaard Museum.

4 Important ethnographic works or works containing ethnographic information of the time were: Elphinstone's classical masterpiece *An Account of the Kingdom of Caubul, and its Dependencies, in Persia, Tartary, and India; Comprising a View of the Afghaun Nation, and a History of the Dooraunee Monarchy*. 1842 (1st edn. 1815, 2nd edn. I-II 1839); Emil Trinkler: *Afghanistan: Eine landeskundliche Studie auf Grund des vorhandenen Materials und eigener Beobachtung*. Ergänzungsheft Nr. 196 zu "Petermann's Mitteilungen". Gotha 1928; Elisabeth E. Bacon: An Inquiry into the History of the Hazara Mongols of Afghanistan. *Southwestern Journal of Anthropology*, 7, 1951: 230-47; *Deutsche im Hindukusch: Bericht der deutschen Hindukusch Expedition 1935*. Berlin 1937; Gunnar Jarring: *On the Distribution of Turk Tribes in Afghanistan*. Lunds Universitets Årsskrift, NF Avd. 1, Bd. 34, Nr. 2. Lund 1939; Bruno Markowski: *Die materielle Kultur des Kabul Gebietes*. Leipzig 1932; G. Müller: Sprachen und Rassen in Afghanistan. *Zeitschrift für Ethnologie*, 71. Jahrg., 1939: 219 ff.; Georg Morgenstierne: *Report on a Linguistic Mission to Afghanistan*. Instituttet for sammenlignende kulturforskning. Ser. C 1-2. Oslo 1926; N. I. Vavilov and D. D. Bukinich: *Agricultural Afghanistan* (Russian with English summary). Leningrad 1929. There are also a large number of travel accounts, especially from the 19th century.

5 The other main topics of the ethnographic studies were: Nuristan, in continuation of Edelberg's early studies (for references see Lennart Edelberg and Schuyler Jones: *Nuristan*. Graz 1979 and Lennert Edelberg: *Nuristani Buildings*. Jutland Archaeological Society Publications, 18. Aarhus 1984).

Collections of folk music (see Thomas Alvad: The Nuristani Harp. *Man*, 54, 1954: 151-4; Thomas Alvad Liste I: Fortegnelse over Nuristanoptagelser, 1947-49 and 1953-54. Danish Folklore Archives, Copenhagen.

Studies of Hazara and Aimaq (see Ferdinand 1959c and 1964). Collections of ethnographic artefacts during the memorial mission for the Department of Ethnography, National Museum of Denmark, from the Kabul area, Hazara, Aimaq and West Afghanistan, Turkestan, Pashtun nomads, Laghman, and Nuristan: E 1701-2108.

Later collections were made by Lennart Edelberg in the Kabul area and in Nuristan 1964 and 1970 for the Department of Ethnography, Moesgaard Museum (EA 99 1-154) and by Klaus Ferdinand. In 1960 he collected in Laghman, the Kabul area, among Pashtun nomads in Central and West Afghanistan (EA 58 A 1-36, B 1-21, C 1-39, D 1-166, E 1-74, and F 1-4), and in 1965-66 together with Marianne Ferdinand among Pashtun nomads in East Afghanistan and in the Kabul area (EA 127 1-157, EA 127 B 1-45, and C 1-7). Finally, in 1975 he worked together with Flemming Bau, Birthe Frederiksen, Gorm Pedersen, et al. (EA 271 1-186, EA 404 1-10, and EA 405 1-150, EA 407 1-16) and in 1977 together with Birthe Frederiksen, Asta Olesen, and Gorm Pedersen (EA 415 and 464 (tent)).

02,1 Omara Khan, an old Tara Khēl nomad .. (G.P., Laghman, April 1975).

INTRODUCTION II

THE TERM NOMAD - A CLARIFICATION

This book deals with nomadism in Afghanistan, and more specifically with the nomadism and nomad trading as it has been practised by the Zala Khān Khēl, a small segment of the larger Pashtun society. The scientific literature possesses no uniform use of the terms nomad and nomadism. Before proceeding to the description and analysis of Zala Khān Khēl it is therefore necessary to discuss briefly some of the different usages, and to define the content of the terms as used in this work.

The phenomenon which we seek to clarify has often been termed pastoral nomadism, with the aim of characterising its two material aspects, namely animal husbandry (pastoralism) as the economic aspect and the capacious notion of movement (nomadism) as a key feature of this form of livelihood. The two words have practically identical meanings; pastoralism coming from the Latin *pastor:* herdsman, and nomadism from the Greek *nomas:* one who lets cattle graze. The use of the word nomad has changed over time, however, so that in many contexts - both in general use and in the scientific literature - it is associated more broadly with the movement of persons and groups of people. It is still used of the movement of pastoralists, but also widely employed, without any connection with pasture or animal husbandry, of for example hunters and gatherers, certain categories of agriculturalists, itinerant craftsmen, entertainers, service people, boat people, and migrant workers (see for example Briggs 1960, Krader 1959, Lerch 1986, Nemeth 1986, Olesen 1988, Rao 1982a and 1987, Salzman 1972 and 1983, and Sopher 1965). In this book the word nomad will be used in its traditional sense of pastoralists who base their livelihood on migration as a part of the subsistence technique. Nomad(ism) and pastoral nomad(ism) will be used synonymously.

Zala Khān Khēl call themselves *kūchey.* This is a Pashto word derived from Persian *kūchi,* which is used to designate wandering people. In the East Afghan context *kūchey,* however, is only used about pastoral nomads and not about any of the other itinerant groups (Ferdinand 1969a). In this book the term *kūchey* shall be used synonymously with the terms nomad and pastoral nomad. When East Afghan nomads stress that they

02,2 Winter grazing in the East Afghan lowland (G.P., Laghman, April 1975). pp. 50-1

02,3

02,3-4 Nomad boys of Tara Khēl, East Afghanistan (G.P., Laghman, April 1975)

are *kūchey* it has a further dimension. The term is of course used to indicate a particular livelihood, but, when used by the nomads, it also carries the connotation of being free as against settled and bound peasants. The settled farmer, on the other hand, may use the term *kūchey* derogatorily as he often regards the nomads as being unreliable and uncivilised people.

Many attempts have been made to establish a suitable classification or typology of pastoral nomads based on selected aspects of nomadism. Patai focuses on the composition of flocks and herds and talks of the camel breeders as "true nomads" and the sheep-and-goat breeders as "semi-nomads" (Patai 1951: 404-5). Bacon, in a discussion with Patai, uses the same terms, but based on criteria of variations in extent of agriculture and form of dwelling. It is Bacon's view that "True or full nomads are people who dwell the year round in portable dwellings and who practice no agriculture", whereas "Seminomads plant a few crops at their base camp before moving out on the seasonal migration, but they normally live in portable or temporary dwellings the year round" (Bacon 1954: 54). It is not obvious what justifies the focusing on one aspect of nomadism rather than the other, and it appears in general problematical to attempt any classification at all on a foundation of some few selected aspects. Each aspect is relevant, of course, but in the light of the socio-economic complexity in which nomadism is found it is necessary to have a broader approach to the subject. "... the price of simplicity is inaccuracy," says Salzman in rejecting ideal types (Salzman 1971: 185). And he further argues:

> "These ideal types make classification easy, but they oversimplify in three ways: First, too few criteria are taken into account in the conceptualisation. Second, these criteria are assumed to vary together, rather than independently of one another. Third, variation is thought of in terms of discrete breaks and radical differences, rather than gradual curves and subtle shadings."

The variables which Patai and Bacon isolate should be seen in another connection:

> "Given these variables, the important task is to study the dynamics of their relationship to each other, rather than to make a case for the *a priori* analytical primacy for one or two of them." (Salzman 1974: 270)

The necessity of analyzing the relationship between the variables is illustrated by a large quantity of empirical data, including Salzman's own material from Baluch in southeastern Iran (Salzman 1971 and 1972). Salzman talks of "multi-resource nomadism" (1972) and emphasises thereby the economic complexity of the nomad community. The analysis of Zala Khān Khēl will stress this very necessity of understanding the relationship between more factors than those which enter into a simple definition of nomadism.

THE PRESENTATION

The analysis of Zala Khān Khēl will follow a historical sequence from the end of the last century till today. In this period of time Zala Khān Khēl came into being as an identifiable tribal group, but also their livelihood as nomads and nomad traders developed and transformed dramatically in an interaction with the larger tribal and state society of which they are part. In the course of events their nomadism deteriorated to such a degree that it is reasonable to question whether this group of people should be characterised as nomads today. It is at the same time clear that, if we are to understand Zala Khān Khēl's situation today and understand the transformation they have undergone, then we are compelled to start with nomadism as the point of departure for the analysis.

Accordingly, Chapter 3 shall describe the basic conditions of nomadism in general and of Zala Khān Khēl's nomadism and nomad trading in particular. On this background we shall analyse the first processes of change, expansion, and constraints, of which we have knowledge from available sources - up to about the middle of this century. This period can be characterised by the fact that Zala Khān Khēl remains a united and relatively homogeneous group.

Chapter 4 gives a description of the changes which began in the 1950s, the point in time when the socio-economic differentiation of Zala Khān Khēl leads to a geographical division. The various ways in which nomadism comes to an end is for some of the Zala Khān Khēl bound up with the rise of new attractive economic opportunities, while for others it offers but negative economic perspectives. In the end Zala Khān Khēl splits up into rich and poor sections of households, and as such they are visited in 1975-76, the main period of the field-work in Afghanistan.

Chapter 5 gives an account of the situation in 1975-76, of the locations, the activities, and the daily life of the households. The main course of the socio-economic transformation of the Zala Khān Khēl society is traced in Chapter 6, which includes an analysis of the genealogy and of the dynamics of its division. Chapter 7 describes the situation of Zala Khān Khēl as refugees in 1986, based on data collected in Pakistan at that time.

First, however, Chapter 1 shall outline the setting by an introduction to Afghanistan - "the land of the nomads" - its history and people, and Chapter 2 will be an initial presentation of Zala Khān Khēl. This presentation will provide an account of the course of the field-work, of the problems I met, and the ways in which I dealt with these. Apart from contributing to the initial presentation of Zala Khān Khēl, this will furnish an understanding of the analysis and perhaps especially of its limitations. After this, an outline of the history of the Zala Khān Khēl is provided followed by a description of the genealogical system of the Pashtun tribal society and a placing of Zala Khān Khēl in that system.

1,1 Nomad winter camp in the East Afghan lowland (G.P., Laghman, April 1975).

CHAPTER I

THE LAND OF THE NOMADS

Afghanistan is harsh and beautiful with rugged mountains and dry deserts, fertile river valleys and green plains. Land-locked, the country is situated between Iran and Pakistan and with the Central Asian republics of the former Soviet Union to the north. The dominating mountainous core of the Hindukush, the westernmost extension of the Himalayan range, divides the country into four major geographical areas: the central and northeastern highlands and mountains with many permanently snow-covered peaks, the highest being Naochak (7,485 metres); the eastern and southeastern mountains and lowlands bordering the Indus plains of Pakistan; the southern and western steppes and deserts, an extension of the Iranian Plateau; and the northern plains, Afghanistan's share of the vast Central Asian steppe-lands. The climate varies from subtropical to continental temperate and alpine. Situated in the easternmost part of the Mediterranean winter rain area, Afghanistan has generally dry and hot summers while winter is cold with heavy snowfall in many places. The summer monsoon rain of the Indian subcontinent is felt only in the eastern parts of the country.[1]

Afghanistan covers an area of 652,225 square kilometres equivalent almost to the size of Germany and Poland together, or to the size of the state of Texas. The vital need for irrigation limits the cultivated area to only 10 to 12 per cent of the total area. Forest covers less than 3 per cent, while close to half the area is pasture. The remaining is barren soil, mountain, and desert.

The history of Afghanistan reflects great events in the history of Asia - and for that matter in the world history. A crossroad of Asia, Afghanistan is the place where a branch of the ancient Silk Route passed east-west connecting China with the Mediterranean world, and where age-old caravan trails cut north-south over several mountain passes linking the commercial centres of Central Asia with the Indian sub-continent.

For millennia the area has been a melting pot with political and cultural influence floating in from all corners. Alexander the Great left a mark on the area when he passed through with his army in the fourth century BC. Buddhism flourished in Afghanistan in the first centuries AD before this religion spread towards East Asia. Islam reached Afghanistan in the mid-seventh century, and has remained a dominating factor in the life here till today. Chinghiz Khān swept through the country in the beginning of the thirteenth century leaving behind him not only massive destruction but, according to legend, also men, who are said to be the

1.2 Shrines marked with flags and banners are found all over Afghanistan; they are places of worship and often believed to hold spiritual power capable of, for instance, curing illness or help childless women to become pregnant (G.P., Laghman, April 1975).

ancestors of the Mongol Hazara people of Central Afghanistan. Turco-Mongolian, Persian, and Moghul empires fought over and controlled parts of the area in the centuries after Chinghiz Khān.

It was not until the eighteenth century that Afghanistan came into being in a shape resembling the one we know today. In the power vacuum between the Moghul Empire of India and the Safavid Empire of Persia, Pashtun[2] tribes living in the southern and western parts of what is present-day Afghanistan gathered to form their own political union. They elected Ahmad Shah Durrani, an ex-officer of the Safavid army, as king in Kandahar in the year 1747.

The independence was to be of a short duration, however. Having suffered from centuries of Asian despotism, Afghanistan was soon to face a period of European imperialism. In the nineteenth century Tsarist Russia expanded southwards into Central Asia, and the British began to move west through India. Afghanistan was squeezed in this Great Game of the imperial powers, and was invaded twice by British armies (First and Second Anglo-Afghan Wars of 1839-42 and 1878-80) in a British attempt to counterbalance what they saw as Afghan and Russian threats to the British interests in India. The net result was that Britain gained control over Afghan relations with other countries.

Modern Afghanistan began to take shape during the reign of Amir Abdur Rahman Khān (1880-1901). Britain and Russia drew the frontiers of the country - the eastern towards India, known as the Durand Line (named after the British negotiating delegation's leader, the Secretary for India Sir Mortimer Durand), in 1893 and the northern towards Russian controlled Central Asia in 1895. Afghanistan became a buffer-state between the two empires. Based on the power of a standing army the Amir began a moderistion of the state apparatus and a strengthening of political control. His means were often harsh for which reason he acquired the name of The Iron Amir. He launched internal colonial wars against several population groups who had traditionally resisted subjection by the central powers of Kabul. Thus the central highland of Hazarajat, the homeland of the Hazara people, was conquered in 1892 after which the Amir distributed land in the area to Pashtuns. Among these were many nomads, who thus acquired fertile pastures in an area previously inaccessible to them. The Amir also broke the tribal power of the Pashtuns, and he exiled individuals and tribal sections or moved them forcibly to North and North-West Afghanistan. Resettling Pashtuns in the northern parts

1,3 . Important dates in the history of Afghanistan

1747	The Pashtun tribes gathered and Ahmad Shah Durrani is elected paramount chief. Afghanistan is being formed as a state.
1838-42	1. Anglo-Afghan war.
1849	British-Indian troops conquer Punjab and move forward to the Suleman mountains.
1878-80	2. Anglo-Afghan war.
1880-1901	Amir Abdur Rahman Khān, the 'Iron Amir', reigns over Afghanistan and embarks on a modernisation through strengthening the state apparatus and through internal colonisation.
1892	Hazarajat is conquered and subordinated central government.
1893	The frontier with British India is fixed.
1895	The frontier with Russia is fixed.
1919	3. Anglo-Afghan war.
1947	Partition: Pakistan is created after British withdrawal from British India.
1961-63	The Pashtunistan conflict with Pakistan.
1973	Military coup. Daoud Khān dethrones King Zahir Shah and declares Afghanistan a republic with himself as president.
1978	Military coup on 27. April. PDPA overthrows Daoud and takes power in the Saur revolution. Resistance starts and the first Afghans flee.
1979	In December the Soviet Union invade Afghanistan with about 100,000 men.
1989	Soviet troops withdraw from Afghanistan in February - in accordance with international agreement. PDPA stays in power in Kabul and fighting continues.
1992	In April Kabul falls to the *mujāhedin* and a coalision government is installed.

1,4 The lowland of the Alishang valley (G.P., Laghman, April 1975).

of the country was in itself a part of the Amir's colonisation of those areas.

In 1919 the king, Amanullah Khān (1919-29), demanded full sovereignty of his country. Confronted with British hesitations, he launched attacks on a British border garrison. This Third Anglo-Afghan War lasted only a month. Being still in the aftermath of the First World War, the British agreed to sign a treaty by which Afghanistan gained control of her own foreign affairs and did finally become independent of colonial powers. Even though Afghanistan never was a colony as such, it is true to say that the country was shaped by the European colonialism in Asia.

When Britain withdrew from India in 1947 the former empire was divided into an independent India (predominantly Hindu) and an independent Pakistan (predominantly Muslim). This event, known as Partition, gave Af-

1,5 Only 10 to 12 per cent of the surface of Afghanistan is cultivated, water for irrigation usually being the limiting factor. Where water is available fields are carefully organised. The patchwork-like layout of this vegetable field secures that water is led to each and every plant (G.P., Bamiyan, May 1976).

ghanistan a new neighbour to the east. The relations between Afghanistan and Pakistan soon became inflamed due to the unsolved Pashtunistan issue (see more below) - a disagreement about the tribal territories separated from Afghanistan by the Durand Line cerated by the British. Conflict culminated in 1961-63 when Pakistan asserted its frontier so restrictively that it in practice was closed. Being landlocked, as already mentioned, Afghanistan depends heavily on transit facilities through Pakistan to the sea-port of Karachi. Afghan import and export therefore suffered severely from the conflict - as did many Afghan nomads, who could no longer pursue age-old patterns of grazing their flocks in the Indus lowlands in Pakistan. The political tension cooled down when the Afghan prime minister, Daoud Khān, was removed from his post in 1963.

1,6 The tea house is an omnipresent part of Afghan everyday life. In a good tea house boiling water is always ready in the brass samovars (G.P., Laghman, April 1975).

Daoud Khān reappeared, however, at the political scene. In 1973 he led a successful military coup against King Zahir Shah, supported by one part of the factionalised leftist People's Democratic Party of Afghanistan, PDPA, and declared Afghanistan a republic. But Daoud Khān's regime lasted only five years. Soon after he came to power he began to ouster the leftist elements of his government. The factions of PDPA reunited and on 27 April 1978 they toppled Daoud Khān in yet another military coup, known as the Saur revolution (after the Afghan month in which it occurred).

This event marked the beginning of what has now been more than a decade of war and misery in Afghanistan. Internal rivalry and factionalism soon reappeared in the PDPA. In support of the fragile revolution, and no doubt also to pursue its own geo-political interests, the Soviet Union invaded Afghanistan in De-

1,7 Tea is served (G.P., Taywara, July 1995).

cember 1979. What began as small local uprisings against the Kabul regime gradually turned into a proper resistance movement with many factions, known as the *mujāhedin*. Under the common banner of Islam they took up armed fighting against the Soviet backed regime and against communism. Meanwhile, the war drove more than five million Afghans into exile in neighbouring Iran and Pakistan and dislocated another two million as internal refugees.

In February 1989 the Soviet Union withdrew the last of its troops from Afghanistan. It was the general opinion among exile Afghans that the Kabul regime, being without the direct Soviet military support, soon after would have to surrender to the *mujāhedin*. But PDPA remained in power in Kabul and fighting continued. Only in April 1992 PDPA was finally defeated in Kabul by the joint military forces of *mujāhedin* and a former government-loyal militia which

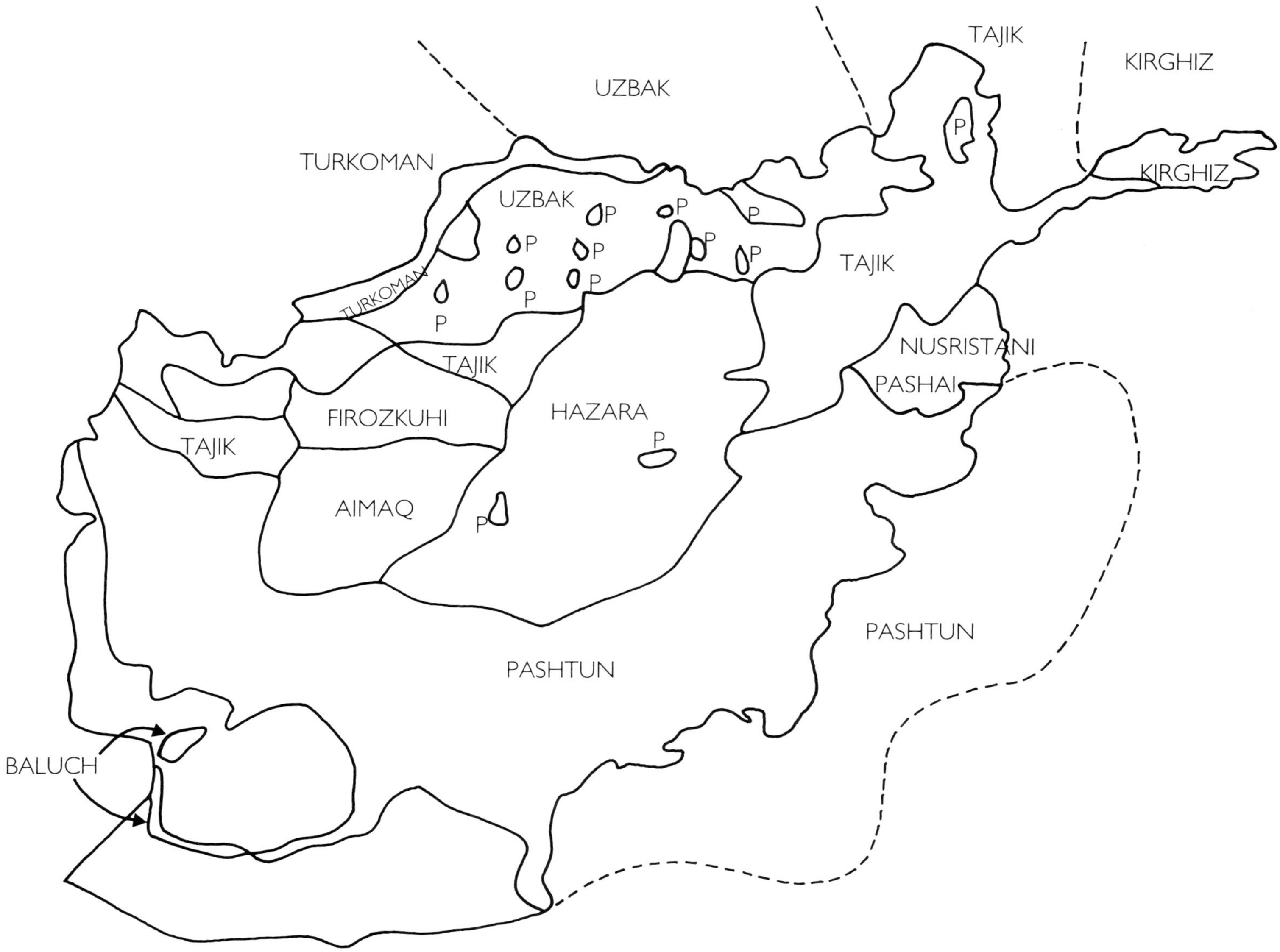

1,9 Distribution of ethnic groups in Afghanistan. The map indicates only roughly the locations of the major ethnic groups. Note that the homeland of many of the major groups stretches into the neighbouring countries to all sides. More details on ethnic distribution can be found in Orywal 1983 (TAVO map of ethnic groups of Afghanistan) and 1986. For an interesting comparison reference shall also be made to the TAVO map of languages and dialects of Afghanistan (Behnstedt and Kieffer 1984).

1,8 Tea is prepared for the traveller at a roadside tea house (G..P, Khost, June 1992).

1,11 Armoured vehicles and other heavy military equipment conquered from Soviet and government forces are now used by local leaders and warlords in the rivalry for power (G.P., Khost, June 1992).

1,10 The British had several confrontations with the Pashtun tribesmen, and the outcome was not always in favour of the Imperial Army. The Pashtuns had the advantage of guerilla warfare, as they were lightly armed, mobile, and knowing their fastness in the rugged mountains of their homeland.

1,12 Agriculture is dominated by traditional techniques. Here oxen are used for threshing (G.P., Samangan 1978).

had changed side in the power struggle. Since then Afghanistan has been ruled by a coalition of former exile parties. This, however, has not yet brought fighting to a halt. With the common enemy defeated, rivalry and a fight for the central power among the political parties and the warlords intensified.

The people of Afghanistan, who numbered about 15 million in the late 1970s, is a complex of ethnic groups with an equivalent number of languages[3]. The largest single group is the Pashtun with about seven million people; second comes the Tajik with about 3.6 million. The Hazara and the Chahar Aimaq each numbers about one million, and the Farsiwan about 0.6 million. All these groups speak Iranian languages - some of them with Turkish loan words. Representing Central Asian cultures, the Uzbak, numbering about one million, and the Turkoman, with about 0.4 million people, speak Turkish languages. The rest of the population is made up of many smaller groups such as Brahui, Baluch, Nuristani, Arab, Kirghiz, Qizilbash, Hindus, Sikhs, and Jews, who speak different Iranian, Turkish, and Dravidian languages and dialects. The approximate distribution of the groups in Afghanistan is shown in the map, *Fig. 1,9.*

As a result of last century's colonial frontiers, most ethnic groups of Afghanistan are found also in the neighbouring countries. As a matter of fact, many of them, such as the Turkic peoples to the north and the Baluch to the south, constitute sections of larger ethnic groups with social and cultural strongholds outside Afghanistan. The Pashtuns, the largest ethnic group of Afghanistan, have their homeland divided between Afghanistan and Pakistan. About seven million Pashtuns live in Afghanistan and an equal number in Pakistan. It is an on-going debate among the Pashtuns whether the Afghan Pashtun-area or the Pakistani Pashtun-area is their proper homeland. This issue was crucial to the border conflict of the 1960s, also known as the Pashtunistan conflict, i.e. the conflict about "the Land of the Pashtuns". Afghanistan claimed all areas inhabited by Pashtuns to be naturally and traditionally a part of Afghanistan - as they had been before the British colonial advance.

Since the election of Ahmad Shah Durrani in 1747, all rulers of Afghanistan, amirs, kings, and presidents, have been Pashtuns. The language of administration, commerce, education, and literature has, however, been Persian, the *lingua franca* of the area. The Afghan version of Persian was officially named Dari (literally "language of the court") in the Constitution of 1964. However, among common people Persian is still called Farsi (i.e. Persian), and people with Farsi as their mother tongue are referred to as Farsiwan.

The Pashtuns are commonly referred to by the Persian term Afghans. Afghanistan, i.e. the Land of the Afghans, thus actually means the land of the Pashtuns. Many non-Pashtun people in Afghanistan still use the term Afghan to designate Pashtun, whereas they refer to themselves be it as Uzbak or Hazara. Only in recent history has it been attempted to furnish a common identity as citizens of the state of Afghanistan against ethnic and tribal identities by promoting the term Afghan as a common designation for all citizens of Afghanistan regardless of their ethnic affiliations.

The economy of Afghanistan is typically one of a developing country; it is largely based on agriculture and animal husbandry which engage about 60 per cent of the workforce and contribute two-third of the Gross National Product. The village- and town-bazaars play an important economic role as trading centres for agricultural products and as centres for craft production. Traditional handicrafts are widespread, highly developed, and often very refined. Most craftsmen earn a living within the agricultural sector by producing agricultural tools; others are known to the world as makers of the fine Afghan carpets, which together with dried fruit and nuts, wool and hides, are major export articles. The industry is largely based on agricultural and pastoral products, but it is little developed and occupies only a few per cent of the total workforce. Also mining is of minor significance; deposits are known but access to these is for the most part too difficult to make mining profitable. One exception is natural gas which is found in North Afghanistan and make up the most important export article.

I,13 A Khawazak Pashtun nomad trader (G.P., Chaghcharan, July 1975).

1,14 A Matani Pashtun nomad trader (G.P., Chaghcharan, July 1975).

1,15 A young Uzbak labourer (G.P., Samangan, 1978).

1,16 A Tajik farmer (G.P., Samangan, 1978).

I,17 Old Stanizai Pashtun nomad (GP, Guldarah, May 1996).

1,18 Stanizai Pashtun nomad with his child (GP, Guldarah, May 1996).

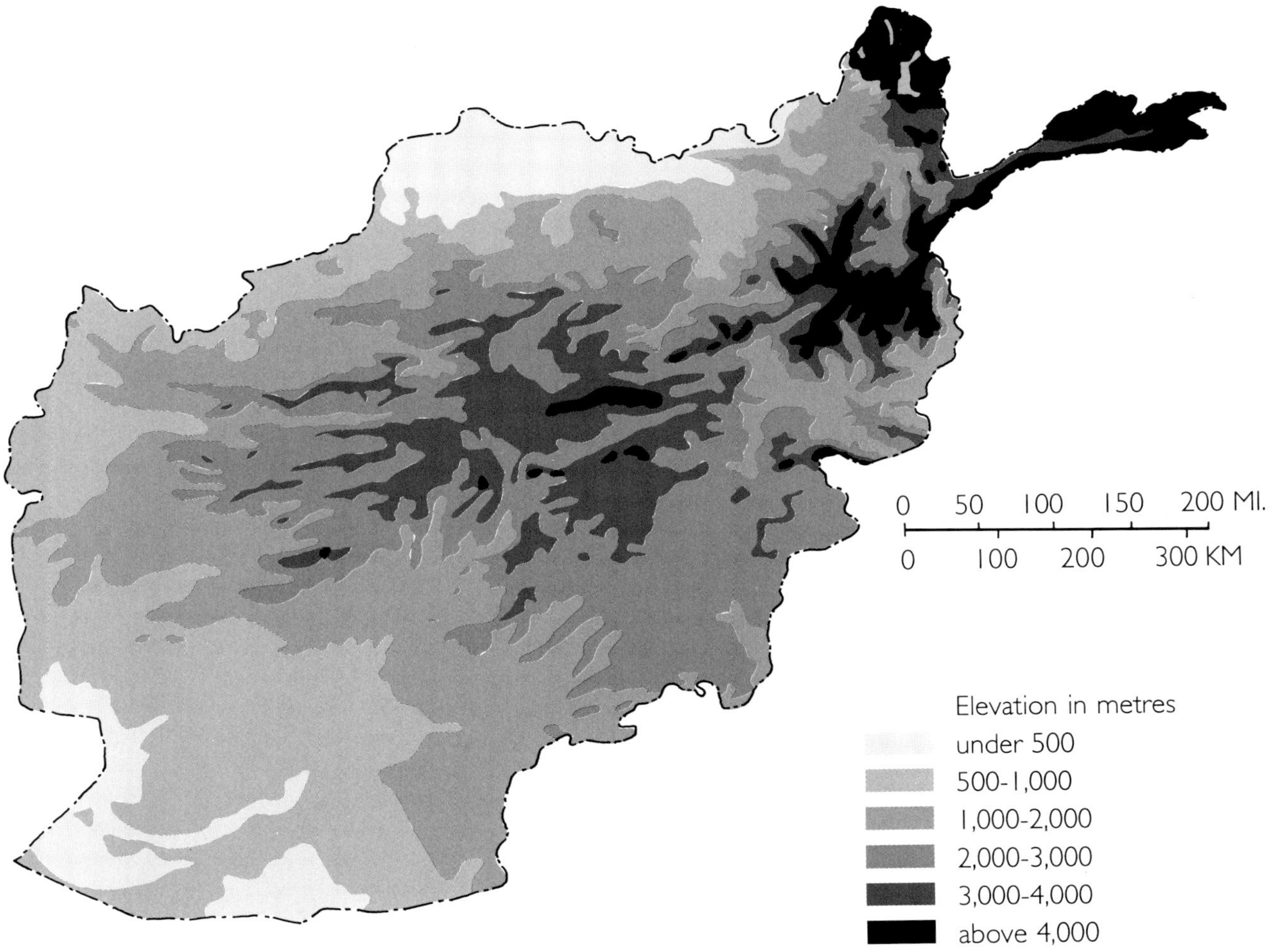

1,19 Relief of Afghanistan.

NOMADISM

Pastoral nomadism, based primarily on the utilisation of sheep, goats, and camels, is a striking feature of the Afghan economy, and throughout history the country has had a relatively large nomadic population. Pastoral nomadism as a form of subsistence and a way of life has left its mark on Afghanistan, and the nomad population has played a considerable role in its political and economic development. We have, however, no precise picture of the nature and extent of nomadism through the course of Afghanistan's history, but, based on general knowledge of the West Asian area, we may assume that the size of the nomadic

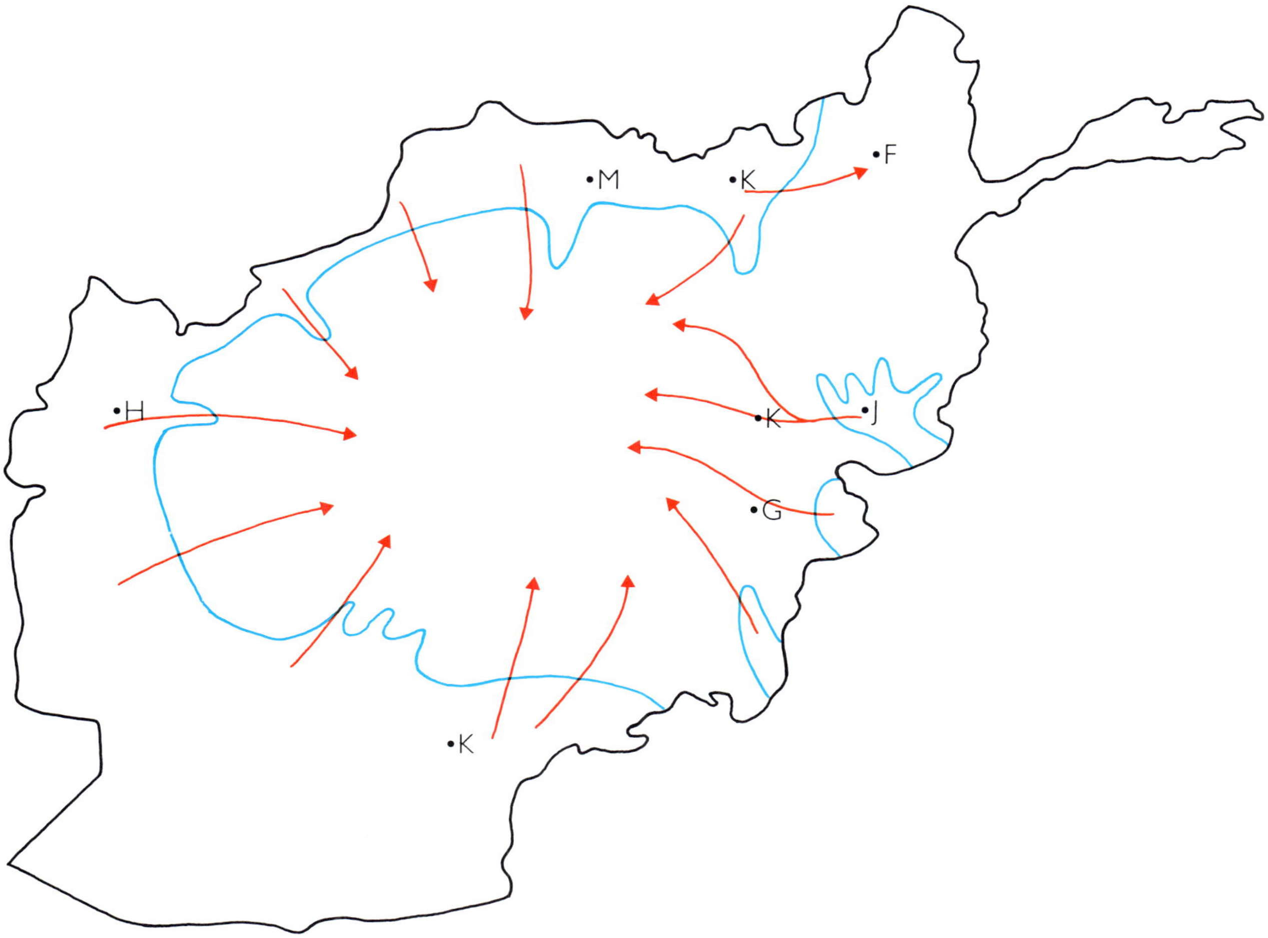

1,20 Nomadic movements. Compared with the relief of Afghanistan (*Fig. 1,19*) it will appear that the nomads' summer pastures are located at an altitude above 1,000 metres, the highest being as far up as 3,500 metres above sealevel. The map only shows the general direction of nomadic movement. For more details of these movements reference is made to the map in Jentsch 1973 and to Balland's very detailed and comprehensive map (of 1989).

population has fluctuated, depending on factors such as the ratio between population and resources, and the political situation.

Only from the beginning of the 19th century does information start to flow to the West. Mountstuart Elphinstone, a British envoy to the royal Afghan winter residence in Peshawar in 1808-09, is among the first to give us substantial insight into Afghan society. In *An Account of the Kingdom of Caubul* (1815) he describes in general terms the Afghan nomadism and the various nomad tribes. Of particular interest in the present context are his notes on the process of sedentarisation, which he registered among some of the East Afghan Pashtun nomads. Among the early sources are also the

1,21 The black goat's hair tent of the East Afghan Ghilzai-type. Tara Khēl, Ahmadzai, summer camp at Dasht-i Desabs near Kabul (G.P., Sept. 1975).

narratives by the British servicemen Alexander Burnes and Charles Masson, who give scattered accounts of nomad tribes, migration routes, and pasture areas of Afghanistan (Burnes 1834, Masson 1842).

From the end of the last century more source material is available to illustrate the conditions of nomadism in Afghanistan. This material derives especially from the British imperial administration in India, which regularly gathered information on the internal conditions in Afghanistan and subjected Afghan nomads to the rule of the British crown when they spent the winters on their grazing grounds in British territory. It comprises a large quantity of published travel accounts, memoirs, and reports, in addition to comprehensive archives, which are now accessible at the India Office Library and Records in London. Also the National Archives of India in Delhi and smaller archives in Pakistan, notably in Peshawar and Lahore, contain interesting source material concerning the Imperial times.

1,22 The black goat's hair tents of the western Durrani Pashtuns are generally larger than those of the eastern Ghilzai Pashtuns. Timuri nomad camp (G.P., Herat, April 1976).

One of these sources, J. A. Robinson's *Notes on the Nomad Tribes of Eastern Afghanistan* (1935), proves crucial to the study of East Afghan nomadism. In 1932-34 Robinson undertook a detailed investigation among Afghan Pashtun nomads wintering on British-Indian territory, and tribe by tribe, section by section, he gives a general account on their numbers, economic activities, migration routes, camping localities, and their genealogy. Originally confidential and restricted, Robinson's work has now become a standard reference source on the topic.

Contrary to most other countries with pastoral nomads, Afghanistan has within the present century seen a period with marked expansion of nomadism. Caused by a unique merging of interests of the nomads and the Afghan state (which shall be discussed in details later in the book) this expansion began in the 1890s and went on for about four decades. Since the 1940s and 1950s Afghan nomadism as a whole has not

1,22 A dome-shaped reed construction is used as winter dwelling among Arab nomads wintering on the banks of the Amu Darya river in northern Afghanistan (G.P., Imam Sahib, March 1976).

expanded, more likely the opposite, but still within the last few decades processes of nomadisation, i.e. of settled people turning to nomadism, have been reported (Glatzer 1982).

The image of Afghanistan being "the land of the nomads" still holds value. Based on the unpublished data of the 1978 Afghan Nomad Survey Balland writes that out of 325 administrative units of Afghanistan only 37 are reported not to have nomadic populations permanently or temporarily, and those 37 units only cover 8 per cent of the country's surface. Balland adds, however: "Incidentally, such a large spatial diffusion of nomads all over Afghanistan may well account for their frequent overestimation." (Balland 1988a: 266)

The number of nomads in Afghanistan has never been known with much accuracy, since statistical information has been limited in both quantity and reliability. For the 1960s and 1970s

1,23 At their fixed winter quarters some nomads live in permanent houses to which they return year after year (G.P., Laghman, April 1975).

general estimates give the figure of about 2 million. However, the estimates have varied from only 1 million (Janata 1975) to 2.5 million (UN 1979 statistics).[4]

The ethnic complexity of Afghanistan is reflected in its nomadism. Nomads are found among a range of ethnic groups such as Baluch, Aimaq, Turkoman, Kirghiz, Arab and, previously, Uzbak and some northern Hazara and Tajiks. By far the greatest part of the nomads are Pashtuns, who thus belong to the largest and dominating ethnic group in Afghanistan. It is estimated that 90 per cent of all Afghan nomads are Pashtun (Jentsch 1973).

Most of the nomads base their livelihood on Afghanistan's extreme differences in altitude and the seasonal climatic variations. Upland pastures, generally above the altitude of 1,000 metres, are exploited in the summer and lowland pastures in the winter. This necessitates two

1,24 Kharoti Pashtun men in front of their black goat's hair tent. This particular tent was later acquired by the author for the ethnographic collections of Moesgaard Museum (G.P., Jalalabad, March 1976).

major migrations annually, which follow traditional routes with little variation from year to year. The migrations vary from a few kilometres for some up to 400 to 500 kilometres in each direction for others (see maps *Fig. 1,19* and *Fig. 1,20*).

Being people on the move the nomads use portable dwellings. Nomad tents of different forms are known in Afghanistan; the two major types are the circular *yurt*, made of felt and used mostly by people of central and northern Afghanistan influenced by Central Asian Turkish cultures, and the rectangular black tent, made of home-spun woven goat's hair and used predominantly by the Pashtuns, but also by Baluch and some other ethnic groups of Afghanistan. Many nomads now make use of modern-type

1,25 After shearing, the wool of each single sheep is twisted into a tight bundle for easy storing and transport (G.P., Herat, April 1976).

cotton canvas tents during the migrations. These tents are easier to handle when shelter has to be set up and taken down daily, but the traditional, more spacious and comfortable types are preferred when the nomads are more stationary. Most nomads return to the same sites for winter camping year after year, and where there is little need for moving the flocks some nomads live in houses or huts or in constructions combining a permanent stone wall with a black tent roofing.[5] The animal flocks mostly consist of sheep and goats while some also have cows. One-humped camels (dromedaries), donkeys, mules, and occasionally horses are used as transport animals. In the northeastern corner of the country also the two-humped Bactrian camel is used.

I,26 -7 Nomad women of Tara Khēl at a wedding celebration (A.O., Dasht-i Desabs near Kabul, Sept. 1975).

1,28 The flocks of an Arab nomad camp are gathered for shearing (G.P., Herat, April 1976).

NOTES

1 The factual information for the general presentation of Afghanistan in this section has been derived predominantly from Louis Dupree's comprehensive book *Afghanistan* (1980). Other sources have been Balland 1985, Barfield 1978 and 1981, Dupree 1978, Dupree and Albert 1973, Encyclopḥdia Britannica 1992, Encyclopḥdia Iranica 1985, Ferdinand 1962, Kakar 1971, Orywal 1986, N. Tapper 1973 and 1983, and UN and World Bank statistics.

2 The terms Pashtun (the people) and Pashto (the language) are the English (and Persian) standardised versions. Depending on dialect the people call themselves Pakhtun (in Kabul and eastern parts of the country) or Pashtun (in southern parts of the country, around Kandahar). The language, which belongs to the Indo-European family, is locally called Pakhto (the 'hard' dialects) and Pashto (the 'soft' dialects), respectively. It may be added that in British-Indian terminology the Pashtuns are refereed to as Pathans.

3 The UN 1979 statistics give the figure 15.55 millions as the total population of Afghanistan (*Demographic Yearbook*. UN 1982). Since then the land has been ravaged by war and the size of the population today can only be estimated with great uncertainty. During the 1980s the government in Kabul published statistics which show a steadily rising population. The 1985 figure thus shows 18.136 millions (*Population and Vital Statistics Report*. Statistical Papers Series A, vol. 39/1. UN 1987) and by mid-1991 the figure was 20.979 millions (*World Development Report*. World Bank 1993). How the 5 million and more Afghans who in those years were living in exile were regarded is not stated. Sources among Afghans in exile reported in 1986 that almost one million Afghans had lost their lives in Afghan prisons or as a result of military action since 1978.

4 During the preparations for the 1978 Afghan Nomad Survey defining a nomad appeared to be a problem. Focusing on tent-dwellings, the risk was to count more people than the actual pastoral nomads. The Survey was furthermore rendered difficult by the instability following the revolution in 1978. The results of the Survey have not yet been published, and in the UN statistics' 1979 figures there is no separate information on nomads. However, two different UN publications give the following information on the 1979 population of Afghanistan: 15.55 million total (*Demographic Yearbook*. UN 1982) and 13.05 million exclusive of nomads (*Population and Vital Statistics Report*. Statistical Papers Series A, 36/4. UN 1984). We should be able to calculate from these two figures that the nomad population of Afghanistan is about 2.5 million, but the background for the origin of this figure makes it advisable to continue to allow for a considerable margin of error in statistical information from Afghanistan.

5 For a closer study of tent types of the nomads, see Andrews (forthcoming), Faegre 1979, Feilberg 1944, Ferdinand 1959a, 1960, 1964, and (forthcoming, b).

CHAPTER 2

ZALA KHĀN KHĒL

STUDYING THE ZALA KHĀN KHĒL

Zala Khān Khēl is one of the nomad groups who used to undertake the long spring and autumn migrations between the Indus lowland in Pakistan and the central highland of Afghanistan. By the mid-1970s, the time when I started my field-work in Afghanistan, only few written sources had made any reference to this tiny segment of the Pashtuns. J. A. Robinson gathered information on Zala Khān Khēl during his research in 1932-34 and briefly notes their existence and place in the Pashtun tribal structure (Robinson 1935). Another source is K. Ferdinand who from the studies in 1953-55 and 1960 describes meeting individuals who are Zala Khān Khēl (Ferdinand 1962 and 1978b). Ferdinand never studied Zala Khān Khēl, but some of his informants on nomad trade and nomad summer bazaars in the central highland of Afghanistan were in fact from this group, even though he speaks of them as Gardez Khēl of Taghar (the reason for which shall be given later in this chapter). Thus, my knowledge of Zala Khān Khēl was in the beginning of my stay with them limited to a few historical fragments, and I knew little of their present-day situation, way of life, and society. I was informed that some Zala Khān Khēl households had settled recently as wealthy lorry-owners close to Kabul, and it was through contacts to these households that my field-work among Zala Khān Khēl started.[1]

I knew of the importance of the lineage system among Pashtuns and this led me to believe that a genealogical survey could give me data which I could use to get an introduction to Zala Khān Khēl and an outline of the genealogical connections between my future informants. In consideration of the importance of the segmentary descent system for the conduct of its members I also expected that a genealogical survey would in itself be able to contribute to the study of Zala Khān Khēl's history and socio-economic development and to point the way to what information I should seek and where I could find it. We are not talking of a kinship study as such, but rather of the simple establishment of a diagram to which I could turn in various ways in the course of my collection of data and my work on analysis.

My expectations concerning the usefulness of a genealogical survey turned out to be justified - though in a way that I had not expected, a way which contained certain problems. As will appear, circumstances decreed that my work with genealogy should be the decisive instrument throughout the field-work. With hindsight I can see that I passed through three phases in this work: the first phase, where I believed that collecting genealogical data was to be a preliminary sideline - just to get started; the second phase, where it turned out that I could not get any information on anything other than genealogy - and therefore concentrated on this field; and the third phase, where the genealogical collection became a means which made it possible for me to acquire data of the type that I was really looking for. The three phases will be described in some detail, together with some of the problems met working with all three of them.

I had been introduced quite briefly to some "elders" of the prosperous Zala Khān Khēl households, who had settled as lorry-owners in Qala-i Niazbeg, but my first real contacts were with a couple of young men from these households whom I and my Afghan counterpart used to meet for some time at a *tea house* in the western Kabul suburb Kote Sangi, where many Zala Khān Khēl had their lorries stationed in a *serāy* i.e. within a closed courtyard. After the introductory courtesies I began to speak of my interest in Zala Khān Khēl's history and livelihood, and expected that this interest would be both understood and accepted. I would like to meet as many of their relatives as possible and learn how they lived and so on, I explained.

However, the young men were not very anxious to talk about themselves and their way of life. They would much rather talk about Europe, as they had plans of earning big money as emigrant workers there. The reciprocity in our exchange of information rapidly became very imbalanced - in their favour. I therefore began cautiously to question them on genealogy. For, apart from my desire to get an outline of the Zala Khān Khēl genealogy, I thought that it might cause my informants to talk a little more about the things that interested me.

2,1 Hajjī Gulbat (right), a man of thorough genealogical knowledge, with a relative in the narrow alley of Bazaar-i Omaid (G.P., Kabul, May 1976).

It only worked to a very limited degree. For it turned out that my young informants constantly avoided all talk of present day conditions, and that their knowledge of Zala Khān Khēl's history and genealogy was, for Afghans, decidedly limited. Moreover, all conversation about the life of the Zala Khān Khēl women was completely barred. "They are of no importance", the young men said, with some embarrassment at having been asked about them at all. This attitude to providing information about women was met with in all informants throughout the field-work.

Talking to these young men thus failed to give an opening. I therefore tried with some of the Zala Khān Khēl men who frequented the *serāy* to look after their transport business, but with little better results. The conversations were always very brief, and they excused themselves on the pretext of various jobs that they had to do. The genealogical survey still covered nothing more than a handful of households.

There is among Afghans a widespread reserve towards strangers, and a reluctance to give information concerning themselves. It is rooted partly in the historical fact that Afghanistan has followed a policy of isolation based on its role as buffer state between the empires of British India and Tsarist Russia, partly in the desire of the individual groups to keep themselves as independent as possible of the central government and, in consequence of this, to avoid giving information which in any imaginable way could reach the authorities and perhaps be used as a basis for taxation, conscription to the army, or other unpleasantness.

The lorry-owners resisted my attempts to get information on other issues, but they did acknowledge my interest in genealogy, and they found that permissible enough - provided that women were left out of the picture. They told me that, since I so much wanted to get to know their genealogy, there was no point in my making do with the small bits that they could give me. Instead they would introduce me to a relative of theirs who had a good knowledge of that sort of thing. And this relative was not one of the prosperous lorry-owners but a more ordinary cloth-tradesman with a stall in Bazaar-i Omaid in the old bazaar of Kabul - and thus far away from the lorry *serāy*. So I was removed from the danger area, and thus began the second phase of my field inquiry.

The 50-year old cloth-tradesman, Hajjī Gulbat, had, truly enough, a wide knowledge of Zala Khān Khēl's genealogy. While I had previously only acquired information from young men about the current members of their own and closely related households, Hajjī Gulbat would give me a considerable amount of impressive genealogical data. He was able to explain family connections between a large number of households and outline the descent some sixteen generations back in time. Only when it came to names of people in the youngest generations living elsewhere in the country it began to be difficult for him. Here and there Hajjī Gulbat would himself draw attention to uncertainty with regard to a name or a placing, and he pointed to disagreements among the older people concerning details in the genealogical framework - as for instance with a group of detached relatives settled in Khoja Khān in the province of Baghlan. Hajjī Gulbat was awe-inspiring. I visited him repeatedly, made copious notes, and was thankful to have met a Zala Khān Khēl who was willing to talk to me.

But then the problems caught up with me here too. For it appeared that Hajjī Gulbat, in this phase of my work, was of the opinion that the one and only thing I was to learn anything about was genealogy. Whether he possessed the same spontaneous reservation against talking about other matters that the lorry people had shown, or whether there was an actual agreement among Zala Khān Khēl not to let me get to know too much, I do not know. But the consequence for me was the same: my informants tied me up to one particular subject, and it was only

2,2 Hajjī Gulu, a knowledgable "elder" of the land-owning Zala Khān Khēl (right), in conversation with the interpreter Azim Safi (G.P., Dahana-i Ghori, March 1976).

exceedingly limited insight I could get into the matters that really interested me.

Hajjī Gulbat's information had, however, given me some actual knowledge of the geographical distribution of Zala Khān Khēl, and with that as background I chose to leave Kabul and try my luck with Zala Khān Khēl in other provinces of Afghanistan. I naturally hoped to be able hereby to break out of my bondage to a single subject and to get some "proper" contacts with Zala Khān Khēl, so that I could start the collection of real field-data.

At first this move did not get me out of the "genealogy trap". I visited a large number of households, but wherever I went I was referred to some few designated "elders" who took care of the duties of hospitality, and who only told me what they wanted me to know. The pattern stayed the same: I had not only been allotted a subject by my informants, I had also been allotted a handful of key informants, who in the main only would talk about genealogy. Need I say that I was desperate at times.

Yet, what was there to do except to exploit the niche which I had been assigned - and just hope that the ice would break sooner or later? In other words I became an unalloyed collector of genealogy. My diagrams with symbols and lines grew steadily, and I checked and double-checked them through repeated visits to various Zala Khān Khēl groups. The final result was a genealogical system 130 households broad and sixteen generations deep.

But the system was not complete. Here and there were holes, and there was, for both the Zala Khān Khēl and myself, an unsolved problem of genealogically placing a small subsection which had been "lost" for 3 to 4 generations. It was when I started the hunt to fill up these holes that I began to feel the possibility of changing my repertoire of questions in the direction of the field of social, political, and economic history as originally intended. And it was here that I entered upon the third phase of my work with the genealogy.

Obviously, I was being steered and restricted by my informants as to what I could occupy myself with, where I could go, and to whom I could talk. But the situation in which I found myself was naturally not a hermetically closed system. The ideal participant-observation, where everyday life is shared with the group whose situation is being studied, had not been achieved, but all the same I had for some months been going about among Zala Khān Khēl, and had thereby gained an impression of various aspects of their, that is to say, of the men's way of life. Nor had the various conversations which I had had in the course of this time been entirely uncontaminated of other kinds of information. Although there had been little opportunity to collect economic data systematically, for example, remarks had fallen and commentaries been made by the wayside which concerned this subject. In the course of the first and second phases I had thus succeeded in collecting a modest amount of data which lay outside the genealogical. It was information concerning business dispositions, problems with the lorry business, or with agriculture, and it was commentaries on the dispositions of other Zala Khān Khēl. As my knowledge of the genealogical system gradually extended the relationships between particular people, households, or sub-groups emerged. I found that the genealogical diagrams provided a basis for structuring my supplementary information, and I was able to pursue a line of investigation which was not directly steered by my informants.

What precisely caused the thaw of the former attitude towards me among Zala Khān Khēl, and with it the start for me of a third phase, is difficult to say, but a contributory fact seems to have been that I became knowledgeable after all and that I made use of my information. Another reason was certainly that they developed a certain admiration for the genealogical diagram that I had worked out. Admittedly, many of the "elders" had an astonishingly wide knowledge of their genealogy, but none of them had a really systematic view of the whole field such as that which I was now in a position to present. For example, none of them knew the total number of households in Zala Khān Khēl. Thus my informants began to pose questions to me on genealogical connections, and they found it both impressive and entertaining that I could leaf through my stack of papers and quickly inform them whether Rauf was a fourth cousin or an eighth cousin of Abdul.

It has certainly had a bearing on Zala Khān Khēl's attitudes towards me that, in this and similar ways, I could now contribute to the general conversation. As a consequence, particularly among the younger people, the atmosphere of impatience and often of rebuffal which had previously characterised my visits to Zala Khān Khēl gradually disappeared. It was now possible for me in connection with the completion of the genealogy to exceed the boundaries for my interests which had previously been imposed on me. To retain legitimacy in my work, I still had to practise my new data search in close association with my work with the genealogy. For to the Zala Khān Khēl it was the genealogy which was my speciality - although they had accepted that my diagrammatical skeletons were given more flesh on their bones. For example, it was now acceptable to inform me not only about the fact that Mahmud had 4 sons, but also that these 4 sons on Mahmud's death divided the family's 42 *jārīb* of land between them, and that this land had been bought 20 years before for so and so much, etc. I could not have obtained this information in the reverse order.

I have here described how my informants more or less steered my way through the field-work. If the collection of genealogical data initially was my line of investigation they saw to it that it became the only way forward. Even though in the third phase of the field-work I extended my control over what kind of data I wanted to collect, I was forced to do so within narrow limits. However, the genealogy-bound data from the third phase did make it possible for me to establish a historical sequence with respect to the economic, political, and social development that had taken place, and they allowed me to carry out an analysis of the transformation and genealogical subdivision of Zala Khān Khēl. But let there be no doubt that a course of field-work such as I have here described gives the anthropologist problems. A bulk of data, especially from the first two phases, remain unanalysed because it could not pass a later evaluation or could simply not be evaluated, and a quantity of data remained unattainable because of the limited applicability of my genealogical method in a wider context of investigation. For instance, as already mentioned, I was systematically cut off from directly obtaining information about and from female members of the Zala Khān Khēl community. As shall be discussed later, this caused limitations in the analysis of the social dynamics. Also, quantitative data, especially those related to economic conditions and individual activities, were not lavishly handed out by my informants. Consequently, my analysis does not bring about a detailed picture with focus on the individual or the household, but rather takes the shape of a broad description focusing on groups and on overall trends in the history of Zala Khān Khēl.

ZALA KHĀN KHĒL AT A GLANCE

Before the more detailed description and analysis of Zala Khān Khēl which follows, this section presents at a glance the history and present-day situation of Zala Khān Khēl.

Until only some few decades ago the households of Zala Khān Khēl have wandered on foot between the lowlands of the Indus in Pakistan and the central highlands of Afghanistan (see map, *Fig. 3,16*), with their flocks of sheep and goats, with camels as beasts of burden, and with the black tent (in recent times supplemented by the lighter tents of cotton canvas) as their mobile dwelling. For generations the camels' loads have, in addition to the normal possessions of the households, comprised trade goods. For Zala Khān Khēl is one of the many groups of nomads in East Afghanistan for whom trade and caravan transport between the Indian subcontinent and Afghanistan have played an important role. They were trading nomads, nomads who exploited their yearly migrations to transport goods between the different regions and to carry on trade within them.

Zala Khān Khēl are Pashtuns, and speak Pashto as their mother tongue. The women normally speak no other language, while most of the men also speak Dari. In the middle of the 1970s the group consisted of about 1200 individuals distributed over 130 households. Some of these were nuclear households, but many were extended households, typically with a depth of three generations and a breadth of two or more brothers with wives and children. Like the greater part of the inhabitants of Afghanistan they are Muslims, and adhere to Sunni-Islam of the Hanafi observance. The myths of the origin of the Pashtuns tell that their common ancestor, Qais, received enlightenment from the Prophet Mohammad in person. They do not therefore regard themselves as converts, and consider themselves as possessing a special quality as Muslims (Caroe 1958). A closer identification of Zala Khān Khēl within the ramifications of the patrilinear Pashtun system of descent will be given in the next section. Here it will suffice to record that Zala Khān Khēl as such is a kin-group whose independent identity goes no further back than to the beginning of this century.

Until the middle of this century all Zala Khān Khēl lived the life of nomads and trading nomads. They formed a unity under the leadership of a selected *malik*, who coordinated joint tasks as regards the exploitation of grazing grounds, and who represented the group in its relations with the peoples around them, including the State authorities. Cracks began to appear in this unity as conditions both for nomadism and trading nomadism gradually worsened in the course of the 1940s, 1950s, and 1960s. The creation of Pakistan in 1947, and in particular the Pashtunistan conflict in the 1960s, produced problems, as has been said, in the crossing of the eastern frontier of Afghanistan. This limited the possibilities of finding winter grazing grounds for the animals, and set restrictions upon the trading activities of the nomads. These latter restrictions were aggravated by growing competition from a modern transport sector and by State interference in the trading and import/export activities of the nomads within the borders of Afghanistan. In these years of upheaval Zala Khān Khēl sought new paths, and in the 1970s a new pattern began to emerge.

During the winter months many Zala Khān Khēl lived in camps near Jalalabad in the province of Nangarhar in the eastern lowlands. Some of them possessed large black tents, but most of them lived in modest huts constructed of leaves from a local marsh plant. The camps were physically and socially organised like the traditional nomad winter camps, but apart from a single tethered milch-goat and a few hens there were no animals. The men engaged in local trading on the grain market, but only with small success as they were new to that branch. Some took local paid work as unskilled labourers. It was simply a question of managing as best one could, after they had had to give up the last remnants of pastoralism and nomad trade in 1973, and after the customary winter pastures in Khost in the Paktya province and near Thal in Pakistan had been abandoned.

2,3 The lowland of the Alishang valley after harvest and ploughing (GP, Laghman, Dec. 1995). pp. 94-5

Most of the households in the winter camps were poor in these years in the middle of the 1970s, when I began my fieldwork among them. Many of their closest relatives had in the past few years accepted the consequences of their gradually deteriorating situation in Afghanistan, and had settled in Pakistan as paid workers. Those remaining, however, still broke camp at the beginning of spring, and travelled by lorry to Ghorghori in the central highlands. On the way they established brief spring camps in the regions around Kabul.

In Ghorghori Zala Khān Khēl had old grazing rights, but they no longer had much use for them, as they could not operate a coherent pastoral nomadism because of the lack of winter pastures. However, it was during the summer months in the highlands that the poor households kept the pastoral traditions to some degree alive. They bought up sheep and goats in the western regions, and drove them later in the summer to Kabul, where they were sold for slaughtering. Not every household, however, had the economic resources to buy animals, but had to content themselves with employment as herdsmen for other buyers. Some of the poor households carried on a little small-scale trade during the summer, while some had an income from land leased to local Hazara farmers. But in general the economic return remained at a modest level, and the households moving back to Nangarhar in the autumn before snow closed the passes in the highlands were still poverty-stricken.

In the course of the summer there came also better situated Zala Khān Khēl to Ghorghori. They inspected their leased lands and houses - for some of them had in fact built modest permanent dwellings in the region - but otherwise engaged themselves little in any economic activity. The general course of development had forced these households also out of both stock-raising and nomad trade, but they were better founded to survive the changes. For in the 1950s they had bought farmland in Dahana-i Ghori in the province of Baghlan north of the Hindukush mountains, and this land now formed their most important economic asset, and had moreover given them a new area in which to spend the winter. These households had not become agriculturalists in the sense that they themselves were cultivating the soil. The land in Dahana-i Ghori was leased out, but the good prospects of income from agriculture in the area resulted in many of the landowners showing an active interest in increasing the yield. In the case of a single household this had resulted in the acquisition of two tractors.

The landowners spent the winter months in Dahana-i Ghori. For some years after the acquisition of land they lived in their black tents, but thereafter they all built permanent houses, which allowed them better to endure the frequently cold and damp winters in North Afghanistan. The tents were put into storage, but were taken out again each year for the summer move. I could determine that Dahana-i Ghori was in the process of becoming the new base of operation for this portion of Zala Khān Khēl. More and more households were choosing to drop the long summer journey to Ghorghori, and instead would pass the summer in the neighbouring mountains by the Salang pass. This gave them the possibility during the whole year of travelling easily both to Dahana-i Ghori and to Kabul in order to look after their business there.

Investment in farmland is one of the classical means for prosperous nomads to place their profits, and this possibility was, as we have seen, exploited by Zala Khān Khēl. Some were in addition able to invest in lorries, and for a little group of households lorry-operation had become a new and profitable specialisation. They had given up completely their migratory pastoral way of life, and were settled in Qala-i Niazbeg, a village on the western outskirts of Kabul. They were industrious and busy people in one of the promising business spheres of modern Afghanistan. They formed transport associations, some of which (as for example Taghar Transport) became prominent firms in the Afghan transport field. The lorry-owners seldom drove their own vehicles, delegating this work to employed drivers. The most important work of the owners consisted in obtaining transport opportunities.

While the adult men in the transport branch had in many ways the outward appearance of prosperous nomads, the new settled town existence moulded in a different way the lives of the youths and children. They went to modern schools, some of them going on to advanced education, while all of them began to direct their aims towards the opportunities afforded by modern Afghanistan - a situation which only in exceptional cases applied to the youths and children among the other Zala Khān Khēl.

Such was Zala Khān Khēl, as we meet them in the middle of the 1970s. This kin-group of former large-scale trading nomads had been split into three categories, each on the course towards a new way of life. This is no isolated phenomenon. On the contrary, the social and economic transformation of Zala Khān Khēl is representative of the processes of change to which the Pashtun nomad societies have been subject. To some degree the changes in the Zala Khān Khēl community have their own characteristics, but the general lines of their development can be recognised among many West-asiatic nomad peoples. For that reason they are well worthy of study in order to obtain an insight into the mechanisms and factors which form and characterise societies such as those of Afghanistan. A common destiny also links Zala Khān Khēl with other nomads when we look at the events which occurred after the end of the 1970s. For in the case of Zala Khān Khēl, as of millions of other Afghans, events did not follow the course of development which was laid down in the mid-1970s. The political upheavals, and the war which broke out after the Saur revolution in Afghanistan in April 1978 and the Soviet occupation of the country in December 1979, drove the whole of Zala Khān Khēl into exile in Pakistan. Only a very few of the households have been able to live, as refugees, on the official distributions of food-stuff rations alone, and they have been forced to seek sources of extra income. The Pakistani authorities have imposed strict limitations on the use by refugees of local grazing grounds, thus obstructing the practise of pastoralism. Most Zala Khān Khēl have therefore engaged themselves in trade and in businesses of various kinds, while some of the young men have sought good and quickly-earned incomes as migrant workers in the Gulf states.

Despite the changes during the past decades all Zala Khān Khēl still call themselves *kūchey* i.e. nomads. For all of them this is naturally an expression of the fact that it is only a few years since they were in full reality migratory stock-raisers and trading nomads. For the more prosperous, those who in the 1970s had become established in profitable new enterprises, there may be no more to it than that; but for the large group of impoverished Zala Khān Khēl the *kūchey*-identity has a greater significance. They regard themselves as nomads on the waiting list - nomads who have temporarily been forced out of their occupation, and who hope for better times *as nomads.*

GENEALOGY AND IDENTITY

The Zala Khān Khēl form an integral part of a great tribal system which comprises all 14 million Pashtuns - those living in Afghanistan as well as those living in Pakistan (see map, *Fig. 1,9*). By far the majority of the Pashtuns are farmers, but as mentioned it is also among this ethnic group that most of the Afghan nomads are found. Pashtun ideology places all Pashtuns, pastoral nomads as well as settled farmers, within one large segmentary patrilineal system, aptly called "the world's largest family". Their common ancestor is said to be Qais, who, according to tradition, lived at the time of the Prophet Mohammad, and it is through the descendants of Qais that the basis is laid for the comprehensive kinship system.

It must be admitted, however, that the origin of the Pashtuns is lost in obscurity, and that the connecting links of the lineage system often are uncertain and in many cases manipulated.[2] Nevertheless, out of this mist of uncertainty emerges today a number of large Pashtun groupings, sometimes called *tribal confederations*, of which two are dominant in Afghanistan - the Durrani in the western part of the country and the Gilzai in the eastern part. Both of these hold large sections of nomads, and it is among the latter that we find the Zala Khān Khēl.

Before we find the place of Zala Khān Khēl within this segmentary lineage system, a short sketch of how the system is built up will be in its place. The descendants of any particular male person may identify themselves as a kin-group by adding *-zai* (son of) or *-khēl* (kin) to that person's name. Thus the descendants of Ahmad can for example call themselves Ahmad*zai*, and Suleman's descendants may call themselves Suleman *Khēl*. In principle, each new generation could give rise to new kin-group names, but in practice it appears that certain levels in the lineage system achieve greater importance than others. A particular ancestor may lend his name to a kin-group because he was a great and prominent leader, or a particular kin-group name may be taken into use because people wish to emphasise solidarity among the descendants of a certain person - in opposition to other groups.

As the ramifications of the lineage system branch wider and wider, and the Pashtuns are numbered in their millions, innumerable groups, large and small, have arisen, each with its name. Any person can moreover use several different kin-group names referring to different levels in the lineage system, all depending on which solidarity of interests he or she wishes in any given situation to emphasise. The Pashtun genealogy is constantly expanding and changing. The significance of a particular kin-group name, or rather the feeling of solidarity within any particular group, weakens as the group grows in number and generational depth. The group may experience a development during which some members become settled, for example, while others remain nomadic, or conflicts of interest can arise. The various subgroups will then gradually begin to use new kin-group names, derived from more recent ancestors.

Ghilzai, who is said to have been a great-grandson of Qais, is the genealogical starting point for one of the larger Pashtun groupings, the Ghilzai (known by the name of the ancestor in this case without any affix attached). For Zala Khān Khēl today the fact of being Ghilzai is of no practical importance, and one seldom hears reference to this level in the genealogy. It is of greater importance to them to be *Ahmadzai*, descendants of Ahmad.

Ahmad, who is placed 14 generations back in the genealogy, became the focal point with his

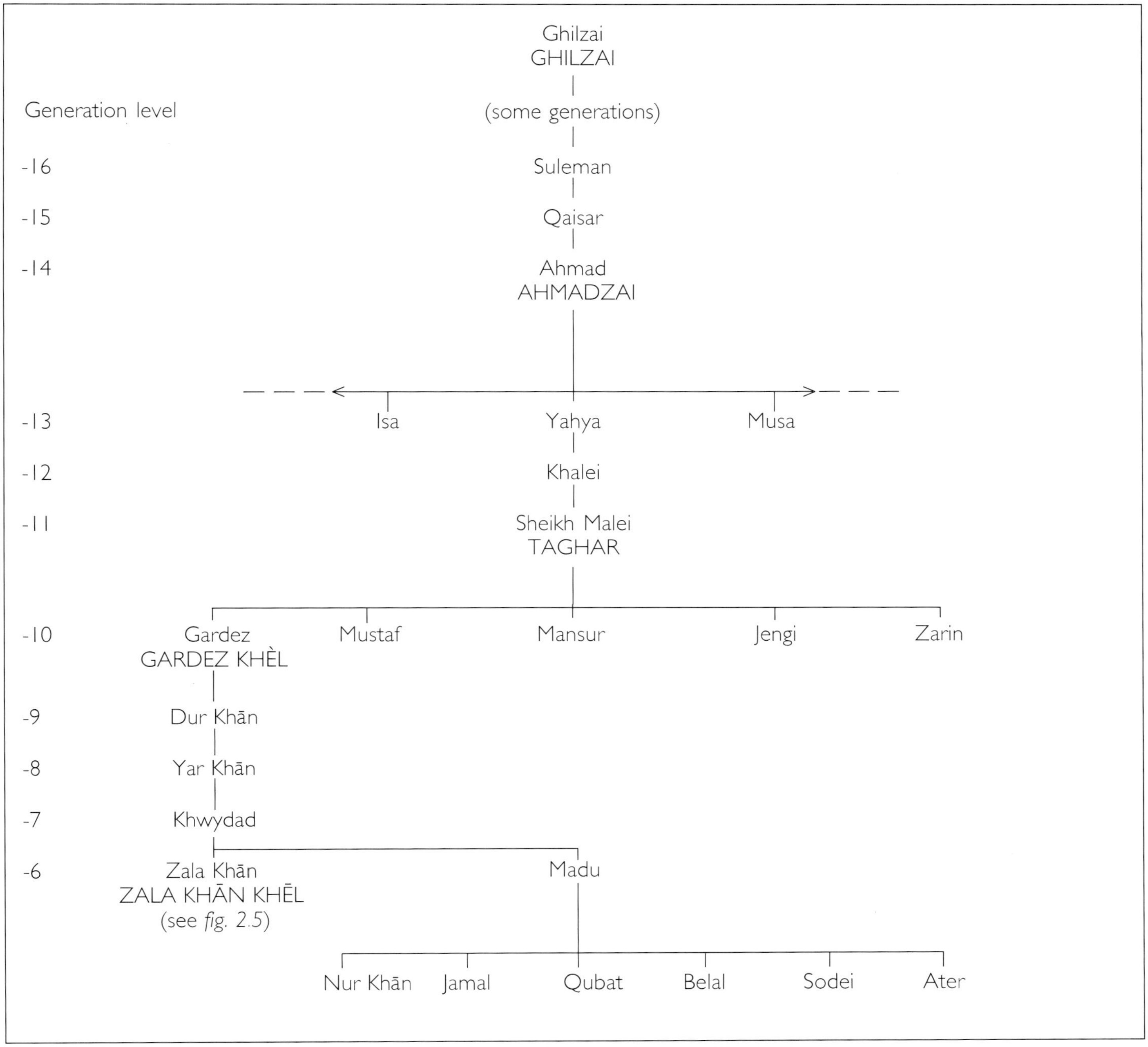

2,4 Zala Khān Khēl's line of descent from Ghilzai to Zala Khān.
It is generally believed that Nur Khān was a grandson of Kwaydad whereas a few informants claim him as a son. The names written with capital letters are kin-group names which to a greater or lesser degree are used by Zala Khān Khēl today. Of Ahmad's thirteen sons only three have been mentioned here - the three who have founded *khēls* which today hold large numbers of nomads. The generation level is read backwards from the generation which today has most male members aged 25-50 (Based on information from Zala Khān Khēl)

13 sons of a kin-group system which today is widely ramified, containing many influential subgroups - *khēls*. The line from Ghilzai to Zala Khān is shown in *Fig. 2,4* as well as the genealogical levels which the Zala Khān Khēl generally refer to, i.e. the levels which hold meaning to them. They apply *Ahmadzai* occasionally as an overall kin-group name, but in everyday speech *Taghar*[3] and *Gardez Khēl* are more commonly used. The kin-group name *Zala Khān Khēl* is more rarely employed, probably because the need to specify a particular degree of solidarity at this level has not been so marked, as the family diversification after Gardez has been small.

Zala Khān Khēl is genealogically a young group within the overall Pashtun system, but we do not know precisely when the designation Zala Khān Khēl began to be used by members of the group itself nor by its neighbours. One important source of information is Robinson's general outline of the genealogy and the economic activities of the Pashtun nomads of East Afghanistan. Here we find Zala Khān Khēl differentiated as one of two sections of Gardez Khēl, with the information that Zala Khān Khēl consisted of 120 households and was under the leadership of Masto Khān (the other section being Nur Khān Khēl - see *Fig. 2,4*) (Robinson 1935: 59, 66). At this time, then, the identity of Zala Khān Khēl is established, but an assessment of the genealogical ramification suggests that this category had probably not existed more than one generation previously - thus coming into being around the turn of the century.

It is noteworthy that while Robinson gives the number of 120 Zala Khān Khēl households in 1934, I recorded no more than 130 in the 1970s. Considering the general population growth rate one should have expected the latter number to have been much higher. There is no way to clarify this apparent discrepancy, but one likely, though simple explanation is that Robinson counted more households as Zala Khān Khēl than those who strictly speaking were so. This argument is supported by the fact that the coming into being of Zala Khān Khēl was at that time very recent and that it therefore may not have been clear to neither Robinson nor his informants who were actually Zala Khān Khēl and who were, for instance, Nur Khān Khēl. As the following will show, there is still today uncertainty about the genealogical placing of some peripheral households.

The genealogy is in the nature of things a system of classification where every individual in principle is given his or her objective placing. However, identification with a particular *khēl* and use of that *khēl*'s name has also social and political aspects. Any particular *khēl* consists of individuals of common descent, but that *khēl* only achieves 'life' to the degree in which these individuals acknowledge their membership. The formation of a *khēl* at a relatively recent level of the genealogy, and identification with that *khēl*, are an expression of actual communal interest between households and individuals. It can therefore occur that individuals who, genealogically speaking, could be ascribed to a particular *khēl* do not consider themselves nor are considered by others as members of that very *khēl*, because they have gone their own ways and live spatially separated from their relatives. An objective descent-group is thus not always identical with a *khēl*.

Four generations back in Zala Khān Khēl's lineage we find 16 forefathers (see *Fig. 2,5*). The descendants of seven of these led, up to the the 1950s, a common way of life as nomads and trading nomads within the traditional bounds of such activities; and it is these very people, who have developed an identity as Zala Khān Khēl.

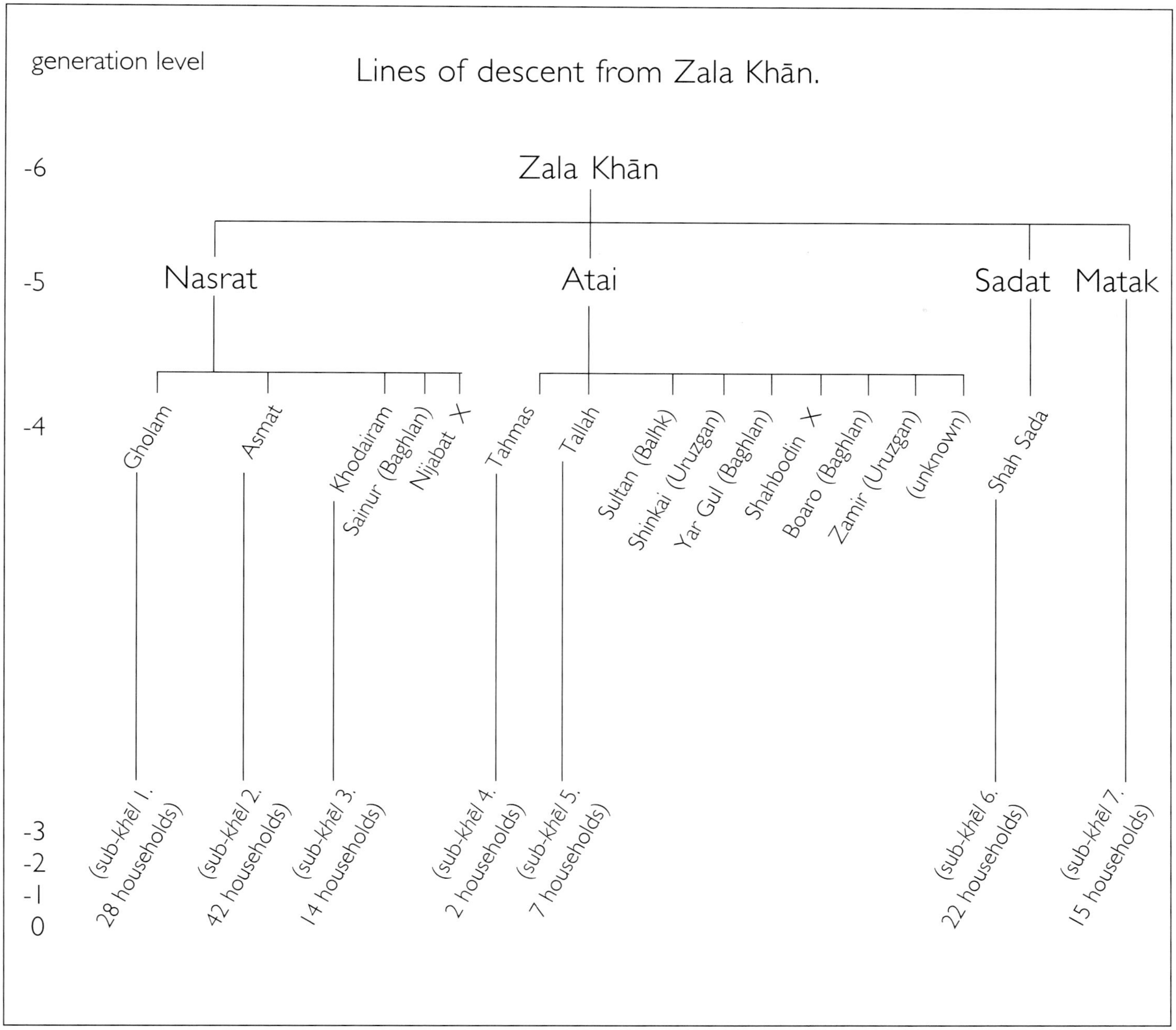

2,5 Lines of descent from Zala Khān.
While all descendants of Zala Khān genealogically can be termed Zala Khān Khēl, only some of his descendants (sub-*khēls* 1-7) actually use the designation to mark a social and political coherence. The remainder broke away about 100 years ago and are now settled in the provinces cited. X denotes absence of male heirs with consequent demise of the line of descent. The number of households is as in 1976.

2,6 Nomad trade in the central highland was the common background for the identity of Zala Khān Khēl (K.F.,Abul, July 1953).

In 1976 they comprised 130 households. Two of the 16 forefathers left no male heirs, while the descendants of the remaining seven for various reasons separated themselves or were separated from the rest of their kin. In the 1970s they were found in the provinces of Uruzgan, Balkh, and Baghlan, where they lived a settled life. They had not taken part in the nomad trade in the central highland of Afghanistan, which in the first half of the present century became a distinctive mark of Zala Khān Khēl's way of life, and they have no share in the pastures in Hazarajat which the Amir divided up among various nomad groups after the conquest of the region in 1892.

The separation of households took place towards the end of the last century, according to my informants, and thus occurred before an actual Zala Khān Khēl identity established itself. A visit to the detached households that now live in the village of Khwaja Khān in Baghlan, revealed that these households called themselves Gardez Khēl, without reference to the later bifurcation of this lineage. Informants from some of the households told how their forefathers - Sainur's three sons - quarrelled with the rest of their kin and were forced to flee more than a hundred years ago. Two of the brothers went north to Turkestan. There they continued to live as nomads until about 1910 when they got the opportunity to buy the land in Khwaja Khān which the households own today. The third brother left for Nangarhar, where his descendants are said to live as religious eccentrics (*malang*). One very old man from another household told how his father, together with certain other Gardez Khēl, was forcibly moved to Balkh at the end of the last century under the regime of Amir Abdur Rahman Khān. The father was later exiled to Bokhara. On the death of the Amir in 1901 he returned to Afghanistan and later acquired land in Khwaja Khān, where his descendants are now settled farmers.

When a section of Zala Khān Khēl began in the 1960s to spend the winters on newly acquired land in Dahana-i Ghori in Baghlan it came to the attention of the detached households in Khwaja Khān, and they visited their newly arrived relatives. This spurred some of the "elders" of both groups to hold a meeting to unravel the genealogical connection between them. It was agreed during this to consider eight households as the descendents of Zala Khān, while there was some uncertainty as to whether the remaining three were descendents of Zala Khān or of Nur Khān.

This meeting after generations of separation did not lead to any reunification of the families or the forging of new economic ties. The genealogical curiosity had been satisfied, but the two parts have not since had anything to do with each other. "They are farmers in Khwaja Khān," say Zala Khān Khēl, "and we are *kūcheys*" i.e. nomads. It is the common history in the first half of this century which is of decisive importance to the Zala Khān Khēl identity, and it is the 130 households which share this identity, who are the subject of this study.

NOTES

1 The data which provide the basis for the description and analysis of Zala Khān Khēl were for the most gathered in the course of field-work in Afghanistan from June 1975 to July 1976. A stay in Afghanistan from April to December 1978 allowed for collecting additional information and in particular for monitoring the early phase of development after the military coup in April 1978. The data on Zala Khān Khēl in exile were gathered during field-work in Pakistan in November to December 1986, while a visit to Pakistan in November to December 1988 allowed for a general follow-up on the situation of Afghan refugees and of nomads in particular. The rehabilitation of Afghan refugees from Pakistan was monitored during a visit to Pakistan and the eastern provinces of Afghanistan in June to July 1992.

The field-work in 1975-76 had the following course of time: After the reconnaissance tour in Central Afghanistan in July 1975 I made the first contact with the lorry-owning Zala Khān Khēl in Kabul in August 1975. The late summer and the autumn of 1975 was spent in Kabul with the lorry-owners, and in Bazaar-i Omaid and the surrounding country, visiting the migratory Zala Khān Khēl while they had brief autumn camps there on their way to Jalalabad. From December 1975 to March 1976 attention was concentrated on the winter dwelling places of the migratory Zala Khān Khēl - partly in Dahana-i Ghori and partly in Jalalabad. After the break-up in the spring Kabul and its environs were again the scene of my work, with new visits to the settled groups and to the spring camps of the migrants. In the month of May 1976 I made a tour via the Ghorband valley to the central highlands in order to obtain general information on the nomads' spring migration - without, however, reaching as far as the Zala Khān Khēl summer pastures in Ghorghori. The description of conditions in Ghorghori is therefore based only on Zala Khān Khēl's own information and on data from K. Ferdinand's visit there in July 1975.

2 Dealing with studies of the Pashtun society one is often faced with the obscure complexity of the tribal system. On one hand the tribal system provides a handy reference, but on the other hand it becomes obvious that the system is not throughout coherent. No studies appear to have gone to the bottom of the Pashtun tribal system, but one book - Olaf Caroe's *The Pathan* (1958) - shall be mentioned here as a comprehensive account of Pashtun history and tribal organisation, including a presentation of the different myths of origin of the Pashtuns.

3 The kin-group name Taghar exemplifies the type which relates to an important person. Concerning the origin of the name Taghar the following is told by Zala Khān Khēl: Sheikh Malei was a great leader and a very respected gentleman, whose advice was often sought, both by his own relatives and by others. He was moreover very hospitable, and many people therefore came to his tent. Here he always spread out kelim rugs (*taghar*) for his visitors, and thereby acquired the sobriquet Taghar. This name was thereafter carried forward as a kin-group name.

3,1 Girls in a Stanizai nomad camp (G.P., Guldarah, May 1976).

CHAPTER 3

EXPANSION AND CONSTRAINTS

PASTORAL ECONOMY AND NOMAD TRADE UP TO THE 1960s

THE COMPLEX SOCIETY

Nomadism occurs in many variations, but true of nomadism everywhere is that it must be seen as an interaction of many factors. These are partly related to the fundamental conditions of pastoral economy: topography and climate, size and quality of grazing grounds, presence of water, composition of flocks and herds, and the internal social organisation of the nomads. And they are partly related to the larger-scale society to which the nomads belong: access to grazing grounds, occupational relationship to other population groups such as agriculturalists, craftsmen and merchants, opportunities for economic activities in addition to those offered by pastoralism itself, and - last but not least - the political situation, local, national, and international. All these factors are interconnected and shape the pastoral way of life to a greater or lesser degree.

Ideally an understanding of nomadism therefore requires a broad regional analysis: All the above mentioned elements in a given area, or a region, must be submitted to analysis, in order to understand the contribution of the individual elements to the overall picture and the connections between these elements. Only in this perspective can we fully appreciate the role of each element (cf. Barth 1973). However, such a regional analysis demands a more comprehensive set of data than is available for the present study, but the principle will be borne in mind, and serve to induce a suitable caution in the presence of the many facets of the subject.

We have no sources earlier than the last century that throw light on Afghan nomadism specifically. But we are in a better position when it comes to an assessment of the general characteristics of the society in which nomadism existed and developed. Some of these have since far back in history been common to a large stretch of country extending from North Africa via the Middle East to India - an area known for its nomadism. One of the most important features is that we here have *complex societies* characterised by a well developed and differentiated structure as far as population, occupations, politics, and economics is concerned. A mosaic is built up, as Barth describes it, with groups of different backgrounds of language forming categories which cross one another:

agriculturalists	nomads	townsmen

plainsmen	mountain-men	desert-men

tribal community	national community

The basic structure is built upon a threefold occupational division into:

agriculturalists	nomads	craftsmen

This division has a high degree of specialisation within each category and a consequent high degree of inter-dependence between the categories binding them together into a loose grand-society (Barth 1968).

Nomadism is part and parcel of the complexity, and it is integrated into the structure of the society in a variety of ways. The areas in which the nomads move are either interwoven with or surrounded by the settled communities. Connected with this is the fact that the occupational specialisation of the nomads leads first and foremost to a traditionally close relationship (including one of opposition) with the agriculturalists, to whom they sell pastoral products to obtain essential agricultural produce. Corresponding relationships are found with craftsmen and merchants in order to obtain other wares and services. A noteworthy characteristic of the complexity is also that nomads normally make a living by other means in addition to pure animal husbandry. Agriculture to varying extent, trade, and seasonal work in settled environments are examples of this.

Just as it is impossible satisfactorily to elucidate the origin and early history of the Pashtuns, so no detailed account can be given of the distribution between nomads and non-nomads among the Pashtuns over time. The latter has fluctuated in accordance with political, economic, and demographic conditions at various periods. Adding to the complexity is the fact that the nomads have ethnic ties and often close relatives among the settled population. The ethnic cohesion and the common lineage system thus transcends the dividing line between nomads and settled people.

The role of the Pashtun nomads in Afghan politics has been strongly marked by these close relationships. Since the country came into being in 1747 government has been in the hands of Pashtuns. This has, however, by no means meant an absence of antagonism between nomads and the state. Since the end of the last century there have been efforts on part of the central government to break the political power of the Pashtun tribes - nomads as well as settled folks - by means of more or (particularly) less voluntary movement and settlement (N. Tapper 1973 and 1983). The relationship between nomadic and settled Pashtuns and the fact that they all share a common lineage system, has meant that the clash of interests between nomads and the state has often been expressed as part of the general political balance between the Pashtun tribal groups and the state (Kakar 1971 and 1979; Poullada 1962 and 1973; R. Tapper 1983).

The nomads (in common, for that matter, with many other population groups) would prefer to be left alone by the government, but here, too, it is a characteristic of the complexity that they appear as protagonists and antagonists to the other political forces of the country. To the degree that East Afghan nomads have made yearly migrations into the neighbouring regions to the east of Afghanistan (British India and, since 1947, Pakistan) this situation becomes even more complex.

The ecological basis of nomadism

Nomadism in Afghanistan is thus part of a complex social, occupational, and political structure, and it can be but poorly understood if analysed in isolation. However, as a basis for the subsequent analysis it is necessary to give at this point

3,2 Dry-farming fields (the light areas in the foreground) at an altitude above 3,000 metres. The yield is small, but the wheat grown at such fields is said to produce the best flour for bread (G.P., Bamiyan, May 1976).

a short description of certain factors underlying nomadism in general.

Pastoral nomadism in this part of the world relies on the exploitation of seasonal variations in the growth of pasture between various regions, and the subsequent movement of flocks and herds. In East Afghanistan this gives rise to two yearly migrations between relatively well defined winter areas in the lowland and summer areas in the highland.

The grazing grounds exploited by the nomads lie in a zone between the arable land and the barren plains or mountain sides - either as uninterrupted areas or interwoven with the arable land. Agriculture in the region is largely dependent upon irrigation. This means the agri-

3,3 The border line between the arable land and the dry steppe land is clearly demarcated by the colour differences in the landscape. Below this line the agriculturist governs and above it the pastoralist (G.P., Wardak, June 1975).

culturalists' endeavours are curbed by the physical possibilities of canalising water. In principle this results in relatively stable boundaries between the spheres of interest of the two forms of subsistence - though changes have occurred in recent years (to which we shall return). Conflict cannot be avoided, however. There are areas where the agriculturalists use non-irrigated land for dry farming, *lalmi*, dependent on the moisture content of the soil after the winter rains, and there are grazing grounds used by settled groups for their own animals. Nomads are not the only stock-raisers. Clashes can also occur when nomads during their migrations cross or move close to cultivated land, where their stock damage the crops. In some places the nomads' ac-

3,4 The border line between the arable land and the dry steppe land is clearly demarcated by the colour differences in the landscape. Below this line the agriculturist governs and above it the pastoralist (G.P., Ghor, July 1975).

cess to grazing grounds is without problems in relation to their settled neighbours. It may be based upon time-honoured custom after generations of use or it may be legally formalised, but often it is determined quite simply by the balance of power between the nomads and their neighbours.

The stock consists largely of sheep, goats, and cattle, with preponderance of the first two. As pack-animals camels, horses, and donkeys predominate. While nomad groups normally use and even own grazing grounds in common, the animals are owned by the individual household, the smallest economic unit in the nomad community. During their stay in the winter and sum-

3,6 A shepherd boy of western Afghanistan (G.P., Obe, May 1976).

mer areas and during the migrations between these areas the households band together in units of varying size and composition in order to ensure optimal exploitation of the grazing grounds and of the labour force, and in order to give the necessary external physical protection and internal social security. While the protection of the grazing grounds and their distribution is normally arranged by larger units within a tribal structure - often under some form of common leadership - the responsibility for the stock of a household rests with that household alone.

A basic principle of the nomad household's economy is subsistence production, in the sense that its production is primarily geared to meet immediate basic requirements of food, clothing, shelter, and so on. The animals supply wool, skins, milk, and meat though only rarely the latter, if it involves the slaughter of sound beasts.

3,5 Shepherd boys of western Afghanistan (G.P., Obe, May 1976).

3,7

3,8

3,9

3,10

3,11

3,7-11 The work of the nomad women is carried out inside or immediately outside the tent. Weaving and bread making in a Musa Khēl household (G.P., Logar, Aug. 1975).

3,12 Utilisation of pasture is not reserved for the nomads alone. Also settled farmers raise animals, and some of them have large flocks often competing for fodder with the flocks of the nomads (G.P., Samangan, 1978). pp. 114-5

3,13 Stanizai Pashtun shepherds (G.P., Kabul-area, May 1976).

These products are at the same time trade goods, used to obtain other foodstuffs such as grain, tea, and sugar, as well as to buy such tools, household goods, and luxury wares as cannot be produced by the nomads themselves. Livestock is also sold to some extent for slaughter in the towns or to other nomads or settled people, though sale in the view of the nomads is less attractive, as it is synonymous with a reduction in the household's capital. A number of nomads have, however, of late turned their attention to the national and international livestock markets, and for some groups this has even become a specialisation.

Economic security for the nomad thus rests in maintaining a flock of livestock of a certain size in order to provide for the daily needs of the members of the household and at the same time to reproduce itself. Conversely, a certain amount of labour is required - in other words a certain number of household members - for the traditional division of labour to function. The greater the number of livestock, the greater the work. As it is the job of the men and boys to look after the

3,14 During summer the nomads utilise high-lying pastures. This camp of Mohmand nomads, just west of Bamiyan and with the peaks of Koh-i Baba in the background, is situated at an altitude of about 3,000 metres (G.P., July 1975).

animals on the grazing grounds, the number of persons in the household available for such work places a limit on the size of the flock, as each herdsman can only manage a certain number of animals. Similarly, the number of women in the household is of importance for the manufacturing processes in the home. Problems of labour shortage, particularly for shepherding, can be solved within a subgroup of households, which may join forces to look after their combined flock while retaining individual ownership. Shortage of labour for shepherding can also be alleviated by employing a shepherd from outside the household, normally from another nomad household. Such an employee may be requited with a fixed number of animals, for example a certain percentage of the flock he is to herd, or with a proportion of the yield in the form of lambs or kids.

For economic security it is, however, not enough with a flock whose average daily yield precisely corresponds to the needs of the household and its own reproduction. A surplus over and above this is required, to compensate for the

3,15 1975, Ark 10 nr.3 Along their routes of migration nomads may work as harvest labourers (K.F., Logar, Aug. 1975).

3,15 Nomads often make an additional earning with their camels in local transport business (K.F., 1974)

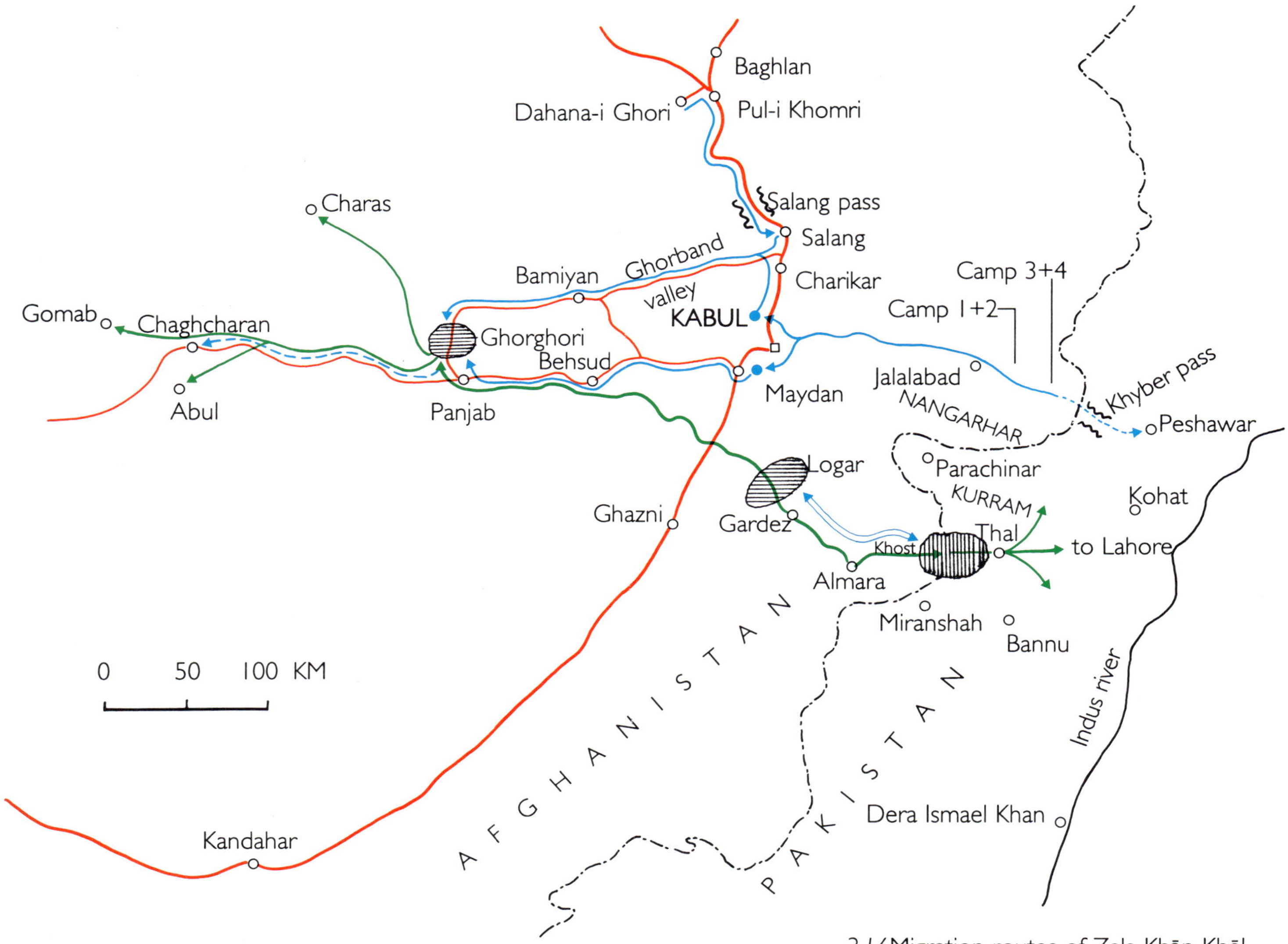

3,16 Migration routes of Zala Khān Khēl

- International boundary
- Asphalt road
- Gravel road
- Kabul
- Town/village
- Pastoral migrations towards the end of the last century
- Pastoral migration and trading routes from the end of the last century till the 1960s
- Trading and purchase routes from the end of the last century till the 1960s
- Spring migration (1976)
- Labour seeking (mid 1970s)
- Animal purchase (mid 1970s)
- Spring camp of 1976
- Winter pasture
- Summer pasture

TYPICAL TRADING GOODS

Afghan highland

- horses
- sheep and goats
- fur
- hides and skins
- wool/woollen goods
- carpets
- fresh fruit
  - grapes
  - melons
  - apples
  - pomegrates
- dried fruit
  - raisins
  - figs
  - mulberries
  - apricots
  - apples
- nuts
  - almonds
  - pistachio
  - pine
  - walnuts
  - apricot kernels
- ghee and qurut

Indus lowland (and other parts of the Indian subcontinent)

- sheet copper and tin
- iron-wares
  - pots and pans
  - nails
  - fittings
  - locks
- razors
- lamps
- kerosine oil
- matches
- cotton cloth
- woollen cloth
- silk
- second-hand clothing
- needles and thread
- shoes and sandals
- saddlery
- dyes
- salt
- tea
- sugar
- spices
- soap
- weapons

3,17 Typical trading goods of East Afghan nomads and the areas between which they are exchanged (Sources: Zala Khān Khēl, other trading nomads, and Robinson 1935).

losses to which the nomad is unavoidably subjected through sickness among his livestock, changes of weather, theft or straying of animals. A surplus is also desirable as a reserve which can be realised in case of extraordinary expenses occasioned perhaps by ceremonial events such as weddings or funerals. The greater flock one has, the better one is equipped to withstand purely economic as well as social and political challenges. The nomad's aim is consequently to maximise his flocks and herds. It is against this background that it is considered inexpedient to sell livestock to meet the day-to-day requirements of the needs of the household, or to slaughter them for one's own consumption.

The aggregated economy

The nomad's opportunities to achieve economic security for his household are not confined to animal husbandry alone. It seems in fact rather

3,18-9 Second-hand clothing (the Khwazak to the left) and a variety of petty utensils (the Matani to the right) are typical trading goods of the nomads. These two Pashtuns are among the few nomad traders found in the central highland in the summer of 1975 (G.P., Chaghcharan, July 1975).

3,20 Khwazak nomad trader (G.P., Chaghcharan, July 1975).

the rule than the exception that the nomad household be engaged in several of a whole series of possible economic activities. Such activities can be related in various ways to animal husbandry, as the following salient examples demonstrate.

An immediate adjunct of the pastoral economy is that the nomads exploit their proximity to other population groups to obtain by trade or barter essential wares from agriculturalists, craftsmen, and merchants. In its simplest form it is the surplus production from stock breeding that the nomads use, and at this level obtaining products such as tea, grain, and sugar is directly connected with the pastoral economy. The nomad, however, often goes further in his exploitation of the trade opportunities, and trading activities more indirectly connected with the pastoral economy can arise. They consist in the nomad acquiring goods for the surplus of his pastoral products over and above what his own household needs. One opportunity for such trade can lie in the fact that the nomads migrate between regions with different patterns of supply and demand. A ware may be bought in the lowlands and sold at a profit during the migration or in the highlands - or vice versa. Such a trade, based on migrations conditional upon pastoral nomadism, can under favourable marketing conditions develop into a more specialised form, where buying and selling no longer bear any relation to animal husbandry; and it is precisely this development which many Pashtun nomads of East Afghanistan have undergone - among them the Zala Khān Khēl.

Transport activities are another example of an economic activity, which is closely bound up with nomadism. Such engagements are found, for example, in the winter areas, where the households often do not move for several months, and where the transport capacities of the animals can be hired out. One can talk of an indirect connection with the stock-keeping economy in so far as a resource which is primarily meant for use in that economy can be periodically released and used for another activity. As was the case with trade, transport activity can develop into a larger-scale and more permanent engagement, which no longer has relation to the pastoral economy, as for example caravan transport - cf. Frederiksen's analysis of the Hazarbuz of Mohmand (Frederiksen 1978 and (forthcoming); Frederiksen and Pedersen 1978).

Work for wages is also prevalent. It can take many forms, among others that within the actual sphere of animal husbandry already mentioned, where men and boys from one household are employed as herdsmen by another household. During seasonal reduction in stock-keeping activity men may also look for work as labourers or agricultural workers. Work of this nature may sometimes be far from the household, and in recent years true migrant labour of longer duration, involving total disassociation from stock-raising activity, has become a possibility for earning a living exploited by some men.

Agriculture should finally be mentioned as playing a role in the economy of many nomad households. Some of them cultivate the soil themselves while others receive a yearly contribution of agricultural products from land they have leased out.

Such economic activities are characterised by their being carried on at a varying degree of association with pastoralism, some being directly or indirectly bound up with it, while others are completely independent. All activities, however, must be seen in relation to the total dispositions of the household, whereby they naturally are all related to each other. But it is when the time dimension is taken into consideration that it becomes interesting to see the total dispositions in relation to the actual pastoral economy. By taking our point of departure in nomadism, which is the traditional basis of their economy and organisation, it is possible to analyse the development undergone by both single households and larger and smaller groups of nomads. As the examples above suggest, the importance given by the households to the various activities may alter. It is through analysis of such changes - seen in relation to economic and political development in a wider national and regional perspective - that we shall approach the Zala Khān Khēl.

ZALA KHĀN KHĒL'S NOMADISM AND TRADING

The source material on the specific history of Afghan nomadism is scanty, as already mentioned, and we know little of the background for what led to the division of the Pashtuns into nomad and settled groups. The Ahmadzai as a whole has been characterised as a predominantly nomadic Pashtun group at an early date (Elphinstone 1972, II: 157), and the Zala Khān Khēl is described by Robinson as one of the Ahmadzai groups that most persistently has maintained its nomad status (Robinson 1935). The sources also suggest that the trading activities of the East Afghan nomads are of very ancient date, without giving us any information as to the origin of the phenomenon. Nomad trade has been a part of a widespread trade network which has united the Indian subcontinent to Afghanistan, further north to Bokhara and other Central Asian emirates, and further west to Persia. Rai talks of activities "from time immemorial" (Rai 1922: 1), and Robinson risks the assertion that these activities probably date back to the 11th century (Robinson 1935: 23). Enriquez describes the Pashtun nomads as "militant merchants" who for centuries have fought their way with families and caravans (Enriquez 1910: 138). Elphinstone gives a detailed account of trading and caravan activities, in the course of which he makes the very apposite point that nomads, possessing transport animals (camels) and migrating as pastoral nomads from one region to another, "naturally turn their attention to commerce" (Elphinstone 1972, I: 378). The interweaving of commerce and nomadism may thus have a long history among East Afghan nomads.

Pastures and economic potentials

The nomadism of Zala Khān Khēl has followed a traditional pattern of East Afghan nomadism. Winter was passed on grazing grounds in the eastern lowlands, either those which today lie within the frontiers of Afghanistan or in the Indus plain further to the east. Here the climate is comparatively mild at this time of the year, and grazing can be found throughout the winter. Water for the animals is no problem, as the run-off from the mountains of the region is abundant and as winter is also the rainy season. At the beginning of spring the heat is felt in the lowland, the vegetation dries up and is parched by the sun and can no longer support the flocks of the nomads. The spring migration starts towards the highlands, the southeast foothills of the Hindukush mountains or higher up in the central areas of Afghanistan. Here the snow is melting away, and fresh pastures give renewed chances for the flocks. Here there is no shortage of drinking water for the animals either, as snow melts from the higher mountains throughout most of the summer. Towards the end of summer the highlands are beginning to be grazed clean, and with the approach of autumn, the nomads begin the movement once again - and the circle is completed.

Towards the end of the last century Zala Khān Khēl had relatively short migration routes within the East Afghan provinces of Paktya (Khost) and Logar (see map, *Fig. 3,16*). These regions, together with the province of Nangarhar, are traditional abodes of Ahmadzai, and it is here that many Ahmadzai have in the course of time settled (Broadfoot 1885, Elphinstone 1972, Robinson 1935). We have no detailed information about Zala Khān Khēl's rights to pastures here, but as the later development will show, it appears that they did not own land to which they could return later. Some Zala Khān Khēl at one time expanded their migrations to include winter grazing grounds around Thal further to the east and summer grazing grounds on the upland plain around Ghazni.

The trading activities of Zala Khān Khēl are in main outline as follows: during their stay in the winter grazing areas in the eastern lowlands a variety of goods such as iron-wares, tea, sugar, and textiles are bought in the local bazaars. These goods are taken along on the spring migration towards the highlands, where they are in general demand and can be sold. In the opposite direction they take with them articles such as wool, carpets, fresh and dried fruits which are bought in the highlands and can be sold in the plains (see *Fig. 3, 17*). The buying and selling and the transport of the wares are mainly governed by the location of seasonal grazing areas and the pattern of migrations between these areas. But the opportunities for trade are not determined only by the presence of markets. It is decisive that activities involved in stock-breeding are somewhat reduced during periods in summer and winter when the households are stationary in fixed camps for some months. For this makes it possible to transfer labour from pastoral to other activities. In addition to trade these other activities have typically been, in the winter area, local transport and hiring out as labourers.

Organisation

Let us look at how the Zala Khān Khēl organised their economic activities in former days. The lineage system of the Pashtuns, the underlying principles of which have already been described, provides an important basis for this organisation. At another level these principles are expressed through *Pashtunwali*, the Pashtun code of honour, which demands proper conduct, unity, mutual support, and mutual respect in accordance with prescribed rules. However, this code is not always taken as a guideline for the economic and political dispositions of individuals and households[1]. The genealogical system provides nevertheless an important frame of reference, which gives directions both for the place of individuals in respect to each other, thereby influencing decisions on the rights and duties of these, and for decisions concerning the access of households to resources held in common. In practice the importance of the system varies considerably, and there is much to suggest that it is weakened when there is no longer need to regulate access to common resources - for example when land passes into private ownership.

Among Pashtun nomads the use of grazing grounds commonly owned or commonly rented by a kin-group is an actuality, and perhaps therefore the lineage system is of greater importance among nomads than among settled Pashtuns. As a close-knit sub-*khel* of Ahmadzai, Zala Khān Khēl has lived and migrated together. A certain freedom of the individual households does, however, give room for variations which can result in some households of Zala Khān Khēl choosing to attach themselves to other groups for a shorter or longer period, just as camps of Zala Khān Khēl may well contain households from other groups - often from the closely related Nur Khān Khēl or other Ahmadzai.

The intimate connection between the lineage system's division into *khels* and sub-*khels* and the economic activities of these groups is shown clearly in Robinson's detailed survey of Ghilzai's genealogy and economic practices, in which Ahmadzai is treated in a separate section (Robinson 1935: 57 ff.). From this it will be seen that 20 to 25 per cent of all Ahmadzai are nomads (in 1934). It is also shown where the individual groups spend their summers and winters, and to what degree they are engaged in other economic activities in addition to nomadism while they are in British Indian territory. Unfortunately, we are unable to form an idea from Robinson's information of the factors which influence the formation and continued unification of the lineage groups - other than a certain degree of common economic activity, which may be assumed to include utilisation of common resources, though Robinson is not explicit on this point. With regard to freedom of action within the kin-groups it is clear from Robinson's surveys and his commentaries to them that it is a case of limited exceptions, when certain groups live and migrate together with genealogically "foreign" groups.[2]

With the variations possible within the lineage system Zala Khān Khēl functions as a closed group under the leadership of a *malik*. He represents the group and normally takes care of contacts with the local authorities, with the surrounding settled communities and with other nomad groups with regard to taxes, legal questions, disputes, and the like. In the winter area near Thal, where Zala Khān Khēl rent grazing rights, it is the duty of the *malik* to negotiate the prize of the areas necessary and to clear formalities with the authorities - in former days with the British administration, which levied dues on the livestock and set a time limit on the stay of the nomads in the region (see below).

The basis for title to grazing grounds in the winter area is membership of a kin-group. The same is true of the summer area where the right to utilise grazing grounds owned in common after 1892 (see below) has been distributed among genealogical subgroups, who may then choose to use the grazing grounds in common or to redistribute the rights for the season in question to the individual households.

The two annual migrations between the summer and the winter areas form another clear case of lineage-based organisation. Zala Khān Khēl do not necessarily migrate in one united group, but more often in a coordination of a number of smaller household groups.

The bonds of kinship unite the households so far as the utilisation of grazing grounds and the organisation of migrations are concerned, but in other respects the households remain independent economic units. The flocks and herds are owned by the individual households, and all arrangements with regard to the herding and utilisation of these are household matters. In the case of mismanagement or accident the individual household bears the loss, just as it is the household which reaps the profit when the stock-breeding goes well. The taxes and other dues, which the *malik* settles on behalf of the group, must be paid by the separate households in proportion to the number of their animals. Some informants depict the internal solidarity within a kin-group as a safety net which provides some degree of mutual help and perhaps the lending of livestock to unfortunate relatives. However, this seems to be rarely practised, and for certain, among Zala Khān Khēl such solidarity is limited as this presentation will show.

The organisation of trading activities forms a parallel to that of stock-breeding. In the same way as pastoral dispositions are private household matters, so also buying and selling of trade goods are the affairs of the individual household. It is the household that decides how and to what degree it will and can engage in trading activities, and it is the household that assumes the economic liability and has to pay taxes or duties. But the trading activities are preferably carried on in larger or smaller groups out of a regard for social and physical security. This is particularly true of the long and hazardous transport of goods between the seasonal grazing areas, during which raids and plundering by no means are unknown phenomena, but it also applies to the purchasing and selling tours which extend beyond the summer and winter grazing areas.

Among certain trading nomads it would be the practice for some of the men in the winter months to go on extensive trading tours - "cloth hawking" and "usury" - as far into India as Bombay, Calcutta, and the East Bengal, today's Bangladesh (Robinson 1935: 26). It was mainly nomads who wintered around Dera Ismael Khan, as well as certain settled Pashtuns, who took part in this special form of trading in conjunction with Hindu moneylenders (ibid.). Zala Khān Khēl has not taken part in this trade, but they have ventured further east than Thal in the Indus lowland. Indian textiles - the single item which gradually became of greatest significance both to Zala Khān Khēl and to other trading nomads - were purchased in Lahore. The men from a number of households would travel together to Lahore, but again the purchases were the affair of the individual. No joint purchases were made, the explanation given by the nomads being that such a purchase would in any case not have resulted in any price reduction. This explanation agrees with those given for similar situations later concerning the cloth trade in Bazaar-i Omaid in Kabul (see Chapter 5).

The summer's trade corresponds to that of the winter. The men normally leave the camps in small parties, but the trade remains an individual household affair.

CHANGING CIRCUMSTANCES

Political changes

The home land of the East Afghan nomads underwent considerable political changes in the latter part of the last century. The British colonial administration in India expanded gradually throughout the 1800s. Punjab came under British rule in 1849, and the British thereby reached as far as the Sulaiman mountains. They stood thus at what is today the eastern frontier of Afghanistan and therefore controlled large parts of the lowlands which constituted the winter grazing areas of many nomads and which previously had been under the Afghan crown. Peshawar, which in Elphinstone's time had been the winter residence of the Afghan kings, became one of the chief British headquarters in the area which in 1901 became a new province in the Empire under the name of The North-West Frontier Province.

Concurrently with this - and under the direct influence of the British Imperial power - the Amir of Afghanistan, Abdur Rahman Khān (1880-1901), embarked on a consolidation of the Afghan state. This comprised partly a general building up of the apparatus of government, and partly a strengthening of internal political control. As earlier described, the "Iron Amir" struck at a series of "unruly elements" in the country and he waged internal wars against several population groups - among them the Hazara of the central highland who had successfully kept the Afghan central power at a distance. Hazarajat fell in 1892.

These national and international political developments were of decisive importance for Zala Khān Khēl. They affected the freedom of action of the nomads both in the winter and in the summer areas, but in opposite ways. While limitations were imposed in one case, promising opportunities turned up in the other. Let us first look at the latter.

Changes in the summer areas

The conquest of the central highland of Hazarajat opened this area to the nomads. Parts of Hazarajat were by royal decree, *farmān*, awarded to various nomad groups for their support in the royal campaign against the Hazara. During the years that followed other parts of the

region were gradually, although against the explicit prohibition of the Amir, taken by force from the Hazara and incorporated into the nomads' summer grazing areas. Still other areas were bought from settled groups, which had originally been allotted the land by the Amir (Ferdinand 1962, Mohammad 1915).

The historical facts concerning the campaign against the Hazara in 1892 and the course of events in Hazarajat in the years immediately thereafter are not entirely clear. Among other matters there is a certain discrepancy between the Amir's and the nomads' interpretation of the importance of the nomad tribes in the war. The Amir relegates the role of the nomads to a subsidiary position, while the nomads themselves claim that they were front-line figures in furious battles with the Hazara (Ferdinand 1962, Kakar 1979).

However, the nomads were alotted *farmān* land and the Zala Khān Khēl tell the following about this event: It was the leader at the time, Qutb-Uddin, who received the *farmān* letter,

3,21-2 Mir Ahmad Khān together with relatives on his summer grazing land (K.F., Ghorghori, July 1975).

and the allotted grazing grounds remained in his lifetime a common resource, the use of which was year by year distributed between the households. During this period many households acquired additional land in the region, and on Qutb-Uddin's death (year not given) the new leader, Qutb-Uddin's brother Masto Khān, made a permanent distribution of the *farmān* grazing grounds in such a way that consideration was taken to where the various households had their other land, and to where they normally had their summer camp and grazing area. This allocation has apparently been in force ever since, but it does not appear from my source material, to what extent the grazing grounds have been privatised or to what degree the actual use of the grazing grounds is still a matter of shuffling and adjustment in accordance with the needs of the households. The *farmān* letter was in 1976 kept by Masto Khān's son, Hajjī Hazrat Mohammad, who at that time was considered among some Zala Khān Khēl to be their formal leader. (See

3.23 Young Zala Khān Khēl (K.F., Ghorghori, July 1975).

Frederiksen (forthcoming) for a further discussion on the *farmāns* given to East Afghan nomads - the case of Hazarbuz.)

After the acquisitions of grazing grounds in Hazarajat the migration routes of Zala Khān Khēl became a good deal longer (see map, *Fig. 3,16*). The allotted area lay in Ghorghori a little north of Panjab, about 400 kilometres' travel from the winter areas by Thal. However, the advantages of the new area outweighed the disadvantage of the long migration. For it provided not merely better grazing grounds, it gave admission to a new trading area. Hazarajat was a virgin market which had been hitherto almost inaccessible to outsiders and therefore unexploited by outside merchants (Ferdinand 1970: 129). Exploitation of this new opportunity by trading nomads such as the Zala Khān Khēl was at first sporadic, but with the establishment of the first nomad summer-bazaar in Kerman around 1919 trade began to boom (Ferdinand 1978b).

While in the central highland the nomads needed agricultural produce to supplement their diet. To understand the background for the trade which arose between Pashtun nomads and Hazara farmers one should be aware that the nomads could not easily acquire such products from the Hazara by the usual barter with pastoral products. For the Hazara were practically speaking self-sufficient in such products, their economy being based on mixed agriculture and stock-keeping. The only exception was the wool produced by the nomads, which the Hazara could use in their extensive weaving activities (Ferdinand 1970: 128-9). Ferdinand describes how three types of nomad trade developed in Hazarajat: local trade between the nomads and the Hazara in limited areas; long-distance trade, where some of the men leave the summer camp and the flocks and herds for a period and travel with loaded camels towards a more distant trading markets; and the short-lasting nomad bazaars which arose in the eastern Hazarajat and later further west in the Aimaq region (Ferdinand 1962: 130 ff.). It appears from Ferdinand's material that Zala Khān Khēl and other Taghar nomads were active over a broad band of trading activities in the central highlands. They were singled out as particularly prominent in connection with the holding of nomad bazaars, where, in addition to being considerable traders, they also occupied positions in the leadership of the bazaars (Ferdinand 1962: 149 ff. and 1978b: 142 ff.). Even the actual founding of some of the nomad bazaars is attributed to prominent persons among Zala Khān Khēl, according to my informants.

Ferdinand points out that to many nomads one aspect of trade with the Hazara - the giving of credit - was of particular significance. The Hazara were not always solvent, and the nomads therefore gave them credit, but on harsh terms and at very high interest. When after a number of summers the buyer was unable to pay the ever-increasing sum and ended in bottomless debt the nomad would first take over his livestock and later his land. This land would be leased out, in some cases to the former owner, and the nomad would thereafter receive a fixed proportion of the yearly yield. It appeared, writes Ferdinand, that it was predominantly the prosperous nomads - often *khāns* and *maliks* - who were able to give this kind of credit, and some of them became large landowners in Hazarajat. In addition to the grazing grounds allotted to them they now also possessed farmlands, which gave a surplus both for consumption in their own household and for further trade (Ferdinand 1962: 132 ff.). Such utilisations of opportunities in Hazarajat had a considerable influence on the Zala Khān Khēl community. Zala Khān Khēl's economy was in an ascending spiral.

3,24 Two generations of Zala Khān Khēl (K.F., Ghorghori, July 1975).

3,25 Hazara children (G.P., Bamiyan, July 1975).

It is also a part of the overall picture that the Hazara were, and to some degree still are, regarded as second-class persons by the nomads. The Hazara were the conquered and oppressed people, who were being punished for their opposition against the Amir. They differed from the Pashtuns in being a separate ethnic group, and they were (and are) moreover a Shia-muslim minority in the Sunni-dominated Afghanistan, which was (and is) an easily used excuse for mobilising animosity against them among the surrounding population groups. During the campaign of conquest the Amir even went so far as to get the priesthood in Kabul to declare religious war - *jehād* - against the Hazara (Kakar 1971: 165; Mohammad 1915: 8). This sanctification of the war was, incidentally, reciprocal (Mohammad, loc. cit.). The Amir's awarding of land in Hazarajat to the nomads as well as to settled Pashtuns was a move in the royal policy of oppression (Kakar, op.cit.). The nomads were already strongly organised and well armed groups, whose presence in the highlands could help to prevent the Hazara from recovering their strength. The nomads had thus a government-sanctioned political and military predominance which made exploitation of the Hazara in trade relations even easier. In further support of nomad activities in the highlands the government offered in certain periods particularly favourable import regulations - so long as they kept away from the town markets (see further on this point Ferdinand (forthcoming, a)).

For many Zala Khān Khēl trade developed to such an extent that livestock rearing gradually became of less importance. Economic decisions were increasingly determined by the trading activities. The yearly migrations continued, but with limited flocks and herds which permitted a greater concentration of labour on trading. The centre of gravity was moved further and further away from pastoralism.

3,26 The summer quarters of a Zala Khān Khēl household (K.F., Ghorghori, July 1975).

Changes in the winter areas

The British occupation in 1849 of the regions up to the Sulaiman mountains quickly had important restrictive effects on the nomads, both directly and indirectly. An early result of the legislation and administration of the colonial power - and of its military presence - was a certain political stability. This led to an increase in population, which in turn resulted in competition for arable land in the lowlands. There was pressure on agricultural land, the irrigation systems were extended, and the cultivated areas gradually expanded at the expense of the pastures. With the Imperial administration behind them the settled farmers felt more secure, and they increasingly gave vent to their dissatisfaction with the nomads' presence in the region. This development seems to have started as early as the end of the 1880s (*Census of India* 1931, XV). On top of this came the direct British interference which limited and regulated the movements of nomads in the lowlands. By 1910 it could already be noted that the number of Afghan nomads wintering in British India was diminishing (Enriquez 1910: 122 ff.).

The nomads experienced the coming of the "new times" in various ways. The most far-reaching impact on thir lives was the fact that they became subject to the general legislation whenever they wished to move in British India. This involved, among other things, that they were not allowed to bring with them firearms, over and above a certain quota per group, considered necessary for self-defence. Excess weapons had to be deposited at fixed points on entry and could be taken again on departure from the country. A regulation of this nature has certainly been of great importance to the change mentioned above in the balance of power between nomads and settled.

For the regulation of the nomadism itself taxes were imposed on animals brought down to the lowlands. These taxes varied from area to area in an attempt to control the development. Also out of consideration for local conditions time limits were introduced for the nomads' stay in the various areas. In the Kurram valley, where Zala Khān Khēl resided in the winters, the authorities, out of a desire to protect the grazing opportunities of the local population, prohibited the entry of the nomads before 1st November (Enriquez 1910: 122 ff.).

British dominance was also shown in single episodes which demonstrate the weakened position of the nomads. For example, in 1944 the harvest had failed in the North-West Frontier Province and to prevent the nomads from becoming an economic burden they were requested to bring grain with them from Afghanistan, where the harvest that year had been good. Although it is admitted that communication with the nomads was far from good, and that it was therefore not necessarily the fault of the nomads if they did not bring grain from Afghanistan to the lowlands, the British nevertheless acted rigorously. For the nomads were not only forbidden to buy grain in the local shops; they were also debarred from their buying markets in the Indian lowlands, such as Thal bazaar, unless they brought grain along (India Office Records R/12/1/42 379 Part II). It is probable that this particular episode must be explained in the light of the war situation. Because of the necessity of supplying the British Army it was not possible to shuttle grain stocks around in India to the same degree as in peacetime, in order to compensate for a local harvest failure.

The source material for the British colonial period is comprehensive and varied, and gives opportunities for many interesting studies in detail of the conditions in and around the wintering areas of East Afghan nomads. We shall not, however, here pursue this theme, but merely allow the examples quoted to illustrate the effects which the course of events has had upon the nomads.

Also the Afghan state made its administration more effective, and desired a better control of the trading activities of the nomads. At times there were, as mentioned, favourable import conditions for nomads, and special customs stations were established for them on the traditional migration routes. Thus Zala Khān Khēl had to pass customs at Almara in Khost. Despite the favourable terms there can scarcely have been many nomads who felt it reasonable that they should pay duty at all. To this day it is regarded as good entertainment to tell stories of how one has fooled the authorities time after time and thus shown one's independence of the government. Many informants among Zala Khān Khēl tell with glee how it had practically become the general rule that at least half of their pack-camels loaded with Indian textiles and other trade goods were led by routes avoiding the customs house at Almara and thus escaped the paying of duty.

The Afghan authorities were well aware of this practice and tried to obtain tighter control. A step in this direction was afforded by the Anglo-Afghan Trade Convention of 1921. This agreement gave the Afghan government authority to station trade agents at three places in Indian territory - at Quetta, Peshawar, and Parachinar at the upper end of the Kurram valley, northwest of Thal - with a view to controlling imports into Afghanistan and in the hope of stopping illegal importing by nomads and others (India Office

Records 1922-32). Files (ibid.) contain repeated requests from the Afghan government to be allowed to make the control more effective by stationing additional trade agents at Bannu and at Dera Ismael Khan, and by moving the agent at Parachinar to Thal instead. This last move would mean better possibilities of control in that area, as Thal is the purchasing centre for many Afghan merchants and is moreover a bottleneck on the routes through the region. The documents show that the British did not like the Afghans moving their officials around on Indian territory but do not reveal what agreement was finally reached. What does appear with considerable clarity is the desire of the Afghan government for stronger centralised control. The main purpose of the trade agreement between Afghanistan and British India had, however, quite different perspectives, which affected nomad trade much more seriously than a handful of scattered agents. For the agreement allowed Afghanistan duty-free import and export in transit through India. Many of the goods on which the nomads had based their trade were hereafter imported into Afghanistan by more formal channels (Robinson 1935: 24).

With the creation of Pakistan as an independent state in 1947, changes in the wintering region of Zala Khān Khēl took a new turn. Many of the business associates of the nomads had been Hindu merchants and moneylenders, and in 1947 these Hindus fled to the new India. Trade connections became uncertain and the supply of goods problematic. Ferdinand writes, describing a group of Niazi trading nomads whom he met in Hazarajat in the summer of 1953: "Most of the goods had been bought in Kabul, for the range of goods in Pakistan after Partition in 1947 had become small and poor - altogether one went less to Pakistan than before" (Ferdinand 1962: 136).

The tightening of control and administration which had begun under the British continued under the new Pakistan government, and many nomads stopped crossing the frontier altogether. From data collected by Ferdinand in 1975 it appears that many Mustaf Khēl, the other large Taghar group, which through the years have distinguished themselves as nomads and trading nomads, were among those who ceased to cross the frontier shortly after Partition in 1947.

Frontier problems

The Zala Khān Khēl continued their trade for some years after Partition, but they were soon to feel the consequences of the growing frontier problems. The British had bequeathed to Pakistan the so-called Durand Line as the western frontier of the country with Afghanistan. As mentioned, this line was created in 1893 as a result of Great Game between Russia and Britain (British India), with Afghanistan as a buffer state. Afghanistan was at that time forced to accept the Durand Line as a frontier between British and Afghan spheres of interest, but many Afghan Pashtuns considered the area east of this line, which is inhabited by Pashtuns, as a natural part of their sphere of interest, and as a region which rightly should come under Afghan rule. After 1947 it was therefore a thorn in the side of Afghanistan that Pakistan as a matter of course took over the disputed area. The Pashtunistan conflict developed and culminated in 1961-63, when Pakistan asserted its western frontier so restrictively that it in practice was closed, as already mentioned. This had serious consequences for the Afghan state as a whole, as a large part of the country's imports and exports went in transit through Pakistan; but it had also serious consequences for the nomads who had been able to operate to and fro across the loosely administered Durand Line. In the aggravated situation Pakistan demanded that the nomads should hold passports and vaccination certificates, as well as health certificates for their livestock, a demand which it was virtually impossible to fulfil. As a result Afghan nomads were cut off from important winter grazing grounds, and consequently many of them were compelled to abandon nomadism. The possibilities for using alternative grazing grounds within the frontiers of Afghanistan only existed to a limited extent.

Infrastructural development

The trading activities of the nomads met competition in several forms during the first half of this century. The trade agreement between Afghanistan and British India encouraged trading activity outside the influence of the nomads, but competition also intensified as a modern transport system gradually developed with lorries as the new means of transport. The trading capacity of the nomads lay partly in the fact that their camels could be used as transport-animals, partly in the fact that their pastoral nomadism caused them to travel from market to market. The camel is a born loser in competition with the lorry, providing that there are roads, and in the question of markets it must be realised that they are only exclusive to the nomads as long as there is no alternative transportation. Nomad trade has accordingly possibilities only in areas to which the lorry cannot yet penetrate.

One of the first stretches of road in Afghanistan which could be used by lorries was the Quetta-Chaman-Kandahar road which was opened about 1923. Thereafter camel transport on this route was considerable reduced (Robinson 1935: 25). From 1924 the road between Peshawar and Kabul was passable for cars (Rhein and Ghaussy 1966: 130). In British India a network of roads and railways had been constructed by the turn of the century, but in Afghanistan road-building was first seriously begun after 1930 (ibid.), and many years were to pass before lorries could make their way into the central highlands of Afghanistan. Here the nomads were to have a monopoly for some time yet. Robinson, however, is in no doubt as to the direction in which things are moving. In an as-

3,27-8 In 1935 Robinson clearly saw a tendency in the infrastructural development towards the camel being ousted by the lorry. While this fact has been the case in general, camel caravans are still used in certain areas of the country, as here in the North Afghan plains and in the northern foothills of the Hindukush (G.P., Khulm, Sept. 1978).

sessment of "The future of migration" of the *powindahs* (the British-Indian term used about the Pashtun trading nomads) he writes:

> "In the march of civilisation, nomads all over the world are gradually compelled to settle on the land and resign their nomadic habits, and in this the Ghilzais and other Powindah tribes cannot be considered exceptions. But besides the usual agencies at work which gradually fix the nomad, there are other causes apparent which must cause the Powindah to adopt a settled existence sooner than might otherwise be expected. Competition by mechanical transport is rapidly ousting the camel, and both the carrying trade and import and export trade between India and Afghanistan are passing out of the hands of the Powindahs; the usury and cloth hawking business, once so profitable, have a future by no means bright; and there are signs that even the casual labourer will gradually find it more difficult to obtain employment in India than he has done in the past. Again, grazing areas available for flocks and camels in British India and tribal tracts must tend to become more restricted as the population of India increases and land development proceeds. Thus, the migration which in former times amply repaid the Powindah for all its difficulties and dangers is hardly worth the trouble any longer, and a desire to settle is apparent even among the most confirmed nomads among all the Ghilzai tribes, the Spin Nasar" (Robinson 1935: 30-31).

NOTES

1 This apparently contradictory aspect of Pashtun society is discussed by, among others, Barth (1959a and 1959b) and Christensen (1980 etc.) against a background of data from sedentary Pashtuns.

2 Robinson's work is marked by a desire to produce a schematic survey in outline of certain conditions among the East Afghan nomads which would be of interest to the British administration of these peoples when they were spending the winter in British Indian territory. He gives a relatively static picture of the situation at the time in question (1932-34), and we obtain only a limited understanding of the dynamics in the nomads' formation of groups and in their economic involvement, as well as of the dynamics in the interaction between group formation and economics. Robinson has only been interested in these structures at a certain level.

CHAPTER 4

A TURNING POINT

THE 1950s AND 1960s

TRADING COMES TO AN END

In the previous chapter we called attention to some of the factors which have influenced nomadism and trading nomadism in East Afghanistan from the middle of the last century up to the middle of this century. These factors are all part and parcel of the general macro-structural development. We do not possess sufficient information to enrich this description with one at the micro-structural level. We can throw light on the consequences of the development for Zala Khān Khēl as a whole, but we cannot obtain any graduated insight into the ways in which this development affects the social organisation and cultural perception of the Zala Khān Khēl - how sub-groups and households fare and react to the possibilities and limitations offered. That changes did take place becomes clear, however, when we look at the situation of the Zala Khān Khēl from about the middle of the 1950s. For at that time obvious differences appear in the ways in which the sub-groups and households of Zala Khān Khēl organise themselves - first in regard to economic activities and later in localisation. That no information concerning the earlier situation speaks of internal differences is undoubtedly linked to the fact that until the middle of the 1950s Zala Khān Khēl did not display such kind of socio-economic differentiation. All the households practised nomadism and trade in a pattern of traditional unity and organisation.

In the first half of the 20th century when trade was booming in the central highlands all households upgraded trade and downgraded stock-keeping, but there were differences between one household and another as to how much weight they lent to these activities, the Zala Khān Khēl told me. Some built up a more successful trade than others. They could invest more and make greater profits - compare Ferdinand's statement that it was often *khāns* and *maliks* who had the economic means to engage in the more profitable forms of trade (Ferdinand 1962). Among the less successful the explanation is often heard that the others were more harsh in their trading methods, forcing the Hazara into ruining transactions, charging exorbitant interest rates, and in general paying more regard to their own businesses than to the common interests of Zala Khān Khēl. However that may be, it is a fact that some people became wealthy through trade, and that the economic significance of stock-keeping diminished. Other households achieved a moderate success in trade, while maintaining a stock-keeping activity of a certain importance to the joint economy.

4,1 and 4,2 "After all, that has been our life, and we love trading, but we know there is no money to be made any more here in the highlands." Khwazak Pashtun (G.P., Chaghcharan, July 1975).

From about the middle of this century new demands are imposed upon the Zala Khān Khēl. The tendencies at the macro-structural level are the ones outlined in the previous chapter. What is novel in the situation is that the opportunities and reactions of the individual households to new demands tend to transgress the common framework of social and political organisation which until now has bound Zala Khān Khēl together and which has given them the outward appearance of a homogeneous group of trading nomads. Before a description of the process of differentiation undergone by Zala Khān Khēl is given, some of the important factors of the general socio-economic transformation after Partition in 1947 shall be sketched.

The infrastructural development of Afghanistan was in steady progress from the beginning of the 1920s. Gradually first one and then another region of the central highlands were connected by road to the outside world. Lorries reached still

4,3 The new permanent bazaars of Central Afghanistan receive regular supplies by lorry (G.P., Chaghcharan, July 1975).

more places, and with them came merchants and goods. Some nomads themselves made use of lorry transport, but the most significant thing was that with the coming of the lorry the market was opened to town-based merchants.

In many ways the year 1961 marks the end of an epoch as already mentioned. The closing of the frontier between Afghanistan and Pakistan had severe consequences for both pastoral nomadism and nomad trade. It became practically impossible to cross the frontier with flocks and herds. The nomads' transport of goods across the frontier suffered badly but was not entirely thwarted. It was still possible to find secret paths through the frontier mountains for loaded camels, but, during the two years that the frontier dispute was at its fiercest, more and more of the purchasing was diverted to the Afghan town-bazaars.

Concurrently with the escalating of the frontier dispute the Afghan government put into effect a number of restrictions on nomad trade. In a desire to control imports now they took measures against the nomads' summer bazaars in the western highlands. The bazaars of Abul and Gomao, among others, were prohibited, and in 1961 trade was transferred to Kassi, which was enlarged after 1964 to become the government capital in the province of Ghor, changing its name to Chaghcharan. This was a political move to bring the trade of the nomads within a system which permitted supervision by the authorities (see Ferdinand 1978 and (forthcoming, a)). The extension of Chaghcharan exemplified in one important way the general transformation of the living conditions of the highlands: a permanent bazaar was built, with frequent supplies by lorry from the larger trading centres - in the summer half of the year, be it noted. In the winter the highlands were closed by snow and the roads impassable. Many of the businessmen are merchants from the larger cities, Kabul, Kandahar, and Herat, and they would normally leave the area before the passes were blocked. From time to time the Afghan government also imposed regulations for control of the nomads' imports and their marketing possibilities.

One last factor affected this closing phase of nomad trade: the drought of 1971-72. This catastrophe hit especially hard the western parts of the country, and brought about widespread poverty which drastically reduced purchasing power among the inhabitants of the highlands here. In the summer of 1975 we met only few and small groups of trading nomads in the central and western highlands, and they were all unanimous in their assessment of the severity of the situation. A Khwazak trader, whose tent was erected on the market-place in Chaghcharan, expressed himself thus:

"Our trade has been going down for a long time, and with the drought it is as good as finished. We are here solely to collect outstanding debts from our old trading partners, but it is a difficult job. Some of them can maybe pay a fraction of their debts to us, but most of them cannot pay anything at all. We can see that we have to remit them their debts, and we suffer heavy losses as we have always been accustomed to giving credit in our trade. We have also this year brought a small amount of goods with us up here, but that is purely out of habit. After all, that has been our life, and we love trading, but there is no money to be made any more here in the highlands."

The government has ever since the 1950s been aware of the potentialities that lay with the wealthier nomads. From time to time these nomads have been urged to engage themselves in other sides of the Afghan economy than nomadism and nomad trade. When nomads have engaged in other activities, the state not only receives new economic input in various forms, it also gets rid of part of a "problem-population". The nomads are above all urged to buy agricultural land, in the hope that they will settle down as farmers. But they are also encouraged to invest in lorry transport, which has been of considerable importance to parts of Zala Khān Khēl.

SOCIO-ECONOMIC DIFFERENTIATION

After the middle of the 1950s the transformation of the Zala Khān Khēl society continued to be closely bound up with the macro-structural development of the country. The follow-

4,4 The Musa Khēl were among the first Taghar nomads to settle. Some of them now live in this village of Abchakan in Logar (G.P., Aug. 1975).

ing analysis illustrates this connection, and will at the same time show how a tribally organised group may react when it comes under a certain outer pressure under conditions which make it necessary to seek alternatives outside the confines of nomadism and trading nomadism. We shall witness how it led to the internal dissolution of this tribal group and the gradual settlement of these nomads. The course of events illuminate how an economic differentiation was followed by a geographic dispersion, and it will describe how the socio-economic framework formerly held in common by all Zala Khān Khēl dissolved, and new frames of reference emerged on a foundation of smaller genealogical groupings.

Land purchase

Throughout most of the first half of the present century Zala Khān Khēl's trade in the central highlands was in a state of steady advancement as we heard. Expansion was both geographic and economic. Trading profits were invested in more trade, bringing in its wake a lesser engagement in stock-breeding among those households which turned to trading.

In the 1940s this tendency began to change. The creation of Pakistan in 1947 had a certain influence, but there were also limits to the amount of goods that could be sold to the residents of the highlands and to the other groups who came to the highlands in the summer. A certain measure of satiety was reached. Moreover, competition from merchants based in the towns was becoming still more noticeable. The nomads were no longer the sole suppliers of the market. Among the greater of the trading nomad it therefore became a problem to find employment for the profits that trade had brought in. It could no longer be invested in expansion of the trade and traditional markets.

In a situation like this one might have expected that the profit could be put to use through an expansion of the herds. Such a disposition would fall within the economic and organisational bounds within which Zala Khān Khēl had hitherto operated. However, this solution was made unattractive by the gradual reduction of the winter grazing grounds. For households with a moderate amount of trade and of livestock this raised no great problems, but the more prosperous had to seek new paths for employing their profits. These were found through purchase of land.

Many Afghan nomads have in the course of time acquired agricultural land, and have settled on that land. Elphinstone described this situation as early as the beginning of the last century (Elphinstone 1972), and it is a well-known phenomenon among nomads all over the world at all times. Rowton's studies of West Asian source material dating back to antiquity prove this with notable examples (Rowton 1973a etc.). In his treatise on the Basseri nomads in southern Iran, Barth describes how wealthy nomads invest in land, and how this leads to a gradual settlement of these as landlords and hence to a peeling off from the top of the nomad community (Barth 1961). Among other Taghar groups this process is well under way. Many Mustaf Khēl (see *Fig.* 2.x) are, for example, settled on their own land in the province of Logar.

In 1956 Zala Khān Khēl took the initial step in that direction - they bought land in Dahana-i Ghori in the northern province of Baghlan. The government had encouraged nomads to purchase land in Baghlan, and, after some Mustaf Khēl had done so, Zala Khān Khēl also became interested. The first year 20 households made a joint purchase of 1,200 *jarīb* (about 240 hectares), all of which were divided among the purchasers. The price was about 1,500 afs. per *jarīb* of irrigated land and about 200 afs. per *jarīb* of un-irrigated land. During the following two years more households bought land in Dahana-i Ghori, and some of the first buyers made additional purchases. In 1957 the price of irrigated land had risen to about 2,000 afs. per *jarīb*, and in 1958 it was 3,000 afs. per *jarīb*. After this three-year rush a total of 56 Zala Khān Khēl households had acquired land in Dahana-i Ghori. Two had over 200 *jarīb* (an equal of about 40 hectares) of irrigated and un-irrigated land, a few had about 100 *jarīb*, while some had 20 to 25 *jarīb*, and some only very few *jarīb*.

Not all households had taken the opportunity of becoming landowners in Dahana-i Ghori, however. One reason was that the purchase of any quantity of land required considerable liquid capital, and therefore only the more wealthy could take advantage of the government offer. They were those who had profited most from the nomad trade and now lacked alternative investment opportunities. Another reason was that some Zala Khān Khēl who might have been able to afford to buy land found Baghlan the wrong place to own land because it was on the other side of the Hindukush mountains and far away from accustomed routes. Better wait, they thought, until a better chance is offered in an acceptable area in the provinces of Logar and Paktya or in Nangarhar. As will appear, this waiting gave no result, mainly because those who were able to afford land in the 1950s saw themselves in the meantime overtaken by rising land prices.

The newly acquired land was indeed far away in northern Afghanistan. The climate there was moreover bad, with hot summers and slushy winters, and the region was infested with malaria. Nor had it originally been the intention of the households to settle on their land. The purchases were talked of as a secure investment of money - "your stock can be stolen, but no one can run off with your land" - and the land was completely left in the hands of tenant farmers, *dihqāns*, who supplied both draught animals and seed grain and who therefore according to local practice had a right to half the yield, the other half going to the landowner.

With a few exceptions all the landowning households gave up the last of their nomadic pastoralism, but they continued their trading activities together with the rest of Zala Khān Khēl. The annual migrations took place as before, but daily life became even more variegated for the households, since the landowning households were now completely free of pastoral duties - except for those involving the camels, which were still necessary as pack-animals for merchandise.

Frontier closing, geographical dispersal, and economic reorganisation

With the closing of the frontier in 1961 purchasing in Pakistan practically ceased for two years, and it was impossible to cross the frontier with flocks and herds, as we have seen. The choice which the households had to make in this critical situation illuminates the internal economic differentiation of the group and a consequence was a geographical dispersion. Zala Khān Khēl broke up in units which fell in three categories. At the same time the first regular settling took place[1].

The first category to emerge consisted of the households which had purchased land and which no longer had flocks to take into account. These were largely all the households in sub-*khels* 1 and 4, as well as some of the households in sub-*khels* 3 and 5 (see *Fig. 2,5*). They chose to pass the winter on their properties in Dahana-i Ghori. As has been said, it was not the best of climates, but at least one had not to ask permission of anyone to stay there. For a couple of years yet these households lived in their black goat's hair tents during the winter, but then they began to have permanent houses built on their land. The winters could now be better endured, but the summer was still regarded as too hot, and the migrations continued to Ghorghori in Hazarajat. The summer trading, too, continued, but it was markedly waning.

The second category consisted of the households which still had flocks, large or small, to care for. They were the whole of sub-*khels* 2 and 6, as well as some of the households in sub-*khels* 3 and 5. The closure of the frontier cut them off not only from their buying markets but also from their winter grazing grounds. In common with many other nomads they had to seek new winter grazing grounds within the frontiers of Afghanistan. The possibilities were limited to the low-lying areas of the eastern provinces - especially Khost in the province of Paktya, where the livestock-owning households of Zala Khān Khēl chose to encamp for the winters. Many other nomads were forced to make the same choice, with the result that Khost in winter had a high concentration of both animals and people. The annual migrations continued, necessitated by both the stock-keeping and nomad trade.

The third category which split off geographically was 15 households whose economy for some years had been steadily deteriorating. These households, which together comprise the whole of sub-*khel* 7, had, allegedly, ruined themselves as a result of many years' engagement in a feud with some Daulatzai Pashtun in Pakistan. They owned no land and had entirely given up stock-keeping. Their principal income came from pauper employment, *gharībī*, in Pakistan during the winter. For some years it was the practice of some of the male members of these households to remain in Pakistan during the summer in order to sell their labour, while the remainder migrated to Hazarajat with the rest of Zala Khān Khēl. In the new situation they chose to stay the whole year on the Pakistan side of the frontier, and to drop completely the last remnants of stock-keeping and nomad trade. They moved to Lahore, where they live all the year round on the outskirts of the city. From 1961 they are settled (see *Fig. 6,1*).

Throughout the 1960s the course of events is marked by retrenchment in all the traditional economic areas. The nomads' share of the highland trade declines in importance, while city merchants expand their business in the new bazaars. The once so favourable association of nomadism and trade no longer bears fruit and even though it is still possible to send men and camels on buying trips to Thal they cannot hold their place in competition with the modern trading system. Stock-breeding cannot be sustained under the critical conditions in the new winter areas. Up until the 1970s - with the drought years of 1971-72 providing the *coup de grace* - one household after another abandons both stock-keeping and the highland trade. The landowners are the first to give up trading, while some of the others for some years yet go on trading journeys to Charas in the northern part of the central highlands. This occurs for the last time in the summer of 1973, after which everyone disposed of all their camels, sheep and goats.

While this process is going on, an important step is taken by a small group of the most well-to-do households. They respond to a direct appeal from the government to invest in the country's transport sector, and by the middle of the 1960s they buy their first lorries. Fifteen of these households - all from sub-*khel* 1 - settle permanently by themselves in 1968 in Qala-i Niazbeg, a village just west of Kabul. Thus from the middle of the 1970s we find Zala Khān Khēl divided into four main groups, geographically separated, and each with its own new economic sphere of activity. The four categories are perceived here as forming an order of rank, and at the same time illustrating four different stages in the process of settlement. This should not be regarded as a unilinear process of evolution, in the sense that all parties in the course of time will undergo the same development. On the contrary, it will become clear that the four groups - the lorry owners, the landowners, the landless, and the emigrants - exemplify four tendencies pointing in different directions and governed by differences in the economic starting point. In the next chapter we shall look more closely at the first three groups; the fourth, the households which have taken up residence in Pakistan, could not be covered by this field-work. I shall describe the milieu of the groups, their activities and their development in relation to the common background of Zala Khān Khēl as nomads and trading nomads.

NOTES

1 The reader is referred to Chapter 2, where it is told how sections genealogically belonging to Zala Khān Khēl had previously settled. These sections fall outside our immediate field of interest however, because they became settled before the expansion of nomad trade in central Afghanistan.

CHAPTER 5

ECONOMIC DEVELOPMENT AND DECLINE

ZALA KHĀN KHĒL IN THE 1970s

THE SETTLED LORRY-OWNERS

The land purchases of the 1950s gave a clear indication of the economic differences within Zala Khān Khēl. It was the wealthy who became landowners. The land purchases demanded considerable means, but a little group of households had not tied up all their savings. When the government's transport agency, General Transport (*Riasat-i Omumi Transport-i Dawlati*) - whose director at that time was an Ahmadzai - invited investment in the sector of modern lorry transport, the wealthiest of the households responded favourably - and this time not merely from a desire to safeguard the profits from nomad trade, as was the case when land was bought, but from a desire to enter a profitable branch of business.

Afghanistan has no railway system. With the gradual extension of the network of roads the lorry has therefore become the most important factor in the transport business. Camel transport still has certain niches, but on the national level the lorry has become dominant, and it is manoeuvred with great skill and often with a considerable degree of daring along even the most impossible tracks in the mountainous country. A special lorry-culture has evolved, which is not only expressed in the exuberant decoration of the vehicles (in its own right worthy of separate studies - see for example Centlivres-Demont 1976; Lefebvre 1984 and 1985), but also in the sporting attitude of some of the drivers to their job. It is, however, neither love of folkloristic lorry-decoration nor sporting spirit which inspired Zala Khān Khēl to invest in lorries, but rather the good prospects of profits.[1]

In 1975-76 the modern transport sector is indeed good business, but it demands also heavy investment. General Transport follows up its appeals by easing import conditions for lorries during the introductory period, and by giving favourable loans. In the middle of the 1960s some Zala Khān Khēl households buy their first lorries for 2-300,000 afs. each (equivalent to 4-6,000 US $ at that time). In the first year these households acquires 12 lorries, and it is claimed that several of them were paid for in cash without recourse to loan. The first lorries are all of the widespread English relatively small Bedford type. This type is still common, but it is typical of the enterprising Zala Khān Khēl that the latest lorries to be bought are of a particularly large type for Afghanistan - several of the American make MAK capable of carrying around twenty-one tons or 3,000 Kabul-*sēr*, according to the owners.

After having invested considerable funds in lorries, fifteen households of sub-*khēl* 1 decide in 1968 to do the job completely. They abandon all earlier activities and move to the village of Qala-i Niazbeg on the western outskirts of Kabul on a year-round basis in order to devote themselves exclusively to the transport business. After their settlement the fifteen households continue to expand in their new occupation, and in 1976 they own altogether more than fifty lorries.

Lorry transport

The Afghan transport market is in principle open to anyone, and is exploited by individual free-enterprise operation. All Zala Khān Khēl's lorries are owned by the individual households, who are totally free to look for and take on jobs for the vehicles. However, like many other lorry-owners Zala Khān Khēl has chosen to form transport associations. The most important function of a transport association is the centralised distribution of work to the associated lorries. It therefore runs an office, to which orders can be submitted. The efficiency and dependability which can thereby be built up will at the same time attract customers - particularly the government.

The Afghan government does not itself own lorries for civil transport. One of General Transport's main tasks is therefore to apportion transport work to private lorry-owners. It has been of particular importance for the government to ensure transport of building materials and of grain. From the carriers' viewpoint not all transport jobs are equally attractive. Short trips on asphalt roads are preferred, whereas long trips on poor roads to distant provinces are less attractive. General Transport therefore apportions its jobs in packages, negotiating with a transport association to take a certain number of good trips in return for undertaking some of the bad ones.

Membership of a transport association does not limit the individual lorry-owner's freedom of action. He may undertake the work that the association receives and then drive at certain fixed rates, or he may look for his own jobs and fix the rates himself in competition with other carriers. Membership of an association does not give any advantage apart from the centralised distribution of work. It does not include, for example, any reciprocal insurance. The individual owner is responsible for his vehicle and for its operation, and expenses or losses as a result of mechanical problems or accidents must be borne by the individual owner.

The majority of the lorries belonging to the Zala Khān Khēl in Qala-i Niazbeg are enroled in the two transport associations Ghamai Transport and Shawali Transport. Shawali Transport is also known by the name of Taghar Transport, which is an important name in the Afghan transport business. These associations were started by Shawali and Ghamai, who today are elderly men, and they cover exclusively lorries owned by Zala Khān Khēl. Some households have their lorries in Maydan Transport, where they form the majority. Among the Zala Khān Khēl who now spend the winters in Dahana-i Ghori there are five households who own a total of eight lorries. Five of these are attached to Ghamai Transport, while three have joined the association Syed Khān Transport.

The large-type lorries of Zala Khān Khēl are often hired by the government for special transport jobs. Such jobs may be long inland trips, or prestigious export and import traffic to and from Pakistan, Iran, and Turkey. Some of these vehicles also carry transit goods between Pakistan and Iran.

5,1 Lorries of Zala Khān Khēl parked outside Seray Herati in Kote Sangi (G.P., Kabul, Aug. 1975).

5,2 Also wealthy Musa Khēl nomads of Taghar have chosen to invest in lorries (G.P., Markuh, Nangarhar, Feb. 1976).

The drivers may be younger members of the lorry-owning household, but only on small quick jobs. It is the general opinion that the work as driver is hard and dangerous, and it is therefore mostly left in the hands of employed drivers. Some of these are from other Zala Khān Khēl households, but the majority are not Zala Khān Khēl. In principle these drivers are hired for one job at a time, but in practice there develops a connection of longer duration. For special transport tasks, or when frontiers are to be crossed with consequent paper-work, a young Zala Khān Khēl often accompanies the lorry, but otherwise the work is left to the driver and his assistant - the so-called *kīlīnar*[2], who is always along on longer and more difficult trips. One of his tasks in difficult mountain driving is to hang on to the outside of the vehicle and be ready with a large triangular wooden block on a stick, which is wedged fast under the wheels as an emergency brake during manoeuvring on steep and poor roads. The brake systems of the lorries are not always in acceptable condition, and they are weakened by overloading and frequent use in the mountains. The *kīlīnar*'s "reserve brake" is therefore often essential to life and limb, and a skilled *kīlīnar* is a highly valued fellow-worker - though at the bottom of the hierarchy.

At the top of the hierarchy stand of course Zala Khān Khēl as owners of the lorries, and to describe more closely Zala Khān Khēl's work and the social system in which they move it is necessary to look at the two localities of Kote Sangi and Qala-i Niazbeg, which are respectively Zala Khān Khēl's working and residential surroundings.

Kote Sangi

Kabul's western suburb of Kote Sangi bears obvious signs of being one of the new entrance gates to the capital (see map, *Fig. 5,3*). In earlier times all transport of goods went directly in to Kabul's central markets on the backs of animals or men, and later in small lorries when this means of transport began to come in. The bazaars contained not merely stalls for retail trade but also *serāys* i.e. enclosed yard systems for storage and wholesale trade. With increased trade, increased lorry traffic, and increase in the size of the lorries all this changed. The narrow alleys of the bazaars could not accommodate the traffic, nor were the old *serāys* adequate to cope with the new development. The suburbs around the entrance ways to Kabul accordingly evolved into new centres for storage and wholesale trade, and they became way stations in the transport of goods. New large *serāys* were built, where the lorries had unhindered access and from where the further transport into the bazaars goes by smaller vehicles or by two-wheeled goods-carts, *karachis*, pulled by one or more men. In connection with this development a whole series of service facilities for the lorry business arose - workshops, sparepart shops, and lorry-*serāys* i.e. parking and workshop yards. To these must be added tea houses and small shops dealing in foodstuffs and petty articles, to serve the many people who have their daily work in these areas (a more detailed description of the development of the Kabul bazaar will be found in Frederiksen (forthcoming)).

Such a suburb is Kote Sangi - an entrepot for a considerable part of Kabul's imports and exports, thanks to its position on the western entrance route from Kandahar and Herat. It is a busy suburb full of busy people employed in the modern trade and transport business. General Transport has its main office in Kote Sangi, as have the three main transport associations in which Zala Khān Khēl is involved. These offices, together with the lorry-*serāys*, are key places for Zala Khān Khēl's business activities. Among the lorry-*serāys* the most important is Serāy Herati on the western edge of Kote Sangi, close to Qala-i Niazbeg. It is called after its builder and owner, who came from Herat, and it consists of a two-storeyed building in three wings surrounding a courtyard measuring thirty by thirty metres, the fourth side being closed by a wall. Access for vehicles to the yard is through a portal in the central wing. Serāy Herati was built in 1972 and lies in a peripheral area which is still characterised by building in progress and by unfinished access roads surrounded by open fields. The upper storey of the *serāy* consists of fifty dwelling-rooms, all of which are rented out. On the ground floor there is a row of business premises, some still vacant. For the time being there are two automobile workshops and sparepart businesses, a smithy, a plumber, and a joiner, a butcher, a shop selling fruit and other foodstuffs, and a shop with petty articles for daily use.

The day-by-day responsibility for the *serāy* rests with a *serāydār*, who keeps watch on the area and collects rent for the premises and fees

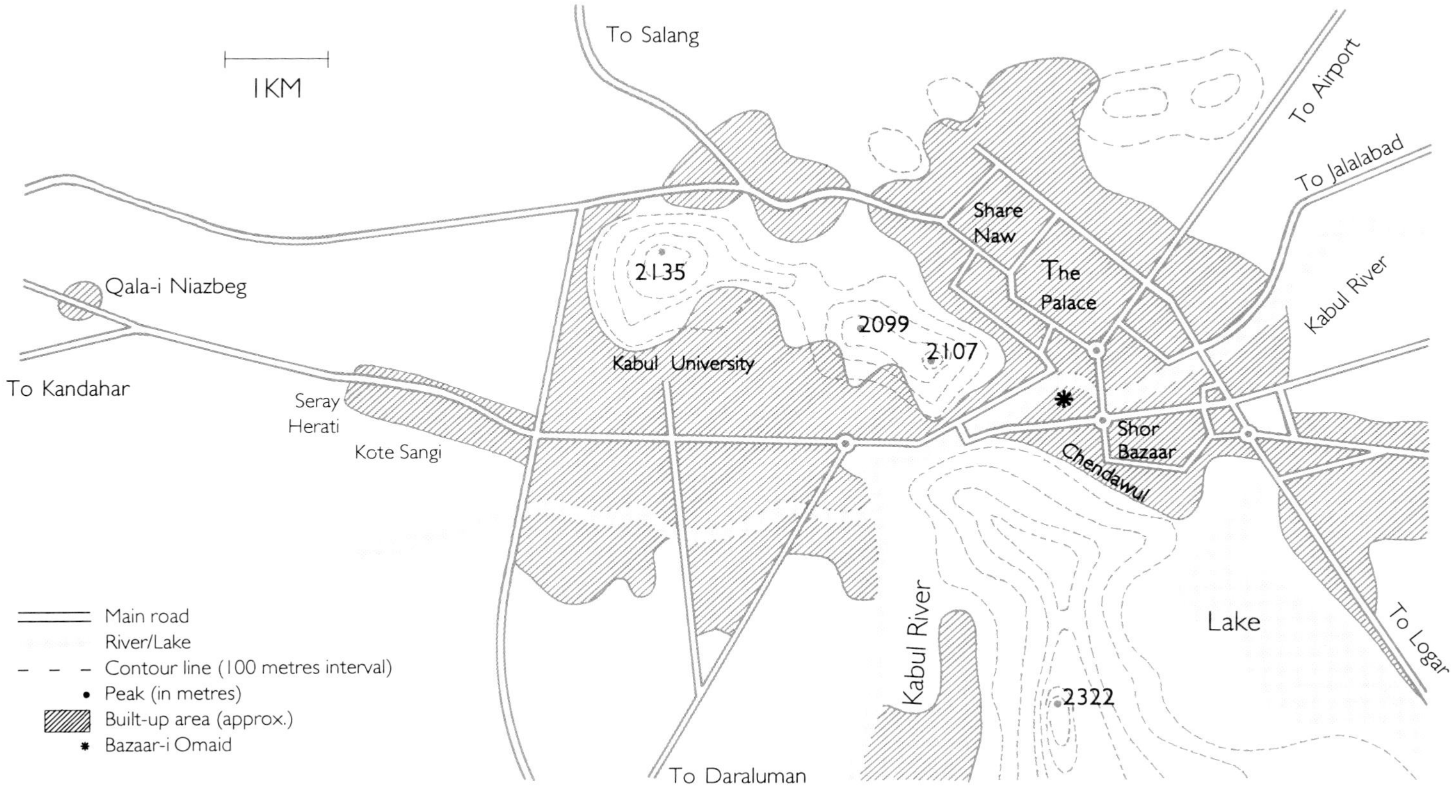

5,3 Kabul with entry roads in 1975.Kabul City is situated at a level of about 1,700 metres between and around three mountain massives raising up to 2,322 metres. The map shows the built-up areas as of 1975 when the city had around 500,000 inhabitants. Since then the number has increased to an estimated 1.4 million as an effect of the war. However, already in the early 1970s scarcity of land caused residential areas to expand up the mountain slopes. Old Kabul is the area south of the river around Shor Bazaar and Chendawul. This is still a busy bazaar area, but traffic and goods transport is hampered by streets being very narrow. Much of the commercial activity, and especially that related to wholesale, has therefore moved out to the entry roads of the city, notably to Kote Sangi where many new *serāys* were being built in the 1970s.

for the vehicles in the yard - 5 afs. per night per vehicle, no matter what the size. He must also see to it that government regulations concerning *serāys* are observed.

The activities in and around the *serāy* are marked by its primary function as a lorry-*serāy*. There are generally two or three lorries permanently in the yard - under repair or chocked up for a longer time. Discarded engine parts and tyres lie around in heaps. Towards evening the yard fills up with large and small lorries, and generally also one or two private cars - and the gate is shut for the night.

The workshops are busy, but tea-breaks are observed, and they take place in the shady portal, which acts as a meeting place for the workers and businessmen of the *serāy*. There is a little sitting-dais with a kelim rug, a couple of plastic folding chairs, some discarded car-seats and a long wooden beam which serves temporarily as a sitting place. Here one relaxes, and discusses all topics - for example a popular hobby to

5,4 The city of Kabul grows up-hill as the population expands (G.P., April 1978)

which the *serāydār* is devoted, caged songbirds. He has one in a little square cage hung from a beam in the portal and another one in a cage on the dais.

Among those sitting here and enjoying their green tea and the bird-song, surrounded by the noise of the workshops, the lorries, and the oil patches, are also the drivers, waiting for their employers - the men from Zala Khān Khēl. Serāy Herati can be used by anyone, but the regular customers are the two Zala Khān Khēl transport associations Shawali Transport and Ghamai Transport. The lorry-owners often visit the *serāy*, but they never stay very long. They come on business, and seldom take the time for a tea-break in the portal. Some come with the local bus which connects the centre of Kote Sangi with Qala-i Niazbeg, while others arrive in their private cars. They are typically from their late twenties to somewhere in their forties, and they are all immaculately dressed in artificial silk sewn in traditional fashion, baggy trousers, a long

5,5 Bazaar area of Kabul city (G.P., April 1978)

shirt, hanging loose and reaching to the knees, carried underneath a waistcoat, and on the head a silk turban wound in a characteristic style. Some wear expensive versions of traditional Afghan sandals, while others prefer modern leather shoes. The contrast with the drivers and the workers of the *serāy* is marked, and no one is in any doubt of the differences in status when the lorry-owners make their entrance.

Their business in the *serāy* is mainly concerned with three things: checking with the mechanics concerning some repair, hearing the drivers' reports of trips they have completed, and making arrangements for future jobs which they have received from General Transport or from private customers. The business is usually quickly completed, and the lorry-owners are out of the *serāy* again. "We are busy men", they say. "We have to keep in contact with General Transport and with private customers all the time, to get transport jobs for our vehicles. We have to check that the mechanics do their job, and we

5,7 New spacious *serāys* were built in the suburbs of Kabul (B.F., Kote Sangi, 1975).

have to engage drivers and arrange the trips with them. It's really quite strenuous work, and not at all enjoyable."

5,6 Cotton-*serāy* in Chendawul bazaar of Old Kabul. In places like this there is little room for expansion of business (G.P., Kabul, April 1975)Cotton *serāy* in Chendawul bazaar of Old Kabul. In places like this there is little room for expansion of business (G.P., Kabul, April 1975).

Comments of this sort are common among Zala Khān Khēl. One of them even claims that he would be willing to sell the whole business and be free of all the trouble, if the right buyer turned up. Such statements should, however, be taken with some reservation, for running lorries is a paying business, and Afghanistan does not offer many investment areas with equally good opportunities for profit.

When the day's transport contracts are safely home, and agreements with mechanics, drivers and others are settled, the lorry-owners call it a day and go home to Qala-i Niazbeg.

Qala-i Niazbeg

A few kilometres west of Kote Sangi, on the main road to Kandahar, lies the village of Qala-i Niazbeg (see map, *Fig. 5,3*). It is now in the process of becoming a suburb of Kabul, and it is here that Zala Khān Khēl bought building sites in 1968 and built their houses. They are built in the normal suburban style, the whole site of each household (around 18 *biswās* - about 0.18 hectares) being surrounded with a wall within which living rooms and outhouses are erected. There is a courtyard, and gardens are laid out so far as space allows.

The houses appear modest, but the interior leaves no doubt that we are dealing with prosperous families. The rooms are furnished in the traditional fashion such as is typically found among wealthy landowners in the country. The floor is covered with hand-knotted Afghan carpets and along three of the walls lie cotton-stuffed mattresses and large cushions in the traditional Afghan seating fashion. The mattresses are covered in cotton material in dark, subdued colours with patterns of small flowers, while the cushions have artificial silk covers in bright clear colours. There are no chairs or tables in Western style. Food and tea are served on a cloth spread on the floor or on small trays. A few pictures, framed and behind glass, hang on the walls - a coloured print with religious motifs and a few photographs of members of the family. In a niche stands a little glass vase with plastic flowers and a cassette-radio covered with a shawl embroidered with flowers to protect it from dust.

Part of the courtyard is planted with young fruit trees, but the most noticeable feature is that the courtyard is also used as storage space and rubbish dumps for old lorry parts; discarded motors lie on the cement terraces and there are heaps of outworn tyres. In one courtyard the past meets the present, for in the middle of the yard the family's old black goat's hair tent has been erected and serves as a cover for firewood and a store for old tyres.

It is easy to travel to and fro between Qala-i Niazbeg and Kote Sangi. There is a bus service together with a constant stream of taxis and other small vehicles, which connect the outer residential areas with Kote Sangi. In Qala-i Niazbeg one meets more Zala Khān Khēl than those who come to the transport offices and the *serāys*. Close by the place where one boards or leaves the bus there is an empty building lot roofed with simple straw matting. Here the men of the village gather, not only when they are waiting for transport to town, but also for relaxation and conversation. Here one can also meet Zala Khān Khēl in all ages, though most frequently the older men and the children. The women do not come here. They follow the Islamic custom of *purdah* and stay within the walls of their homes. Women who are waiting for transport to town stand at a proper distance from the men's meeting place and seek the shadow of a house-wall.

A look into the social categories of Zala Khān Khēl in Qala-i Niazbeg gives a picture of the transformation of the households in recent decades, and at the same time it may provide an indication of the possible directions of future development for this part of Zala Khān Khēl. The men fall roughly into three categories, related to age and occupation:

1) The old men - a little group of eight to ten persons aged over 50 - some of them "very old", as my young informants put it. Five of these men have the right to the title of *hajjī*, a sign that they have been on the *hajj*, the pilgrimage to Mecca. At the height of their economically active life they were pastoral nomads and successful trading nomads, and it was they who correctly

judged the trend of events in the 1950s and 1960s and took the decision to buy land in Dahana-i Ghori as well as lorries and houses in Qala-i Niazbeg. All of them are still the formal head of their extended three-generation household, but they are no longer directly involved in the new economic activities of the household. They mainly stay at home, or in the shade of the building site by the road, where they drink a glass of tea with plenty of sugar and keep an eye on the comings and goings in the village. Their occasional appearances in Kote Sangi are more recreational visits than business calls.

The old men are well dressed in the traditional fashion, but lack the extra polish which characterises the younger men of the households. They are in a double sense "old nomads", who can now lean back and relax. They talk preferably of the great days of the nomad trade and, if the anthropologist brings up the subject of modern transport business, they refer him to the younger folk - after perhaps a passing remark that it was in fact they, the old ones, who started it all.

2) The active men - a group of twenty to twenty-five men aged from the late twenties to somewhere in the forties. It is these men who characterise the households today. It is they who are active in the new lorry business and it is therefore also they who are to be met at the transport offices and the lorry-*serāys*. They have all grown up in black tents as nomads and trading nomads on the annual migrations, and they have spent adult years under these conditions and been active in the final phases of nomad trade.

As we have seen, they adopt the appearance of prosperous nomad traders, attaching importance to emphasising their status through refinement of the traditional costume. Their way of acting, too, is such that they are often deemed arrogant by those around them. When they return home to Qala-i Niazbeg in their cars they drive directly down the narrow alley and disappear behind their walls. If they come by bus they stalk rapidly with a dignified air by the same roads into the village, and make only a short pause, or none at all, at the building-site meeting place. They are busy men, with family responsibilities and a flourishing business, as they are not themselves averse to drawing attention to. The keepers of the tea houses and the small shops along the main road through Qala-i Niazbeg hardly see anything of them except when they come and go on their way in and out of the village. The old ones are queer, says one shopkeeper, and the others are both queer and stuck-up. Zala Khān Khēl is regarded as a newly arrived nomad upper class, who has not really found a place in the little village which, true enough, has become urban-like, but which is still a pronounced agricultural community.

3) The young men - a group of ten to twelve men and older boys under the age of 25. They differ from the previous group in a number of ways. It is not a question of a true generation gap, as they are in fact younger brothers of the active men. However, there is such a large variation in age between the households - and within a range of brothers - that the relationship often resembles rather that of father-son or uncle-nephew.

Their childhood lay back in a time of tents and migrations, but their youth and their growth to maturity has been marked by "the new times" with lorries and settled homes. Most of them dress, wholly or partly, according to modern city fashion, which means Western-style clothes with shirt, jacket, and slim trousers. Meet them in town, and they are always in this garb, but when you meet them at home it is not unusual to find that they have changed into Afghan "house-clothes" of a modest traditional style - a change which is common among Western-inclined city Afghans. They have all gone to school, some even to the 12th grade, and a few have gone higher in the educational system. In the extended households they are formally part-owners of the lorries, but they are not involved in running them, and they neither are given nor assume the same responsibilities as their elder brothers. Some of them say that their future no doubt lies in the lorry business, but for the moment they take it easy, and have plenty of time to stroll in the bazaar, to drink tea, and to talk.

In the consciousness of these young men the nomad and trading nomad past plays but a minor role. They can see and understand their elder brothers' busy daily life in the modern transport business, but they often regard their fathers as oldsters who have no idea of what matters today. The young men turn their eyes to Kabul and modern Afghanistan. When one talks to them over a glass of tea they are very interested in modern techniques, in the world outside, and in the possibilities of studying in Europe or of making a quick fortune as emigrant workers. Not surprisingly, it was among these young men the anthropologist made his first personal contacts with Zala Khān Khēl, as described in Chapter 2.

A stay in Qala-i Niazbeg gives little opportunity to a male anthropologist to familiarise himself with the women living there. As mentioned, the women are subject to *purdah*, the normal Afghan customs as regards public appearance and conduct of women when there are male strangers present. It is therefore not possible for me to describe their situation in the changing conditions of Zala Khān Khēl. The children of both sexes, on the other hand, move freely around as always. They know nothing of tent-life and nomadism, they all go to public elementary schools when they are of the age for it and, in general, they give the impression of being the village or suburban children which they in fact are. They have more actual freedom, however, than many village children, since they do not grow up under conditions which permit or necessitate an early participation in the household economy. Elder brothers and sisters are looking after younger siblings; and children, at least girls, have duties in connection with minor practical tasks in the home. But there are no flocks which need herding, and no need for fetching firewood in the mountains.

THE MIGRANT LANDOWNERS

The town of Pul-i Khomri in the province of Baghlan is situated in the northern foot-hills of the Hindukush mountains. From here the landscape begin to open out into wide valleys and stretches of plains. To the west lies a large shallow valley and on the western edge of this, about 20 kilometres from Pul-i Khomri, lies the little market-town of Dahana-i Ghori (see map, *Fig. 3,16)*. Dahana-i Ghori is reached by a dirt road which in winter is barely passable. The weather at this time of the year varies between snow, sleet, and rain, and heavy lorry traffic churns up the road until it is difficult to distinguish from the surrounding ditches and irrigation channels. When one stretch of road becomes too muddy the route takes an improvised track out over the surrounding fields. Passenger traffic is carried on by small pick-ups with four-wheel drive. Ordinary private cars are a rarity during winter. It is in this area that fifty-six Zala Khān Khēl households bought farmland in the 1950s. Most of them have only small plots, while some are large landowners. Six households live here all the year round,

5,8 During winter the area of Dahana-i Ghori can be dreary, cold, and muddy (G.P., Dahana-i Ghori, Feb. 1976).

while thirty-one households at present choose to be here only for the winter, and seven households only for the summer.

Zala Khān Khēl's lands are scattered over a large area. Some of them have built houses in clusters conveniently close to the road between Pul-i Khomri and Dahana-i Ghori, while other houses are reached only after some kilometres driving by small sideroads or walking by paths and on the embankments between the fields. Of the six households that live here all the year round five own no land themselves. They are servant families, *hamsāyas*, and tenant farmers, *dihqāns*, on other people's land - two of them on land owned by other Zala Khān Khēl. These two comprise an exception, since it is a common attitude that one should not have close relatives employed as tenant farmers. It can bring problems, the landowners say, if the relationship between employer and employed collides with the standards dictated by blood relationship. The exception is occasioned by the fact that the

5,9 Residential area of Pul-i Khumri on a sunny winter day (G.P., Feb. 1976). pp. 164-5

5,10 Shopping in the bazaar of Pul-i Khomri (G.P., Feb. 1976).

two Zala Khān Khēl are landless and poor, and to have them as *dihqāns* is considered a way to provide for them. The sixth family has a little land of its own, and in addition farms the land of others. The large landowners are found partly among the lorry-owners of Qala-i Niazbeg, who at no time live on their land except for short inspection periods, and partly among the thirty-one households who reside on their land in the winter half of the year. It is these households who have built houses.

The houses of Zala Khān Khēl are large *qal'a*s - a construction typical for wealthy landowners with high and massive walls of sun-dried clay surrounding a rectangular area measuring around twenty to thirty metres. The corners are often furnished with towers, and a single portal gives access to the courtyard. From the outside the construction thus looks like a regular defensive structure. Within the protecting walls buildings have been erected, as dwellings, as stores, and as stalls for animals - perhaps one will also

5,11 Dahana-i Ghori, the small but busy market town where Zala Khān Khēl do their daily shopping. The bazaar is dominated by North Afghan ethnic groups using the *chapān* as winter clothing (G.P., Feb. 1976).

find a small mosque. Some *qal'a*s are inhabited by only one household, while others have some or all of their functions divided, and house two or more households of brothers or patrilineal cousins. Some *qal'a*s have outhouses built up against the outer side of the walls, and where several *qal'a*s lie close together a joint mosque has been built, standing free outside the walls.

The state of repair of the *qal'a*s leaves often much to be desired, also as regards the owners' dwelling quarters, which is the only part of the complex with which the majority of Zala Khān Khēl have anything to do since the agricultural work is for most of them left completely in the hands of the *dihqān*s. In one *qal'a* the repair of the roof of the living room has been so neglected that water is dripping at several points, and buckets and bowls are standing around to catch the drips. Apologetic remarks about the state of the buildings fall frequently. "We can't be keeping an eye on our *dihqān*s all the time, so they often neglect the maintenance."

5, 12 The *qal'as* of the Zala Khān Khēl are large, but the maintenance is generally lacking behind (G.P., Dahana-i Ghori, March 1976).

In consideration of the relative prosperity of these households it is surprising that it shows so little in their dwellings. It may be explained by the fact that they only live here some few months of the year, and that residence on their land up here in "Turkestan", as this part of North Afghanistan is frequently called, is so recent a habit that it has not as yet found a permanent form. The living quarters are furnished traditionally with seating arrangements at floor level along the walls. There is seldom any decoration apart from the design of mattress and cushion covers. In many houses the walls are naked and unpainted clay-plastered surfaces. Only in a few sitting-rooms flower motifs in North Afghan style have been painted upon the walls. The clay floor is covered with straw mats and flat-woven kelim rugs which are often quite worn. But the cassette-radio is always there, as standard inventory.

It is normal among Pashtuns who have settled in North Afghanistan that dressing habits gradually change to comply with local fashions.

5,13 Keeping up the style as wealthy landowners is difficult under the muddy circumstances in Dahana-i Ghori (G.P., March 1976).

Changes of this nature are not yet to be seen among Zala Khān Khēl in Dahana-i Ghori. The North Afghan *chapān* (a cloak-like outer garment, normally worn hanging loose over the shoulders) is used by some of the older Zala Khān Khēl, but this is only in accordance with the fact that the use of this garment has spread to large parts of Afghanistan and is for example also used among Zala Khān Khēl and other Pashtuns in East Afghanistan. Otherwise the men are all well-dressed in the same fashion as their relatives in Qala-i Niazbeg, though without the noticeable modern trends among the young. It is not easy, however, to maintain the style, since every step in the area at this time of year is taken through mud and slush, which causes many irritated comments. The women who momentarily appear around the houses are clad in pure nomad fashion, with heavy ankle-length dresses in red and black. Here the new status of the households has occasioned no change, nor has the households' earlier existence as cloth traders

brought new thinking into the women's choice of material or design.

The involvement of Zala Khān Khēl in agriculture on their own land is limited in most cases to a minimal superintendence of the *dihqāns*, and to the obtaining of extra labour at certain periods and arranging for the transport of the harvest. Only a few households have gone any further in involvement in agriculture (for which see the next section). Much time is therefore spent in social intercourse. And as the winter weather is fickle and mainly slushy, this social life goes on for most of the time in the living rooms of the houses. Here one gathers around the stoves, with a blanket over the shoulders. A couple of the old men keep warm with a fur-lined *chapān*. Most of the time is passed in light conversation, but business matters are also discussed. How the harvest is looking, the last of the cotton must be transported to the factory, someone has to go to Kabul and arrange something with the household's lorry there, someone has to straighten out papers at the provincial office, and someone has to make agreements with the local *mir-āb* - the man who looks after the maintenance of the irrigation system and the distribution of the water. During the winter of 1975-76 discussion also concerned rumours that the old nomad bazaar in Charas would perhaps liven up again next summer. There were a couple of tents there last year, they had been informed, and there is talk of more probably coming this year. Perhaps a couple of the young men should go up there and do a little trading.

5,14 Tara Khēl nomads wearing white turbans on the occasion of a wedding celebration (G.P., Dasht-i Desabs, Sept. 1975).

In between one drinks tea and eats. The food is simple and not different from that prepared in ordinary nomad kitchens. Coarse bread, milk products including dried buttermilk, *qurūt*, and animal fats are the most usual. Eggs are sometimes included in the menu, while rice and meat are but rarely eaten. This diet must be based upon habit, for the bazaar in Dahana-i Ghori has no difficulty in supplying other foodstuffs, nor can it be any problem for Zala Khān Khēl to afford it.

The older men take their religious duties seriously, observing for example the obligatory daily five times of prayer. The young men pray only irregularly and send the anthropologist a side-glance and an apologetic smile when their father breaks off a conversation with the explanation that he must go out to pray. As in the days when nomad trade was at its height the prosperous households have still today a mullah in residence - a Pashtun from the East Afghan provinces who has received a long or short, formal or informal religious education. He usually takes part in the ordinary social life of the household. The older men enjoy talking on religious subjects with the mullah, but his most regular duty appears to be teaching the children. There are no public schools within practicable distance and, even if there were, the frequent change of residence of the households would make them difficult to attend. Teaching therefore takes place in the living rooms of the *qal'as*, where the children gather a couple of hours a day. Some of the older children, however, go to school in Kabul, where they stay with relatives, and one of them is receiving higher technical education.

While the mullah is in residence in a single *qal'a*, the barber circulates among several *qal'as* to offer his services. A single barber has agreement with several Zala Khān Khēl households. He completes his task and goes on to the next

5,15 Lorry loads of melons from the fields of Zala Khān Khēl arrive at the whole-sale market in Kabul. With the opening of the Salang road in 1964 Kabul, as well as the export markets of Pakistan and India, became accessible to the cultivators of North Afghanistan (G.P., Kabul, Aug. 1975).

customer. Only if the weather is completely impossible does he stay for any length of time in one place.

It is also dependent on the weather how much Zala Khān Khēl visit one another. Most of the time they spend at home, but when it can be done without getting wet through or too muddy they enjoy visiting each other. As the weather can change rapidly this means that visits can often be protracted. Some days during the winter Baghlan can show itself from a completely different aspect, with high blue skies and warm, almost spring-like air. It is unstable, but people make the most of it while it lasts. People move out of the dark damp rooms and gather in the sun on the verandas or around the common mosques. Fine weather is exploited for various practical activities as well as for larger gatherings and celebrations. Weddings are held among the Taghar in the neighbourhood, and one day in

5,16 The melons of North Afghanistan are highly praised and considered to be of the very best quality (G.P., Kabul, Aug. 1975).

January one of the larger landowners of Zala Khān Khēl holds a betrothal party for his son. For that occasion most of the Zala Khān Khēl men gather, together with many neighbouring Taghar and other Pashtuns. Only a few of the guests are non-Pashtuns.

Agriculture in Dahana-i Ghori

As has been said, Zala Khān Khēl's purchase of land in Dahana-i Ghori was primarily regarded as an investment of the profits from the trading activities. The land was leased out and was for the most left entirely in the care of tenant farmers - partly Pashtuns and partly Tajiks. Some of the Pashtuns are Taghar of Mustaf Khēl, and two are, as mentioned above, Zala Khān Khēl themselves.

5,17 Most fields of Zala Khān Khēl are tilled in the traditional way as here with the use of an ox-plough (G.P., Dahana-i Ghori, Feb. 1976).

One should not underrate the factor that this tenant arrangement gave the owners half the yield as rental, but in the beginning there was no one who dreamed of taking the matter further than that. Neither agricultural work nor residence on the land were regarded as attractive.

When, as a result of the closing of the Pakistan frontier in 1961, a number of households nevertheless began to spend the winter on their land, a gradual change in the situation began. These households became aware of the opportunities which lay in agriculture in this part of Afghanistan, and they became interested in achieving greater yields than they had obtained hitherto. The comparatively poor land, which they had bought relatively cheaply in the 1950s, had undergone important changes. National development schemes had early concentrated on the province of Baghlan. This had included the carrying out of draining and irrigation projects which had increased the quality of the soil and at the same time improved the health of the

5,18 Cotton fields of Zala Khān Khēl in Dahana-i Ghori (G.P., March 1976).

whole area, with the disappearance of malaria. In general this led to the land in Baghlan being now among the most fertile farmland in Afghanistan. Prices have risen correspondingly. Good irrigated land in Dahana-i Ghori now sells for 30-50,000 afs. per *jarīb* - more than twenty times the price of 1956.

The most important crops are sugar-beet, cotton, wheat, and maize, in addition to melons, beans, and other vegetables. Rice is grown in the region, but not normally on Zala Khān Khēl's land. With certain combinations of crops double-cropping is possible. After wheat, for example, beans or maize can be harvested the same year from the same field, or vice versa. Sugar-beet and cotton, on the other hand, exhaust the soil more, and from fields with these crops only one harvest a year is taken.

Even before the region became prime agricultural land a local industry had been established in Baghlan based on the cash-crops cotton and sugar-beet. A cotton-spinning mill was started in

5,19 Only one Zala Khān Khēl household in Dahana-i Ghori, that of Hajjī Gulu, has entered the path of mechanised agriculture. This household has two tractors (G.P., Dahana-i Ghori, March 1976).

1941 in Pul-i Khomri, and a sugar-factory two years later in Baghlan town.[3] Sale was thereby assured for the most important part of the produce. The opening of the Salang road over the Hindukush mountains in 1964 was a further step in the right direction. "Turkestan" was no longer quite the back of beyond. Kabul could now be reached by lorry in six to seven hours, and the market for farm produce - especially melons and vegetables - was thereby widened.

The increasing prospects of good profits do not, however, induce the men of Zala Khān Khēl to grab a spade and get to work in the fields. They seldom venture out in anything which would dirty more than their shoes, and even that seems somewhat extreme. "After all, we are *kūcheys*", they say, with a smile that suggests a certain ironic reservation towards their own views. "All that farming business - it isn't us. We live on *zamīn-dārī* and *dihqān-karī* " - on land-owning and tenant-labour.

The increased involvement of the landowners consists in acquiring knowledge of the special circumstances of cultivation and marketing which apply to agriculture in the Baghlan province, to be in a position to check the work of the *dihqāns* better and to plan an overall strategy. It is characteristic that with but one exception, which shall be dealt with in the next section, none of the Zala Khān Khēl landowners has as yet tried anything new or modern of any sort. Up to now the increased profits are the results only of an increased efficiency in the traditional *dihqān* system and of the benefits of extended marketing possibilities.

Mechanisation and new trends

Where the country is rolling and mountainous, mechanisation of Afghan agriculture runs into difficulties. To exploit the uneven landscape and to permit of irrigation the fields are laid in terraces, and the individual fields are moreover often small - all of these circumstances being hindrances to mechanisation. This is particularly true of eastern Afghanistan. In southwest and northern Afghanistan there are many regions with more open country, where the fields are larger and the possibilities for mechanisation better. It was therefore in these regions that mechanisation projects were established. In northern Afghanistan particular emphasis has been put on the areas around Mazar-i sharif and in Baghlan. The idea of mechanisation was indeed introduced, but it took some time before it was taken up by Zala Khān Khēl. When they first bought the land it was only after Mustaf Khēl had demonstrated that it was a practicable way to go. Now too it is a Mustaf Khēl in Dahana-i Ghori who is the first to buy a tractor, and he is followed in the spring of 1975 by one Zala Khān Khēl household. They acquire a Russian tractor with various implements for a total price of 450,000 afs.

This new acquisition entails a number of consequences for the landowners' attitude to farming and for the relationship between them and the *dihqāns*. For the tractor is to be driven by one of the Zala Khān Khēl men. They do not expect a farmer to be able to drive a tractor, and, even if he could, their general mistrust makes them prefer to look after that matter themselves. Maintenance of the tractor and the appliances also gives work to the men of the household, some of whom have mechanical experience from dealing with the lorries. It is thus now a matter of a more direct and practical involvement in the actual process of cultivation than previously. The *dihqān* is now freed from certain parts of the hard work, but at the same time the consequence is that the terms of his contract are changed. The landowner now also supplies traction, and the *dihqān*'s share of the yield is reduced from the previous half-share to a third. The landowner sees no problem in this reduction of the *dihqān*'s income. "There are plenty of *dihqāns* available, so if he won't accept the new division we just get a new man."

The first year's experience with the tractor is extremely positive. In particular the yield of the sugar-beet harvest is increased quite considerably. Among the other Zala Khān Khēl there is a mixture of admiration and envy, which is increased when the tractor-household goes a step further in the spring of 1976 and gets another tractor. When questioned on the reasons behind this investment they give an answer which can be summarised thus:

"With two tractors it is probable that we won't always have both of them working on our own land. One of them will often be free, and then we can hire it out to others. That sort of hiring gives 130 to 140 afs. for each *jarīb* ploughed. Since we can plough 20 to 25 *jarīb* in a day - 2 *jarīb* an hour on normal soil - that gives us 2,600 afs. or more. We drive ourselves, and pay for fuel. Fuel consumption is about a gallon an hour at 40 afs. a gallon, so it will come to about 400 afs. for a day. In other words there is a possible day's earnings of 2,200 afs."

Even though this calculation is based on optimal conditions, and may well be more an expression of wishful thinking than of harsh realities, it does give some idea of the opportunities inherent in the investment. For comparison it could be pointed out that the calculated possible daily earning of 2,200 afs. is more than double the monthly wage of an unskilled worker at the nearby cotton-spinning factory.

There seems good reason to believe that the tractor-owners among Zala Khān Khēl represent a not very distant future for several households. There is money in being up to date. And at the same time there is a possibility - perhaps a necessity - of a change in attitude towards agriculture. From being landowners Zala Khān Khēl may well become farmers.

A new migration pattern

Whether the landowning Zala Khān Khēl in Dahana-i Ghori are really in the process of becoming farmers (and after the exile will be so) only the future can tell. The example described is as yet only a single swallow. They look at themselves as nomads, and they migrate every spring and autumn - though under somewhat changed conditions; there is no livestock and no nomad trade to pay heed to - only their own health and wellbeing.

Winter can now be endured in "Turkestan", thanks to the houses, but people still flee the heat of summer. Around the first day of Jawza (21 May) the black tents are taken out of the storerooms and loaded on to a lorry, with the family on top, and they drive up into the mountains to spend the next five months there. They describe it themselves as pure and simple holidays - *hawā-khūrī* (literally "to eat air"). As there is no reason to make the long journey up to the old *farmān* land in Ghorghori, many content themselves with driving a good 100 kilometres on the asphalt-surfaced road across the Salang pass to the village of Salang on the southern side of the Hindukush mountains, somewhat over 2,000 metres above sea-level, and there the tents are erected on borrowed land.

The summer camp hence lies about halfway between Dahana-i Ghori and Kabul and, furthermore, it lies easily accessible, close to the main road. This gives good possibilities for keeping in contact with the world outside, and for making small trips as and when necessary. With their greater interest in increasing the yield from the farmland in Dahana-i Ghori they find supervision necessary even in summer. And the short distance between Salang and Dahana-i Ghori makes it possible for the job of supervision to be taken in turn for short periods by the younger men of the households, and thus to be made more bearable. Kabul is also within practicable reach, which makes it easier to look after interests there - these interests being, apart from lorries, cloth-stalls in Bazaar-i Omaid which are run by three of the households (of which more in a later section of this chapter).

THE POOR MAN'S LOT

The closing of the frontier in 1961 caused the well-off households of Zala Khān Khēl to turn to their new fields of investment. They abandoned their old migration pattern, which no longer had any relevance to their new economic interests, and established themselves as settled lorry-owners and as landowners with a new and holiday-like migration. Other Zala Khān Khēl had no such path to salvation in their hour of need. They were still dependent upon a mixed economy in which stock-keeping continued to play a part. For them it was therefore necessary to seek replacements for the winter grazing grounds which they had lost east of the frontier, and just about the only choice was the lowlands of Khost in the East Afghan province of Paktya. As has been said, this was not without problems, since many other Afghan nomads were forced to make the same choice, with subsequent overpopulation and overgrazing. Tension between the nomads and the settled population, and between the nomads themselves, increased and developed into open and frequent conflicts. "Towards the end you had to shoot your way just to get a couple of square yards for your tent", one informant says.

In the following years up to 1973 six Zala Khān Khēl households gave up, and moved to Pakistan on a year-round basis. After the last trading trip to Charas in 1973 the rest also surrendered, with the exception of three households. Only these three households still find space and scope for a continued pastoral nomadism, with winter grazing grounds in Khost and summer grazing grounds in the central highlands. The rest sold all their stock - sheep, goats, and camels - and left Khost with relief, but at the same time with a new problem. They had to find a new place to spend the winter and a new way of making a living.

In the previous sections we have seen that many Zala Khān Khēl chose economic activities and places of residence completely independent of the way of life which nomadism and nomad trade dictated earlier. The households which left Khost in 1973 obtained perhaps a similar "freedom", but without the same opportunities. They had no new economic basis in farmlands in Dahana-i Ghori, and they had no lorries. Some of them owned *farmān* land in Ghorghori, but this land was only of minor economic significance as it no longer formed one end of a pastoral nomadic grazing system - and the families could no longer be proper nomads their winter grazing grounds being gone. This group of households chose to settle for the winter in new surroundings east of Jalalabad in the East Afghan province of Nangarhar.

Divided into five camps they now live on government land, where they receive permission to camp for one winter at a time.

New annual economic pattern

With the abandonment of stock-breeding and with the reduction of nomad trade almost to vanishing point there is little left of the adventure in the central highlands. However, the livestock-market in Chaghcharan continues. Following the closure of the nomads' summer bazaars this market achieved an independent and legal existence. The purchase of animals with especial view to sale at the meat markets of the towns has long been known as part of the economic life of Afghan nomads.[4] Also Zala Khān Khēl has taken part in the provision of meat to Kabul on a basis

5,20 Sohak nomad with his children (G.P., Maydan, May 1976).

5,21 Sohak nomad with his children (G.P., Maydan, May 1976).

5,22 Market days and festivals provide good opportunities for the petty-trade and occasional business of Zala Khān Khēl in the winter area. *Naw-rūz* (New Year) festival (G.P., Jalalabad, March 1976).

of purchase of stock in the highlands - more recently particularly in Chaghcharan. In recent years this business - together with the last remnants of the nomad trade - has been the only fixed point to which the poor households could cling. Profits have been but modest, because they have only been able to make limited investment in this trade.

In the new situation, with winter camp at Jalalabad and summer camp in Ghorghori, the stock trade forms part of a new annual economic pattern, which is chosen by the least well-to-do Zala Khān Khēl as a way of making a living. This pattern admittedly includes an element of migration, but it has otherwise little resemblance to former time pastoral nomadism and trading activities.

Let us start in the new winter area by Jalalabad. Here the main occupation is grain trade, known as *'allafi*. In the beginning of winter a certain quantity of wheat, maize, or rice is bought on the Jalalabad grain market or

5,23 The livestock market in Jalalabad attracts many nomads, and this is one of the places where Zala Khān Khēl can make small business enterprises (G.P., Jalalabad, March 1976).

directly from local producers. The grain is stored in Jalalabad at a certain charge, and after that one merely waits for the rise in price which normally comes with the progress of winter and the consumption of the autumn harvest. The grain is then again put up for sale in the Jalalabad market, and a profit can be realised. This local trade (with both purchase and sale in Jalalabad) is still a very uncertain business for Zala Khān Khēl. Perhaps because they are new to the business, miscalculations of price trends often occur, and sales at a loss are not rare. The position is often that they have to sell at the price they paid, because they have bought too late in the winter, when the prices have already had their rise for that season. They thus lose the cost of storage and transport. The amount of grain in each transaction can vary considerably, but in the course of a winter a household has normally bought and sold 500 to 700 Kabul-*sēr* or around 4 to 5 ton.

5,24 The spring of 1976 some Zala Khān Khēl choose to camp for about one month on the northern outskirts of Kabul (G.P., Karezemir, May 1976).

Two examples shall be given to illustrate a typical trade situation: a household has, a little way into the winter, bought 500 *sēr* maize at 41 afs. Including storage and other expenses they have invested a total of 22,000 afs. They had reckoned on a profit of 3 to 4 afs. per *sēr* - in all therefore 1,500 to 2,000 afs. When by March there was no trace of a rise in the price of maize the household had to sell at the buying price, with the result that they had a loss of 1,500 afs. Another household had earlier in the winter bought 400 *sēr* of maize at 35 afs., and somewhat later 300 *sēr* maize at 41 afs. In the situation just described the last 300 *sēr* would give a loss of about 1,000 afs., while the first 400 *sēr* should bring in a profit of a good 2,000 afs.

These two cases do not necessarily show the normal relationship between success and failure, but they do give a clear indicatioin that the size of investment is very great in proportion to the possible profit. In other words, if you wish to make a decent living out of *'allafi*, you need to

5,25 A day of livestock trading has come to an end, and it is time to rest and chat before night is falling *(G.P.,* Chaghcharan, July 1975).

come up into a somewhat higher level of investment, which is beyond the means of all but a very few Zala Khān Khēl in Jalalabad.

Some few of the Zala Khān Khēl households, though, are in a rather better situation. They live with Nur Khān Khēl and Musa Khēl (see *Fig. 2,4*), and together with them they are in a position to buy grain in considerably larger quantities than the majority of Zala Khān Khēl can afford. Providing that the run of prices has been correctly evaluated this is in itself an advantage, but the possibilities of profit are increased still further because, with the greater quantity of grain, it can pay to hire a lorry and transport the grain to another market - such as Khost, Kabul, or Kandahar - where the prices are higher.

Apart from *'allafi* Zala Khān Khēl engage in practically every transaction which falls within their capability and which promises even the smallest profit. Practically speaking everything can be traded, and the trading is often carried out so inconsequently that it is difficult to esti-

5,26-9 and 5,30-1 p.188 Flocks of animals bought at the livestock market in Chaghcharan are herded through the highland of Hazarajat on the way to Kabul, where they will be sold for slaughter (G.P., Lal, July 1975).

5,30

5,31

5,32 The livestock market in Kabul - the end station for the flocks herded through Hazarajat from Chaghcharan (K.F., Kabul, Sept. 1975).

mate its extent and economic consequences. To a limited degree pauper labour, *gharībī*, is carried out in Jalalabad - some of the younger men take paid jobs as labourers and as helpers on building sites and in the bazaar.

With the total proceeds of the various activities in their pockets the households break up from Jalalabad about 1st Saur (21 April), and make their way to Kabul, Maydan, or Logar, where they have their spring camp for about a month (see map, *Fig. 3,16*). Behind the choice of camp site lies partly the choice of migration route onwards from the spring camp to Ghorghori, and partly certain sympathies and antipathies between the households. With no animals along on the migration, the route no longer needs to follow the old pastoral roads and tracks, which in former days were chosen by all households. The route needs not therefore to be the same for every household, and it may even vary from year to year. Tents, household effects, and people are transported by lorry. In Kabul a small quantity of bazaar-goods is bought - especially tea and Afghan cotton material - with a view to later sale in Hazarajat. The majority expresses the opinion that this trade is rather a matter of "force of habit" than of sound business sense. Today simply nothing is to be made out of selling tea and cloth to the Hazara. There are too many lorry-loads up there already, they say. I have no means of judging the real extent of this trade or its significance for the economy of the households. That it should be completely without significance is questionable, considering that people often work for very modest profit.

Towards the end of May the last stretch of road is covered to reach the summer areas at Ghorghori, where the tents are erected on the traditional sites. From here some of the men go to the stock market at Chaghcharan to buy livestock, after which the animals are either herded through Hazarajat to Kabul or driven there by lorry. It has for some time been practised to transport sheep and goats by lorry. The high body of the lorry is fitted with 'tween-decks to make room for many animals. It is not, however, considered a good way to transport animals, as they become sick and exhausted and lose weight. It is for the most done only with fat stock for the meat markets, while those nomads who still run proper pastoral migration seldom use lorry transport for their own animals. If it is a matter of transporting fat stock from Chaghcharan to Kabul it is often necessary to graze the animals for some time on the outskirts

5,33 Types of *lukh* huts in winter camps in the area around Jalalabad.

1) *Kodei* is a little domed hut with an oval grounc-plan. It is made completely of *lukh*, and it is used as guest house, mosque, and occasionally as dwelling.

2) *Chopla* has a rectangular ground-plan, vertical walls, and a ridged roof made of *lukh*. It usually has a single dividing wall, and is used as a dwelling.

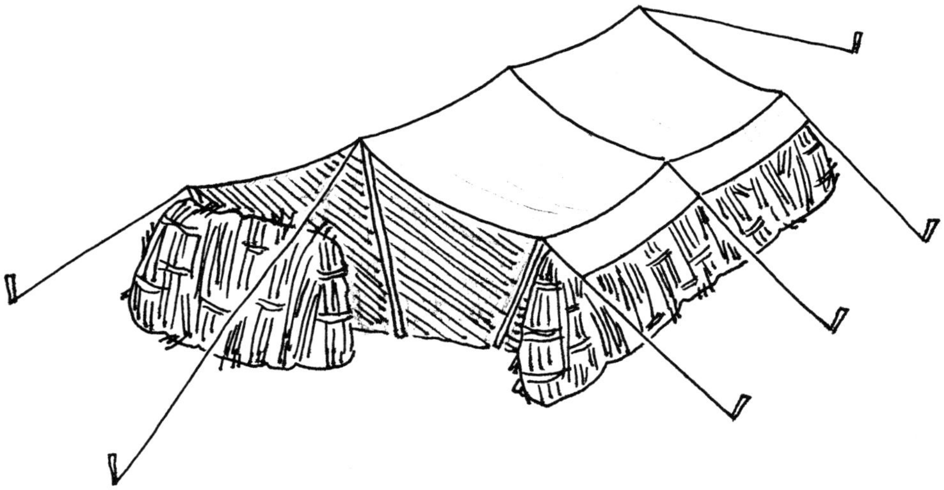

3) *Kher* has the *lukh* leaves erected as walls, while the roof is formed of the top of the black tent. The interior arrangement and the usage is the same as in an ordinary black tent.

5,34 The *kher*-type dwelling in Camp 1 (G.P., Jalalabad, Feb. 1976).

of Kabul, to allow them to regain their strength and put on weight before they are sold. The time won by lorry transport is thereby reduced. The best prices are reached by animals which have grazed their way through the highlands and arrive at Kabul healthy and well-fleshed. The use of lorries is therefore a question of balance between time and price. All the livestock bought by Zala Khān Khēl is sold in Kabul, and no animals are brought down to the lowlands since they have no grazing facilities there.

In September or October the households once more set off for the lowlands, with a stay of some weeks around Kabul or in Logar. On arrival at Jalalabad they can begin the annual economic pattern over again, with the profits from their summer activities as stake.

The original nomad trading was based primarily upon two factors: (1) that the nomads owned the beasts of transport, and (2) that for pastoral purposes they moved between areas which at the same time provided good markets both for buying and selling. The situation we have described here possesses none of these elements. Apart from the transfer of profits there is no longer any interrelationship between the activities in the summer and in the winter areas. *'allafi* is for Zala Khān Khēl primarily speculation in local marketing conditions. Only rarely does it involve transport, and this transport again has no bearing upon or

5,35 Camp 1 of Zala Khān Khēl consists entirely of huts made of *lukh*-leaves. Only in one of these huts the top of the black tent has been used for roofing in a construction of the *kher*-type (G.P., Jalalabad, Feb. 1976).

relation to the yearly migrations. The livestock trade in the summer has its origins in a nomadic way of life, but it has in the course of time been separated from it and has developed into an independent occupation. At this point of time the livestock-buyers in the highlands may just as well be city merchants or butchers from Kabul as nomads. As a matter of fact it is quite often city merchants who buy the animals, and then hire poor nomads to herd them to Kabul.

The winter camps

The way in which the Zala Khān Khēl households manage economically in their winter camps by Jalalabad vary to some extent. Generally speaking, they belong to the poorest of the lot, but the economic differentiation which occurs manifests itself precisely in the choice of winter camp.

The largest camp, Camp 1[5], contains seventeen Zala Khān Khēl households, all from sub-*khēl* 2. In addition, there are a few other

5,36 Zala Khān Khēl men surrounding the interpreter Azim Safi in front of the *kodei*-mosque of Camp 1 (G.P., Jalalabad, Feb. 1976).

Ahmadzai households, including one from Mustaf Khēl of the Taghar. These other households normally live together with Zala Khān Khēl. Camp 1 lies 10 kilometres east of Jalalabad, immediately north of the asphalt road to the frontier crossing of Torkham and the Khyber Pass. Transport to and from the camp is easy, as there is regular traffic of busses and small cars on the road connecting Jalalabad with its surroundings.

The living quarters in Camp 1 are all built of the leaves of a marsh plant bulrush (Lat.: *typha angustata*), locally called *lukh*. It grows on the banks of the Kabul river close by the camp. Local people have government authorisation to harvest and sell this plant, and it is from these the nomads buy the necessary material. The long stiff leaves are used in three different types of structure (see *Fig. 5,33*), and the leaves for each of these cost about 70 afs.

The *lukh*-huts are only able to last a single winter, and they cannot be moved without falling to pieces. In the spring they are pulled down, or they fall apart when the camp is left and the huts no longer maintained. No foundations are made, nor any other more solid construction which could be used the following winter - in contrast to many traditional nomad camps in well established winter dwelling areas, where foundations and walls of stone and clay are built, and used winter after winter.

The immobility of the hut construction gave rise to a problem in the autumn of 1975, when the authorities intervened in the placing of the camp. The nomads had been shown a site for their camp by one official, and had then bought building material and erected their huts in a combined camp, where everyone was living relatively close together. Shortly afterwards another official - a surveyor - arrived. He studied the area, made measurements on the basis of theodolite observations and declared that the camp was placed wrongly in relation to some imaginary line in the landscape, and accordingly had to be moved.

The space on the correct side of the line proved insufficient for all the huts, so that half of them had to move some hundreds of metres away to the other side of a large irrigation canal, while the remainder only had to shift their huts a few metres to satisfy the surveyor. The huts are not designed for this, and as a consequence every household that winter had to live in lopsided, rickety, and leaking dwellings. In addition, the camp was divided into two halves, and the irrigation canal made a long detour necessary going from one camp to the other. No one was ever quite sure, moreover, what significance the surveyor's line in fact had.

All the households in the camp share the same lot in the development here described. In addition to *farmān*-land some of them have small plots of land acquired later in Ghorghori, but none of them owns farmland in Dahana-i Ghori. They own no lorries, and no cloth-stalls. They all make a living as described and they all do fairly badly economically.

The physical layout of the camp and of the individual dwellings follows the tradition for nomad winter camps. But both the arrangement and the activities of the inhabitants are marked by the fact that there are no longer any livestock. All that is left are a few goats which stand tethered by the huts, and some hens which go around and scratch in the dry soil. The possessions of the households are limited to what nomads normally take with them on the annual migrations. Everything can be packed up and moved with no great difficulty. There are no fixed seating arrangements as in the houses of their relatives; instead there are rugs which are rolled out on the ground, perhaps supplemented with bedrolls as supports for the back if greater comfort is desired. It is neat and orderly around the huts, and twigs and large stones have been removed. The little sitting-plateau which everyone has constructed in front of his hut is kept especially clean and tidy. This area measures about two by four metres, is levelled and cleared of all stones, in some cases covered with an even layer of gravel.

The men are often away for some hours every day. They are in the bazaar in Jalalabad or out in the villages, running their grain trade and other activities. Business is not extensive, and much of their time is thus spent in the camp. Here they gather on the small sitting-plateaux, drinking tea and discussing business and what is wrong with this world. The women do not sit with them, but they go around in the camp much more openly than the women do among their relatives in Qala-i Niazbeg or Dahana-i Ghori.

Both men and women are dressed in comparatively simple nomad fashion, without the refinements and modernisations seen among the

5,37 Landscape around Camp 1 (G.P., Jalalabad, March 1976).

men in the richer environments which we have described. The food is similarly modest - usually merely tea, maize-bread, animal fat, and *qurūt*. Rice and meat is scarcely ever eaten in the camp, and the hens unfortunately lay no eggs. The men, however, occasionally permit themselves a meal of rice, *pilaw*, or roasted meat, kebab at a tea house, when they are in the bazaar.

The camp has two small mosques - one in each of the separate halves. They consist of a cleared plateau similar to those by the dwellings, with a little hut of *kodei* type (see *Fig. 5,33*). The plateau is used for joint prayer, and it is the place where guests are received. The hut can be used as a guest-room, but it is normally occupied by a young *tālib* - a student mullah [6], who comes to the camp for a couple of hours a day. The *tālib* will, among other duties, organise one or more joint prayers daily. At the appropriate time he calls to prayer out over the camp, and the men

5,39 Mir Ahmad Khān (in the middle) together with other "elders" of Camp 1 (G.P., Jalalabad, Feb. 1976).

who are at home and wish to take part meet at the mosque, each with his prayer-mat - a shawl, a woven mat, or a little pile rug. None of the men appears to be particularly interested in religious discussion or conversation with the *tālib*, but they value the sense of community to which his call to prayer gives rise. They appreciate, too, the

5,38 The old men pass much time in idleness - in company with their Islamic rosary (G.P., Jalalabad, Feb. 1976).

tuition which he gives daily to the children of the camp. It is traditional religious teaching, and it takes place on the plateau of the mosque - in bad weather inside the hut. It is the only tuition the children in this camp receive, as none of them goes to any other form of school. The *tālib* receives a modest cash payment in addition to food in the camps and villages where he provides his services.

The distance between Camp 1 and Camps 3 to 5 is so great that frequent, not to mention daily communication between them is impossible. But a smaller Zala Khān Khēl camp, Camp 2, lies

3,40 Children of Camp 2 dressed in typical Pashtun nomad fashion (G.P., Jalalabad, Feb. 1976).

only half an hour's walk away on the south side of the main road. Despite this modest distance and the fact that they are close relatives there is no frequent social intercourse between them. The formation of different camp-units reflects to some degree the latest development in differentiation among Zala Khān Khēl, and several of the men in the big camp of poor Zala Khān Khēl express in the present situation little common interest with their relatives in the other and more prosperous camps. The contacts appear to be confined to a diminishing number of situations of wider significance, where the old traditional leader of Zala Khān Khēl still plays a certain role - and that leader, Hajjī Hazrat Mohammad, lives in Camp 2.

It is claimed that a sufficiently big social event, such as a wedding, can still bring Zala Khān Khēl

3,41 Children of Camp 2 (G.P., Jalalabad, Feb. 1976).

5,42 Men and children gathered in front of the little *kodei*-mosque in Camp 2 (G.P., Jalalabad, Feb. 1976).

from the different camps together, but during the winter I stayed among these people no such weddings took place in the Jalalabad area to prove the case. However, in a neighbouring camp, where a large group of Sohak nomads live, a wedding is held one day in February, and here many Zala Khān Khēl are invited - and they come from both the large and the small camp. The background and the later development of the Sohak is completely parallel with that of Zala Khān Khēl. They used to trade in the same areas, and have often been neighbours of Zala Khān Khēl, just as they now are in Jalalabad.

For Zala Khān Khēl in Camp 1, however, the day-to-day social contacts remain largely within the bounds of the camp - apart from the daily visit of the *tālib* and from the men's business contacts in the bazaar and the other places where they conduct their activities. The women only rarely leave the camp. Their contact with the outside world is through the men and the few pedlars who turn up every now and then and offer hairpins, cloth, and sewing articles for sale.

Camp 2 is in many ways representative of the four smaller camps by Jalalabad where Zala Khān Khēl dwell. Unlike Camp 1 these four camps are

5,43 The households in Camp 2 all live in spacious black tents (G.P., Jalalabad, Feb. 1976).

occupied by households that are relatively successful economically. They operate the local *'allafi* on a larger scale and achieve greater profits. Some of them have small plots of land and *qal'as* in Dahana-i Ghori, where they spend the summer. Others have houses in the Kabul suburb of Dasht-i Bachi and spend the summer there. Some have cloth-stalls in Kabul and one or two even in Jalalabad. One household, that of Hajjī Hazrat Mohammad, is a large landowner in Hazarajat. All the households are regarded as comparatively well-to-do, though not to the level of their lorry-owning relatives or the big landowners in Dahana-i Ghori.

Camp 2 has a somewhat different appearance from Camp 1. Six households from Zala Khān Khēl and two from Matani live here. All the dwellings are large black tents with stone walling on the lowest half or whole metre. The tents stand well apart from each other, and there are only a few huts of *lukh* leaves, which are used as storerooms. In the middle of the camp there is a large cleared and levelled area of about six by four metres surrounded by a low clay wall on three sides and a row of stones on the fourth. It is the assembly place of the camp, and is part of the mosque which also comprises a *kodei* hut. As in Camp 1 a

5,44-6 Weaving of tent cloth. The Pashtun nomads of East Afghanistan do not weave the cloth for their black tents themselves. While the thread of goat's hair is spun by the women of the households, the weaving is done by professional itinerant artisans, often people from Wardak. These Wardakis tour the lowland during winter and offer their services to the nomads. They are paid in cash and daily meals. "And we always get good food", they say with a smile. "For somehow the quality of the food, we are given by the nomads, is reflected in the quality of our weaving" (G.P., Jalalabad, March 1976).

student mullah comes daily to Camp 2, where he leads the joint prayer and teaches the children. But some of the children in this camp also go to school in Kabul when they are living there, while a couple of the elder children live in Kabul for the greater part of the year in order to attend school in the upper classes.

Both men and children are well dressed in the traditional fashion, and most of the men bear themselves with the same arrogance as their lorry-owning relatives in Kabul are wont to show. They are busy people, with various doings to look to, and they are away from the camp often for several days at a time. Despite the relative prosperity in this camp it is noteworthy that the food does not differ from that prepared in the poor men's camp. It is the standard nomad menu, with tea, maize-bread, *qurūt*, and animal fat, which is the daily diet - just as it also is among the prosperous landowners of Dahana-i Ghori.

Further to the east - in Gerdai Ghaus, Markuh, and Basawal - lie three more winter camps, with seven, three, and two Zala Khān Khēl households, respectively. They live here together with other nomad groups, including Musa Khēl of Ahmadzai, and form only a small part of the total composition of the camps. All the households in these camps are better off than those in Camp 1,

5,47 Young men of Camp 1 (G.P., Jalalabad, March 1976).

and it is from here, for example, that the more profitable *'allafi* is run, with purchases of greater quantities of grain and with transport to other markets.

An unstable situation

The picture of Zala Khān Khēl's situation in the winter camps by Jalalabad, and the impression of their new annual cycle, is one of uncertainty and lack of stability - most marked for the poor households in Camp 1. Both the locality and the economic pattern are new. There are no fixed rules for the camping site, and no one dare prophesy that they will be in the same place next winter, or that they will be making their living in the same way next year.

The individual household has always been an independent unit with free right to self-determination; but within the framework of restricted variation which Zala Khān Khēl previously held in common. With the dissolution of the common social and economic basis the differences be-

5,48 Mir Ahmad Khān (centre) and our interpreter Azim Safi (right) during an interview session in Camp 1 (G.P., Jalalabad, Feb. 1976).

tween the households grew. The first year after abandonment of pastoral nomadism in Khost some households chose to look for work during winter in Peshawar in Pakistan. The next year other households followed their example, and in the winter of 1975-76 a total of 10 of the poorer Zala Khān Khēl households had winter quarters in Peshawar. From other households only some few of the younger men went to Pakistan to look for winter employment. Some households and individuals still return to Afghanistan when the spring migration towards the highlands starts (though others, as we have described, have chosen to stay in Pakistan all the year). Life has turned unstable, and both anger and frustration are aired when one talks to the men of Camp 1. Mir Ahmad Khān, an elderly respected nomad, expressed his views on the situation in these words:

> "Everything was much better before. We had animals and we traded; we had horses for our enjoyment - it was a good life. Then came the Pashtunistan quarrel between Afghanistan and

5,49 Zala Khān Khēl shop-keepers in Bazaar-i Omaid (G.P., Kabul, May 1976).

Pakistan, and our freedom to move was restricted. Conditions for nomads got worse and worse in this country, and one after the other of us chooses to go to Pakistan. After all, we have to live. We should go to the President and ask whether he knows how many of one group and how many of the other are still in Afghanistan. And when the President finds out how few they are we should ask: Why, Mr President, - why are they leaving the country? We've fought for this country more than once, but what do we get in return? Our way of life is taken away from us, and we get no land. The land reform of 1975 is worth nothing - at

5,50 Zala Khān Khēl shop-keepers in Bazaar-i Omaid (G.P., Kabul, May 1976).

least it doesn't benefit us poor nomads. The big landowners make sham divisions of their estates, so that nothing is taken from them. Just look at our kinsfolk in Dahana-i Ghori. They've been busy making deeds of conveyance to a whole crowd of members of the family. If only we had bought land then... . The government should realise that we nomads are used to a hard life, so ten dissatisfied nomads are more dangerous than five hundred dissatisfied farmers. Because we can fight. If your life was to last 500 years you should never wish yourself a single day as a nomad under these miserable conditions."

5,51 Nazar Khān in front of his shop in Bazaar-i Omaid (G.P., Kabul, May 1976).

Bazaar-i Omaid

In the preceding sections of this chapter I have described the three main groupings into which Zala Khān Khēl is today divided. They are three new occupational categories, and three new localisations. However, this division is not quite so rigid as the description may give the impression of. There are the few overlappings and border cases, transitional forms, and exceptions which do not fit easily into the main categories. In the category of the most prosperous Zala Khān Khēl, for instance, the lorry-owners are dominant, but it should be mentioned that this

5,52 Business and pleasure. Hajjī Gulbat and Nazar Khān, standing in front of their shops in Bazaar-i Omaid, give a high priority to their business, while others are more inclined to favour social gatherings with relatives (G.P., Kabul, May 1976).

category also includes three households who have established a modern import-export business. One of these households is from among the lorry-households, while the others are close relatives from the same sub-*khēl*. These latter two are resident in Kabul and have chosen to concentrate their strength entirely upon international trading business. There is yet another environment where Zala Khān Khēl can be met in circumstances which merit a short description. This environment is Bazaar-i Omaid, also called Omaid Market, in central Kabul.

Bazaar-i Omaid was built in 1970 as a modern concrete structure in a single storey. It consists of seventy small stalls measuring about six square metres, lying on either side of a narrow alley running between an outer four-winged building and an inner rectangular building. The complex has a single entrance portal. Forty of these stalls were bought in 1970 by Zala Khān Khēl. Many of the remaining stalls were bought by other former trading nomads - including Sohak from the neighbouring camp to Zala Khān Khēl at Jalalabad.

Six of the stalls were bought by Zala Khān Khēl who are in an intermediate economic position. They could not afford to buy land or lorries, but they were better off than those of

5,53 Hajjī Gulbat in his shop in Bazaar-i Omaid (G.P., Kabul, May 1976).

their relatives who are now relegated to an existence in minor trade and paid jobs. They established themselves as cloth traders in Bazaar-i Omaid and now run their stalls there as their only, or at least most important, source of income.

The other Zala Khān Khēl who bought stalls in Bazaar-i Omaid were wealthy landowners and lorry-owners, and for them it was mainly a question of investment in the stalls as such. For they go up in price and can be disposed of at a good profit. In 1970 they cost 25-30,000 afs. (the nearer the entrance the more expensive), and in 1976 it is reckoned that they can be sold for 120-150,000 afs. That it is not the cloth trade that was the attraction is shown by the fact that only eight of the wealthy households run the trading from the stall themselves - and the trading is considered, both by themselves and by others, as a sideline, a way of passing the time for the young men who run the stalls.

Bazaar-i Omaid has become specialised in dealing in fairly expensive Japanese textiles - for the most part synthetics but also some high-quality cottons. All the stalls trade in the same products except for one which deals in tape-cassettes, and which is not owned by a Zala Khān Khēl. Purchases go via a Kabul tradesman who is authorised to import textiles from Japan. As with purchases in Thal and Lahore long ago, there is no form of joint purchase. It is impractical for the single owner, they say, and it gives no sort of rebate. So, each stall makes its own separate purchases.

Bazaar-i Omaid is not nearly so hectic as other parts of Kabul's bazaar often are - in fact some people might call it dull. This is partly because the enclosed court is a barrier against the busy life of the city, and partly because the exclusive choice of wares limits the number of customers - who by the nature of things are more well-off city dwellers including the community of foreigners, especially Russians. There is therefore often time for tea-drinking and conversation in the small stalls - especially in those where business is not the primary concern. The stalls and the narrow alley are also a meeting-place for other Zala Khān Khēl than the traders. When they have business in Kabul they look in, drink a glass of tea, and exchange news with the stall-keepers and with other relatives who are passing through. It is not the prosperous Zala Khān Khēl who live permanently in Kabul, who use the bazaar in this way. They hardly ever come here. It is rather those who still move their dwelling-place with the seasons, who get a little news of the various groups via Bazaar-i Omaid. Especially in the spring and the autumn, when the yearly migration passes by the neighbourhood of Kabul many come visiting. The small stalls are crowded, when six to eight men are invited in and served to. Such meetings are given a high priority by the young stall-keepers. Potential customers are often ignored, or referred to the next-door stalls. The older traders are scarcely so slack. They enjoy visits, but do not let them interfere with business - they have to live from it. Rather than having their stall full of tea-drinking relatives they prefer to join the party in the younger men's stalls, when they can see that there are no customers in the offing.

NOTES

1 The following description is written in the "ethnographic present tense", thus giving the situation as it appeared in the period of the field-work in Afghanistan in 1975-76.

2 *Kīlīnar* or *klindar* probably comes from the English cleaner. The *kīlīnar* is in a sort of apprentice relationship to the driver, whom he calls *ustad* i.e. master. Most drivers have started their careers as *kīlīnars*. The taking over of English words in a modern technical branch such as lorry transport is quite typical. A number of English words have found slightly modified forms in Farsi and Pashto - for example *kalach* (clutch), *brik* (brake), *akselator* (accelerator), *eshtereng* (steering wheel), and *diriwar* (driver).

3 For a description of Afghanistan's early industrial development, see *inter alia* Ali 1946.

4 For many nomads the overall development of society has led to an increased interest in local and national markets. The participation of nomads in the provision of meat for the towns is a case in point. While for Zala Khān Khēl this is exclusively a summer activity with buying and selling within the same season, other Afghan nomads with less problematical access to grazing grounds than Zala Khān Khēl have incorporated livestock raising for the market into a more completely nomadic production system. Thus Barfield describes the Arab in North Afghanistan as nomads who have transformed the traditional subsistence production into a production designed for the market. Their stock raising was in the 1970s aimed at the Afghan meat market and even at the export of fat stock to Iran. Barfield points out how this reorganisation has led to a one-sided conception of the animals as production units: what matters is to produce meat, while the animals' byproducts of milk and wool are ignored. This ties up with the fact that the stock-keeping is to an ever greater degree entrusted to specialist shepherds, rather than to a household which in a traditional nomadism would exploit a broader spectrum of the animal resources (Barfield 1981).

5 The designations Camp 1, Camp 2, etc. are not locally used but merely the anthropologist's reference. The camps do not have formal names but are characterised by the locations along the road where one gets off the bus.

6 The education of Pashtun mullahs is concentrated in the East Afghan provinces (and also takes place in Pakistan). Here the students are either attached to a *mulla* in one of the mosques or they receive a more formal education in a *madrasa* - a *mulla*-school. During their apprenticeship they go round to the neighbouring villages and nomad camps and perform religious services.

CHAPTER 6

A WAY OF LIFE COMES TO AN END

SETTLEMENT AND NEW MIGRATION PATTERNS

Nomads are seldom pastoralists only. The livelihood of the individual household is based upon activities in a variety of fields. These activities reflect the opportunities and limitations of the household in a local, national, and international context. Nomadism is part of a dynamic system. The description of Zala Khān Khēl in the preceding chapter is a momentary picture of the situation around 1975-76. To be able to use this picture in an analysis of the dynamics of the society we have added a historical dimension, and to take a position with respect to the processes of change we have selected a point of origin in a situation with a simplified nomadic economy and a traditional organisation, as given in Chapter 3. At the point of time, somewhere in the last century when our information allows the beginnings of an insight into the way of life of East Afghan nomads, the economy comprises more than mere pastoralism. Many nomads are also traders, and have probably been so for centuries; but the guiding frame of reference is that of nomadism - they are trading nomads. Let us from that starting point look more closely at certain aspects of the development which Zala Khān Khēl has undergone.

Towards the end of the 19th century nomadism provided the basis for a trading business of Zala Khān Khēl, as far as we can judge. The migrations between summer and winter grazing areas were at the same time the basis for purchase, sale, and transport of goods between different markets. We have no details about the balance between nomadism and trade, but we do know that, after the opening up of Hazarajat in 1892, trade began to grow in importance - probably with the establishment of the summer bazaars as a point of breakthrough. The nomads received new and better summer grazing grounds, but they also found widened spheres of activity for their trade. From then on through the first half of the present century trade expanded; and for many households it became the dominant part of their total economy, but without breaking their framework of pastoral nomadism. Trading activities were still organised attuned to pastoral requirements, with yearly migrations and with the independence and responsibility of the households in parallel with their independence and responsibility in pastoral activities. The nomadic system was, so to say, taken over from within by a new activity. Zala Khān Khēl continued to be migrant nomads, but

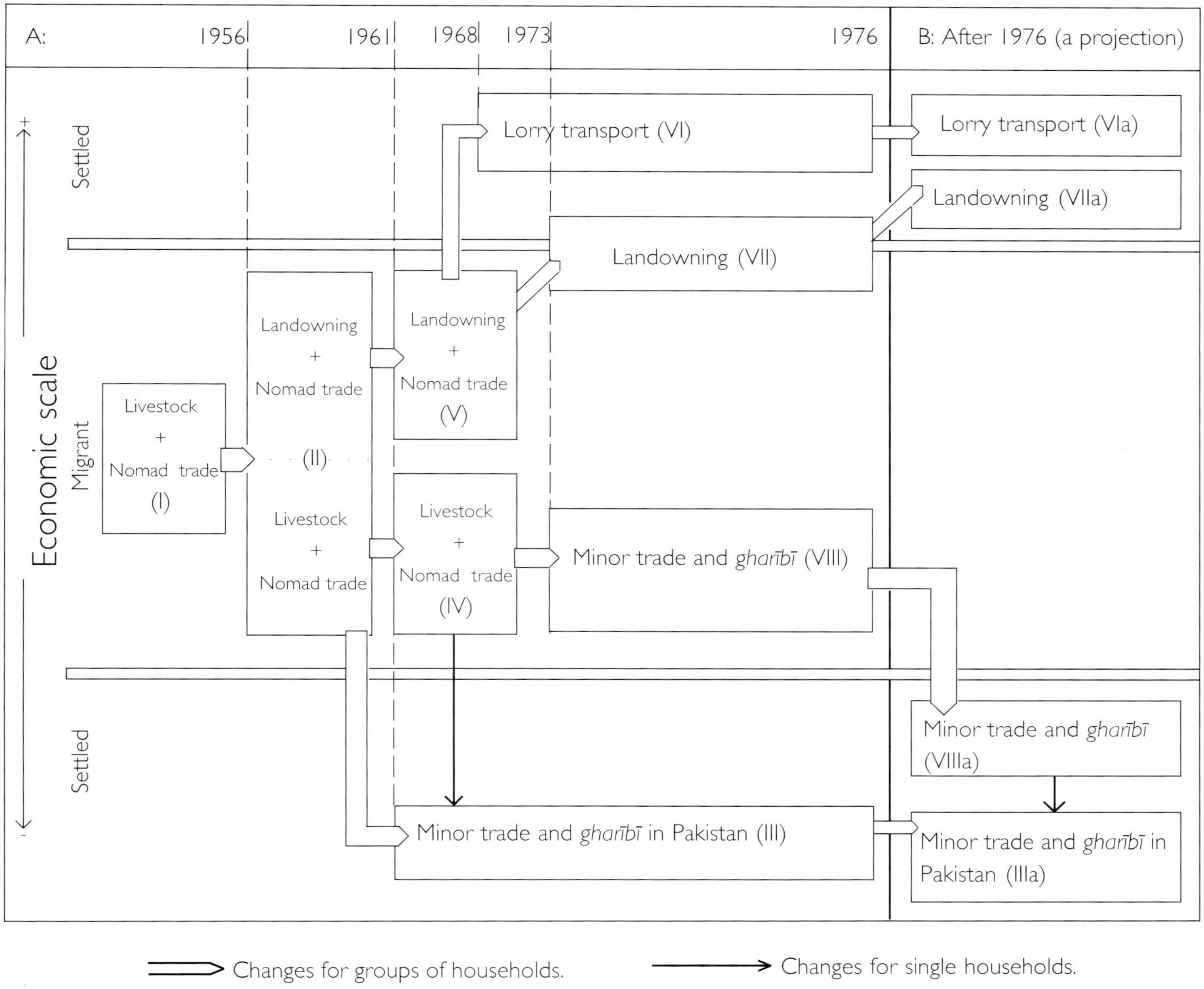

6,1 Zala Khān Khēl's economic and geographic splitting up seen in relation to the process of settlement and the economic hierarchy.

A: The documented development until 1976. From joint participation in nomadism and nomad trade (I) the prosperous break away by buying land, but they all continue their joint migrations (II). Sub-*khēl* 7 settles in Pakistan (III), while the remainder choose new winter stations in Khost (IV) and in Dahana-i Ghori (V). The lorry-owners settle (VI), while the landowners gradually spend more and more time on their estates (VII). The households with winter camp in Khost move to Jalalabad in the winter and establish a new annual economic pattern (VIII).

B: A guess at the course of future development, as made probable by the dominant trends at the end of the field work. The lorry-owners will continue to extend their business (VIa), and the landowners will become permanently settled on their properties in Dahana-i Ghori (VIIa). The households in the vulnerable new annual economic pattern will gradually settle (VIIIa), and many of them will join their relatives in Pakistan (IIIa).

This guess has not proved correct, however, as the revolution in 1978 and the subsequent war has changed the direction of economic and political development and driven all the Zala Khān Khēl households into exile in Pakistan.

we have reason to believe that it was in this expansion phase of nomad trade that the differences between households developed and deepened. It was at that point of time the foundation was laid for the later evident differentiation of Zala Khān Khēl. It was in that phase of economic development that some households became prosperous, while others managed only reasonably well or even poorly. And it is with reference to this development that some of them expressed the opinion that the old Pashtun ideals of unity and mutual support in a tribal organisation were receding (if they ever actually were more than ideals) and replaced by the pursuit of individual ambitions. The system broke up from the inside.

Following the creation of Pakistan and the general modernisation of Afghanistan's infrastructure, we saw among Zala Khān Khēl the first breakaway from the traditional way of life. The purchase of land in Dahana-i Ghori from 1956 onwards brought into the open the differences in the economic situation of the households, while at the same time these purchases of land were dispositions which lay outside the nomadic system as hitherto practised. At the other end of the economic scale, too, a little group of households began to break away by letting members of their households remain in Pakistan for the summer to perform pauper work. They had exhausted their resources in a feud and were forced in an ever-increasing degree to base their economy on other things than livestock-keeping and trade.

The rest of the Zala Khān Khēl kept up the migratory pattern for a while. Single individuals were left behind, but all the households as such carried on the usual migration. The economic differentiation between households was expressed in the fact that for some this migration still covered both stock-keeping and trade, while for others it covered predominantly or exclusively trade. Thus in the 1940s and 1950s no actual settlement had yet taken place, but the pattern of the course which events would follow after the closing of the frontier to Pakistan in 1961 began to appear.

The principles of Barth's model for economic development and fluctuation in a nomad society (Barth 1961) are applicable to the situation of Zala Khān Khēl. This model is based upon the situation among the Basseri nomads in Iran at the end of the 1950s. The general economic developments and government policies favoured the settlement of Iranian nomads, but in the case of the Basseri it was still both possible and reasonable to regard the economic fluctuations which the model includes as fluctuations in relation to an actual nomadism. Poor nomads, who could no longer make a living as independent pastoralists, were forced out of nomadism and had to seek an earning for example as hired shepherds for other nomads or as labourers. At the other end of the economic scale rich nomads faced difficulties in handling large flocks of animals and therefore met a certain limit as to how much they could expand their pastoralism and thus accumulate wealth within the pastoral economy. For them investment in land and subsequent settlement on that land was a convenient possibility. It is Barth's view that the poor and the rich abandoned nomadism with the possibility in mind of later returning to it - the poor when they had accumulated the means to do so, and the rich when in a given situation they might find it politically expedient to choose a migratory way of life rather than a settled one. Nomadism in Barth's view is a possibility which can be chosen.

In the case of Zala Khān Khēl we have seen households with economic success break away, first by reorganising their migrations so that they incorporate their estates in North Afghanistan, and later, in the case of the most prosperous, by becoming fully settled as lorry-owners in Kabul. The paupers turned to a settled existence with *gharībī* in Pakistan, while those in the middle continued for some time yet with reduced livestock breeding and a declining nomad trade. The possibility of a return to nomadism, as foreseen in Barth's model, was, however, an ever-decreasing prospect to Zala Khān Khēl. Since the creation of Pakistan both nomadism and nomad trade have been less and less attractive choices, and by 1976 these choices were no longer possible because of lack of winter pasture and outing from the trading fields by competitors favoured by the general commercial and infratructural development. With the latest reorganisations, which led to winter camps at Jalalabad and the establishment of a temporary and fragile new economic pattern, the last remnants of pastoral nomadism have been abandoned, and the limited trade which is still carried on by some households in the highlands has very little in common with the old trading nomadism. The basis of both nomadism and nomad trading has gone.

A momentary picture taken some time in the 1950s would perhaps have justified an interpretation of the position of Zala Khān Khēl at that time as a matter of certain economic fluctuations in relation to a nomadism which was still possible. The picture of the mid-1970s shows rather that we are dealing with stages in a series of different ways of leaving nomadism. It shows how the economic background of the groups of households under investigation opened up for different economic strategies within the general development of the country. These gradually altered the basis of existence for the whole of Zala Khān Khēl - as well as for many other East Afghan nomads.

We must conclude that, with the exception of the three households which still practise pastoral nomadism to some degree, all Zala Khān Khēl have in 1976 broken with the nomadic way of subsistence. The economics of the households have been transformed, and the migrations which are still undertaken by some groups are without pastoral content. When asked, many pastoral nomads will reply that they migrate between highland and lowland in order always to be where the weather is most agreeable. When we are dealing with a fully functional nomadism this is naturally no satisfactory explanation, but for some of the landowning Zala Khān Khēl it comes very close to the truth. Many of them look upon their own situation as the realisation of "the nomad's dream" - to be free of the daily labour and insecurity of stock-breeding, and to continue the yearly migrations for reasons of comfort, and with an economic basis which has nothing to do with the migrations.

For the poor households in the winter camp at Jalalabad it is not the same realisation of "the dream" which lies behind their continuing migrations. Their migrations have retained a pastoral aspect in the summer livestock trading, but the original nomadic content is gone. The migrations have become a framework around a series of economic activities which are independent of each other and are only tied by the fact that together they have to provide the economic basis of existence for the households. Inspired by Barth's model we can illustrate the development and transformation of Zala Khān Khēl in *Fig. 6,1* as an economic and geographic splitting up seen in relation to the process of settlement and the economic hierarchy.

GENEALOGICAL DIVISION

From the historical sources we can see how sections of Ahmadzai and other East Afghan nomad groups have settled in the course of time (Broadfoot 1885, Elphinstone (1815) 1972, and Robinson 1935). It is in the course of such a process that Zala Khān Khēl has achieved its identity. Taghar's five lineage groups (see *Fig. 2,4*) experienced different courses of development. Most of them settled several generations ago, while Zala Khān Khēl continued as nomads for longer than any other Taghar. As development has been Zala Khān Khēl now exemplifies a continued course of splitting up which step by step has advanced along the lineage system, always interacting with changes in political and economic conditions. Among the Pashtuns it is a well-known pattern for a lineage group to undergo changes which lead to the formation of new lineage groups with more or less different directions of social and economic development, or with the same direction of development at different points of time. Though the changes that have taken place within the Zala Khān Khēl community of course display elements specific to Zala Khān Khēl, the transformation follows this pattern, in so far as a correlation can be found between the new directions of development and the branching out of the lineage system into sub-*khēls*.

Among Zala Khān Khēl there is an awareness that some groups of households are better or worse off than others, and there is also an awareness that these differences occur among definite groups of brothers or cousins. It is most clearly expressed where the differences are greatest, and where the number of households in a sub-*khēl* which are in the same situation is so great as to give a basis for a group identity. This is the case with sub-*khēl* 1 and sub-*khēl* 2, which are the two largest sub-*khēls* with twenty-eight and forty-two households, respectively. All the households in sub-*khēl* 1 left nomad trading with large accumulated profits. They are now prosperous landowners, and fifteen of them are also lorry-owners. The households in sub-*khēl* 2 have in general only done moderately or badly out of nomad trade, and they have no new investments of any significance to turn to. Most of them live in poverty in the new annual pattern with grain trading and wages labour. When people in sub-*khēl* 1 and sub-*khēl* 2 talk of their own situation and of the differences between themselves and others there is a growing tendency to use the terms Gholam Khēl and Asmat Khēl after the brothers Gholam and Asmat, who four generations ago are the genealogical source-points each for his own branch of the family tree (see *Fig. 2,5*). These terms are also used to a certain degree when other parts of Zala Khān Khēl refer to the two large sub-*khēls*. It is the use of such terms which symbolically marks the birth of a new independent *khēl*.

While the tendency is obvious in the cases of sub-*khēl* 1 and sub-*khēl* 2, it does not yet manifest itself for the remaining sub-*khēls* of Zala Khān Khēl. Either they are too small or the economic dispersal within the individual sub-*khēl* is too great to provide a basis for the households to regard themselves (or be regarded) as an independent *khēl*. The new terminology with regard to sub-*khēls* 1 and 2 inspired Hajjī Sadar Khān from sub-*khēl* 4 to comment that, were he to follow the tendency, he would be *malik* for the smallest *khēl* that he had ever heard of. For sub-*khēl* 4 consists only of two households. However, Hajjī Sadar Khān was expressing a common opinion among all branches of Zala Khān Khēl: that the uneven development will give rise to new directions of self-awareness, and that it is likely that all Zala Khān Khēl in a few

6,2 The household of Hajjī Sadar Khān (G.P., Dahana-i Ghori, March 1976).

years' time will use a whole new set of *khēl*-names to locate themselves and others within the lineage system.

This is happening in the case of sub-*khēls* 1 and 2 - here two new *khēls* are in fact established. Sub-*khēl* 7, which is settled in Pakistan, has also an immediate basis for considering itself (and being considered) as a *khēl*. In the case of the rest of Zala Khān Khēl's sub-*khēls* it is still uncertain how a reorientation of the lineage system may occur.

As mentioned earlier, the conditions of the field-work unfortunately made it impossible to obtain a closer insight into the position of women among Zala Khān Khēl. Information concerning marriage relations is only scattered and casual, and for that reason cannot be used to illuminate the relationship between the various *khēls* and sub-*khēls*. We know concerning the tribally organised Pashtun society that endogamy was ideally practised, with marriage to the father's-brother's-daughter preferred. To understand the creation of new sub-*khēl* identities within Zala Khān Khēl it would therefore be relevant to know to what degree endogamy is practised and to which order of size of kinship group it applies. Is the actual subdivision of Zala Khān Khēl an expression of a division into endogamous groups? If this is not the case, then what significance have marriage relationships between households in various sub-*khēls* - and what significance have possible marriage relationships between Zala Khān Khēl and non-Zala Khān Khēl?

We are unable to give an answer to these questions, but can refer to Ferdinand's studies of marriage relationships among Tara Khēl (another East Afghan Pashtun nomad group) for an illustration of the importance of marriage relations as a politically regulating factor among Pashtuns (cf. Ferdinand 1978a and 1982). Ferdinand's interpretation of a large amount of demographic and genealogical data covering several generations is that a newly arrived nomad group establishes itself in an area by contracting external marriage relations. After some generations the number of endogamous father's-brother's-daughter marriages increases markedly, and it can be said that the group now consolidates itself. Ferdinand says:

"The sudden change in marriage preference in the fourth generation must be a clear political strategic decision of the elder generation to establish themselves as a political entity" (Ferdinand 1978a, II: 187).

This illustrates the great significance of marriage relations, and with it the necessity for information on this aspect in order to be able to evaluate in optimal fashion the development of a society such as the Pashtun.

CHANGES IN THE ROLE OF LEADERSHIP

In the wake of the changes of the pastoral economy the role of the leader in connection with usage of grazing grounds obviously becomes of lesser importance. Moreover, the differentiation in development among Zala Khān Khēl makes a common coordination of all economic activities of less and less importance, until it is finally completely meaningless.

"A *malik*? That was something we had when everybody had sheep and goats and camels. Today we don't need a common leader. There isn't anything common for him to lead. Now we manage our own affairs and solve our own problems."

This is the way the general opinion is expressed among the well-to-do Zala Khān Khēl, and if a need should arise for a spokesman they would pick out an "elder" from among their own group, they say. Only a few of the well-to-do feel that the old *malik* Hajjī Hazrat Mohammad can still be addressed as *malik* - and then only as an honorary title, without content. Hajjī Hazrat Mohammad belongs to an intermediate group economically. He is from sub-*khēl* 2 and spends the winter in Camp 2 at Jalalabad. It is therefore not surprising that his social position as *malik* is valued more highly among the poor Zala Khān Khēl than among the rich. While they recognise that the *malik* has outlived his usefulness as an economic coordinator, the poor people still consider him important as a political spokesman and as a legal authority. It is Hazrat Mohammad, they say, who shall plead the case of the poor nomads before the authorities.

While parts of Zala Khān Khēl appear to have written off Hazrat Mohammad as their leader there is much to suggest that parts of the surrounding Afghan society still ascribe him a role as "tribal leader". For example, he takes part in meetings which government officials from time to time hold with tribal leaders. Hazrat Mohammad is apparently also recognised as a leader by other tribal groups. Thus, I was informed, he took part in a *jirgah* in August 1975 not only representing Zala Khān Khēl but the whole of Taghar.

A *jirgah* is the traditional council of the Pashtuns, where decisions are reached by unanimous agreement. Problems of a certain importance within a Pashtun group are normally resolved by a *jirgah* in which only that group's own members take part. If members of two groups are involved a joint *jirgah* of both groups will be held. A problem between people of a single group can, however, be of so serious a character, threatening to extend beyond the group immediately involved, that a *jirgah* is held with participation of several groups. It was a *jirgah* of this latter type that Hajjī Hazrat Mohammad took part in. An Isa Khēl of Ahmadzai (see Fig. *2,4*) had killed another Isa Khēl in a quarrel concerning land in Logar. The affair had developed to an extent where there was a danger of a blood-feud which would involve several Ahmadzai groups. A summons was accordingly sent to Isa Khēl, Musa Khēl, and Taghar to meet in a single large *jirgah*. A representative of each of the three groups came forward - and for Taghar it was Hajjī Hazrat Mohammad. Two hundred men took part in all, and after two days of discussion the *jirgah* decided that the brother of the murdered man was to receive two daughters from the murderer's family.

It is difficult to obtain a clear picture of Hazrat Mohammad's real role in Zala Khān Khēl, but there is no doubt that the role of supreme leader as such has declined in significance in accord with the social and economic transformation of Zala Khān Khēl. The question is whether the new groups will establish their own leadership in the same manner as formerly followed the creation of new *khēls*. The changes in the Zala Khān Khēl community can admittedly be viewed as a continuation of the historical process, which includes formation of new lineage groups, but at the same time this process has reached a stage where the single household is less and less dependent upon economic and social coordination. This minimises the need for formalised leadership, and it is in accord with this fact that some informants say that in concrete cases they would pick an *ad hoc* leader out of their own group.

IDENTITY AND TRANSFORMATION

Despite the many changes the Zala Khān Khēl still talk of themselves as *kūchey*. Admittedly, two thirds of the households still have a more or less migratory way of life, but practically none of them are pastoralists any longer. What has this development meant to the individual in his relationship to the household and to the lineage group, and what can we permit ourselves, against the background of the foregoing analysis, to suggest with regard to future development? We must look at the individual groups in an attempt to answer this question.

The settled lorry-owners in Qala-i Niazbeg illustrate the course of development by the three types which were described in Chapter 5 - the old, the active, and the young men. These types represent three stages in the process of reorientation to the household's background in nomadism and nomad trade. The old men see the situation as the end of a long nomad life - a well-earned retirement as nomads. The active men see the lorry-business and their present occupation as a natural continuation of their existence as nomads. They have changed their line of business, but their new activities follow many of the principles of their nomad way of life. They talk of the developments more as a continuity than as a break. Only with the young men important new tendencies can be seen in conception of the situation and in attitude to the changes. Even though they too call themselves *kūchey* it is with them and with the children that the new activities and changed way of life of the households break through in the form of an individualised attitude to modern Afghanistan. The young men and the children are influenced by new norms and new ideas through modern schooling and education, and through the mere fact of growing up as settled, and it will be with their entry into active business and economic responsibility that the lorry-owning households will become modern transport contractors.

Considering that the households first became settled in 1968 it is not surprising that they still call themselves *kūchey*. Their history is still to an overwhelming degree a history of nomadism and trading nomadism, though it may be a nostalgic reminiscence when they regard themselves as *kūchey*. Whatever the objective reality, in their view of the social order it is still the best to be a *kūchey*. But for the young and for the children this will change. As has been said, they will become more individually associated with a broader range of Afghan society. Many will go into the lorry business, but many will also exploit the greater choice of occupations which their new way of life offers. They are not bound by the dominant economic involvement of the household but have real possibilities of choice, partly through education. Such possibilities are already to some degree being utilised.

It has been mentioned that sub-*khēl* 1, to which the lorry-owners belong, was establishing itself as a new *khēl*. This development should be seen as a dissociation from other sections of Zala Khān Khēl and as an emphasis of internal unity. The greater degree of independence among the young with regard to career opportunities may, on the other hand, prove to carry with it a tendency towards dissolution of the *khēl* identity, which is still only in its formative state. For the independence may lead to an internal differentiation similar to that which Zala Khān Khēl as a whole underwent earlier. However, with the changed placing in society the tendency cannot be expected to go in the direction of the formation of yet another set of sub-*khēl*s, but rather towards a dissolution of the lineage system - towards detribalisation.

The migrant landowners have established a new pattern of migration, with winter sojourn on their estates in Dahana-i Ghori and summer sojourn in Salang or Ghorghori, and according to general opinion this pattern, as we have said, represents an ideal *kūchey* existence. Their relationship to agriculture on their own estates is in the course of development, and a single household has shown that Zala Khān Khēl may have a future as farmers rather than merely as landowners. Such a step is still far beyond the horizon of most of the landowners, but when it will eventually be taken there is much to suggest that it will cause much more change of attitude than the change of business has done to the lorry-owners. To be a landowner is seen as the successful conclusion of a nomad existence. To be a farmer is something quite different, and at the moment incompatible with the conviction of most of Zala Khān Khēl who identify themselves as being *kūchey*.

The young men and children of the migrant landowning households are more traditionally inclined than their contemporaries in Qala-i Niazbeg. Modern schooling and education are not part of their new daily life and are rarely met with. The continuing yearly migrations and varying places of sojurn keep the *kūchey* identity alive and at the same time give a basis of organisation which does not give any immediate encouragement to completely detached individual careers.

For the poor households with winter quarters at Jalalabad the identity as *kūchey* has a somewhat different connotation than for the rest of Zala Khān Khēl. They consider themselves as actual nomads, who have been forced out of their vocation and are now enduring a period of waiting and economic insecurity until better opportunities appear. Although they would naturally like to see themselves as landowners on a par with their relatives in Dahana-i Ghori, a return to pastoral nomadism is for them a positive alternative to the present position - and moreover an alternative which would be economically possible, were it not blocked by the absence of winter grazing grounds. If this absence could by some means or other be overcome they are still prepared to reestablish a nomadic production process - they are, as it were, nomads on the waiting list. In the new annual economic pattern with which these households are experimenting there are far more traditional aspects than in the way of life of the other Zala Khān Khēl households. It is therefore not surprising that we find little inclination towards the modern development of Afghanistan in these households. Their continued economic dependence on the yearly migrations limits the number of alternatives, but with the insecurity which marks the situation of the households, and with the poor prospects for a reestablishment of real nomadism, it is not inconceivable that the poor households will be forced more and more into unskilled labour as a partly or completely settled land proletariat (cf. *Fig. 6,1*)

CHAPTER 7

ZALA KHĀN KHĒL IN EXILE

WAR AND INSTABILITY

War broke out in Afghanistan in the wake of the communist Saur revolution in 1978. The very first reaction of people in the countryside to the news of the change of political power was largely that of curiosity and a little unease, but no major concern. After all, Kabul to most people was far away, and political incidents there were usually considered as a concern of members of the ruling circles only. Thus it was only five years earlier, in 1973, something similar had happened. King Mohammad Zahir Shah was dethroned by his cousin and brother-in-law, Sadar Mohammad Daoud Khān, the former prime minister, who declared Afghanistan a republic. That change had not been felt to any substantial degree. "Monarchy or republic? - that's a question of a fight between two cousins," the situation was interpreted to me.

However, the People's Democratic Party of Afghanistan (PDPA), in power after April 1978, embarked on a reform programme with an unexpected haste and with an incomprehensible use of force which soon became felt throughout the country. With practically no time allowed for political motivation young party members, for the most recruited from among the urban intellectual elite, supported by army units tried overnight to wipe out deep-rooted cultural values and behaviourial patterns of the predominantly rural population. The result was not hard to predict; people turned against the revolution, and after the first incidents of violent government reprisals - for reasons such as the hesitation of some men to allow their wives to participate in adult literacy classes - villagers fled to the mountains and took up armed resistance. The resistance movement, the *mujāhedin*, came into being, and at the same time the first Afghans chose to leave their country.

The war was intensified after the Soviet Union, in support of the Kabul regime, invaded Afghanistan in December 1979. Also the flow of refugees was intensified, and when I first visited the refugee camps in Pakistan in 1986 more than five million Afghans had been driven into exile while perhaps another two million were living displaced as internal refugees. Iran had received about two million refugees, while Pakistan had received over three million. Among the latter were the entire 130 households of Zala Khān Khēl.[1]

The first among the Zala Khān Khēl to be affected by the policies of the new government and by the armed fighting were the landowners in Dahana-i Ghori. The government proclaimed a land reform in November 1978, and officials

7,1 Soviet invasion troups (P.F., J.S., Jalalabad road, March 1980)

started preliminary investigations. At that time armed resistance to the new government was already a reality. In Dahana-i Ghori the officials were met by the local settled population with weapons in their hands. Fighting broke out and some officials were killed. In Pul-i Khomri the police station was attacked and senior officers shot. The government retaliated with reprisals against the whole region. The army and the air force was sent in, with the result that many of Zala Khān Khēl's houses were destroyed. Since then Zala Khān Khēl kept away from their land. Cultivation of the land was either given up or done by casual locals or by men of the resistance - *mujāhedin*. The ruins of the houses were used now and then as hiding places for *mujāhedin*, which regularly led to new attacks by government forces. "There is scarcely a stone left of any of our houses", one of them told me in 1986.

Some of the Zala Khān Khēl businessmen in Kabul quickly came into the purview of the government as suspected opponents of the new regime. One was arrested and has not been seen

7,2 Young armed *mujāhedin* (P.F., Kuna, Feb. 1980)

since, while confiscation orders allegedly were issued on property, stocks of goods, and bank accounts against some of the others. It was feared that arrest warrants were just around the corner, and this led to the first Zala Khān Khēl fleeing to Pakistan in 1979 - before the Soviet invasion.

The landless and poor Zala Khān Khēl were contacted by party and government officials and were promised that the new land reform would soon be to their benefit. Mir Ahmad Khān, from sub-*khēl* 2, relates:

"But when we realised the way in which they stole land from its legal owners, we understood that the land reform was nothing but a crime, and that to accept the land they offered would be un-Islamic. They never made any concrete offer anyway. They only talked about it - it was just propaganda. At the same time, when we understood the communists' crimes against us Afghans - all over the country and not just against us - it became clear that we weren't in safety, and we couldn't live a free life as Muslims."

With the Soviet invasion in December 1979 the majority of Zala Khān Khēl became convinced that the expectations expressed by Mir Ahmad Khān would come to pass. They had to leave Afghanistan, even though only a small minority of Zala Khān Khēl were directly threatened by the situation. In the first week of 1980 one of the men from the winter camps at Jalalabad, inspired by the call from many religious leaders in East Afghanistan, travelled to Kabul and urged all Zala Khān Khēl to flee - and the proposal was acted upon immediately thereafter by the greater part of the households.

The poor families who left from Jalalabad had few worldly goods to abandon. Others left behind businesses, houses, and other property. "We locked up securely after us, but we don't expect to have any property in Afghanistan any more. It's been confiscated by the government," they say. The stalls in Bazaar-i Omaid were also left as they stood, since no Zala Khān Khēl had the time to prepare for a selling. Some of the other shopkeepers in Bazaar-i Omaid had better time to prepare their flight. They managed to sell their stalls to Hindu and Sikh businessmen, who took over more and more of Kabul's business life. The selling price should under normal conditions have been somewhat over 100,000 afs., they say, but they only managed to get 20-30,000 afs. per stall. It was not a seller's market in Kabul.

After the flight in the first week of 1980 only the lorry-owners in Qala-i Niazbeg stayed on. They kept a low profile politically and ran their businesses as before - still with the government as principal customer. It was probably this circumstance that helped to ensure that their business was not affected by the government's work of reform. There was urgent need for a functioning transport sector in war-torn Afghanistan.

One of those who stayed behind recounts how he was contacted by the government and offered money to form a militia - the government's arming of the local people in defence against "the bandits", which was the usual official description of the *mujāhedin*. He, and other Zala Khān Khēl, had no wish to take sides politically and, after having several times rejected the government's charm offensive, they felt its attitude changing. One by one they began to prepare for a flight to Pakistan. They sold lorries and other property and converted their valuables to cash and jewellery. From 1982 they began to flee, and the last Zala Khān Khēl household left Afghanistan in 1985.

Details on how the Zala Khān Khēl fled from Afghanistan was not conveyed to me. The usual explanation was: "We just crossed the border the way we used to do." The fact that many Afghan nomads traditionally had been going back and forth across the border with Pakistan provided a handy excuse for the Kabul regime when the world became aware of a new major refugee problem: The refugees were merely nomads, Kabul claimed, who used to cross the border into Pakistan. The fact that some of them now decided to stay there for more than just a winter season was explained as the traditional fluctuation within nomad societies. The postulated refugees thus should be nothing more than marginalised nomads who adjusted to certain changes in their socio-economic basis by staying in Pakistan, according to Kabul.

Some of the refugees indeed were nomads who in earlier days used to cross into Pakistan for seasonal grazing, in search for labour, or for trading, but evidently the reason for their prolonged exile was a different one from the traditional fluctuation of socio-economic circumstances.

EXILE

All Zala Khān Khēl now live as refugees in the North-West Frontier Province of Pakistan.[2] Just as the transformation of Zala Khān Khēl society in Afghanistan to some extent reflected the changes of the country in general, their situation in exile seems to reflect the refugee situation in Pakistan in general. Zala Khān Khēl live scattered in twelve places, with from one to thirty-one households in each. Eleven of these localities are official and unofficial refugee camps in the districts of Peshawar, Mardan, and Abbottabad (see map, *Fig. 7,3*); and one is a privately-owned house near Peshawar where a single household has rented accommodation. The distribution follows the households' economic means, and is an expression of the degree to which they are dependent on the official refugee aid.

Zala Khān Khēl's division into households is in 1986 practically identical with that of 1976. One household dissolved following a death unconnected with the war, two others split up into independent economic units. In 1976 several households were on the brink of division, judging from their composition and from the direction of their economic engagements, but this has for the most part failed to take place.

Those Zala Khān Khēl who were poor in Afghanistan are also poor in exile. They brought no valuables of any sort, and are completely dependent on help provided by the Pakistan government and by national and international relief organisations. Initially some of them considered reestablishing themselves as migrating pastoralists in their exile, but the prospects for such a subsistence proved discouraging before any attempt was made: In the early 1980s other Afghan nomads in exile tried to establish themselves as migrating pastoralists inside Pakistan. The critical factor was summer pasture which is a scarce resource in Pakistan. It is generally only available in the highlands north and northeast of Peshawar and in some parts of the Tribal Area. Besides, these areas are here already fully utilised by local pastoralists. To protect the pastures from a destructive over-grazing and to protect the interests of the local population the Pakistani authorities intervened with general restrictions on refugees' access to grazing land. As a consequence only few Afghans managed to pursue a pastoral way of life in Pakistan - and for the most under less than attractive circumstances, relegated to the utilisation of very marginal pastures such as road- and railway-sides and embankments (Glatzer 1988, Pedersen 1988a and 1991, and Sweetser 1984.)

Denied access to pastures and being without means or alternative economic possibilities, the poor Zala Khān Khēl have to follow the instructions of the authorities with regard to place of residence in order to receive refugee aid and food rations. They live on a year-round basis in official refugee camps - but scattered because they arrived in small groups and over a period of some years. In Afghanistan they led an existence which to the very end included two yearly migrations. Their way of life was not economically attractive, but at least the households managed to get away from the hot lowland summers and the cold highland winters. As refugees they have lost this last remnant of the nomadic heritage, they complain. Like the majority of the refugees they must endure the hot summers of the Pakistani plains. They must also endure the crowded housing of the camps, the poor facilities or absence of facilities, and the gradual reduction in the refugee rations, as the case is. This last factor has forced many of them to seek supplementary income through local wage labour or petty trading.

Refugee camps in North-West Frontier Province of PAKISTAN.

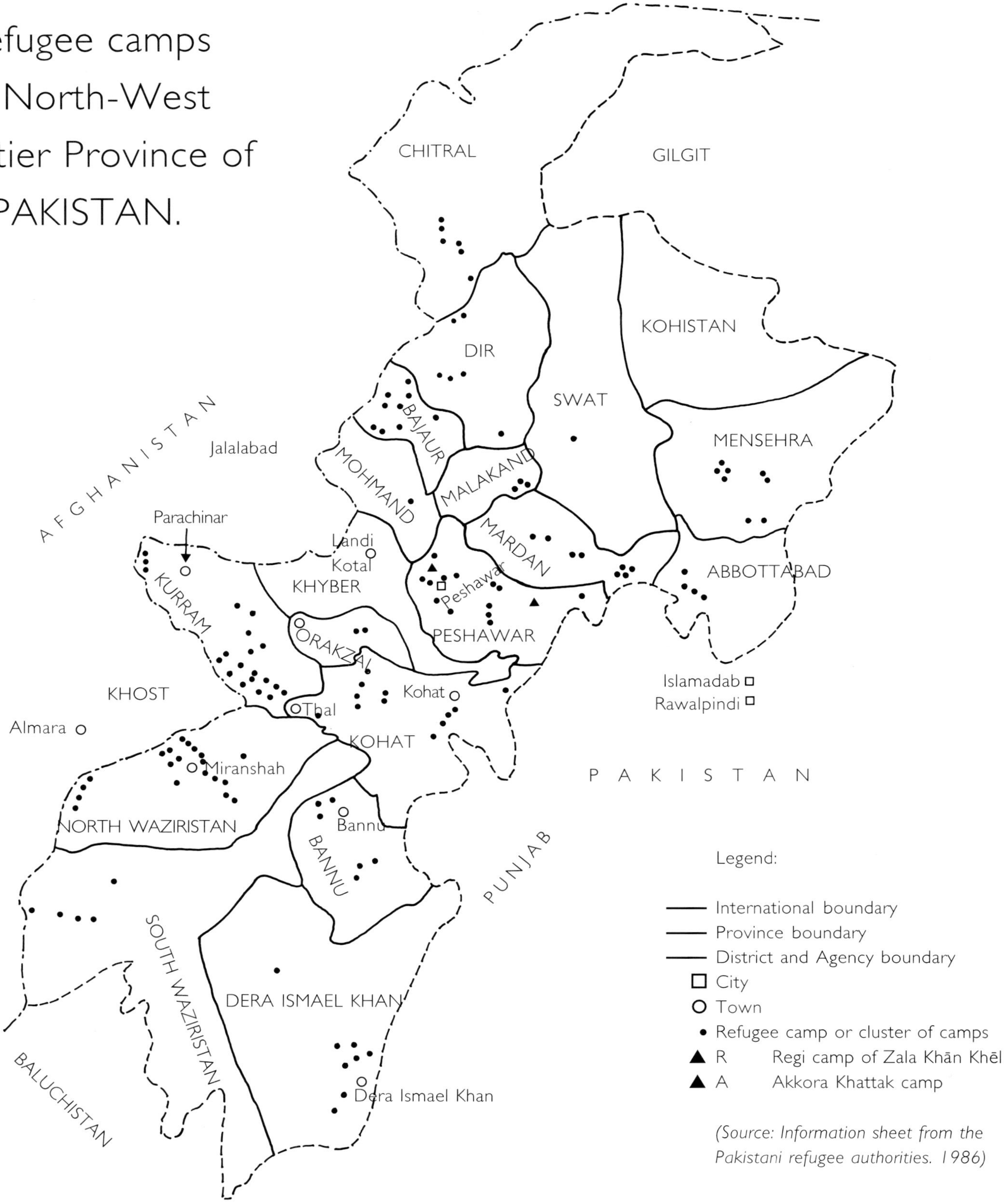

7,4 Although registered as refugees some Zala Khān Khēl live outside the official refugee camps as they do not depend on refugee aid. In their private camp of Regi they enjoy larger tents and first of all they enjoy a considerable freedom of choice. (G.P., Peshawar, Nov. 1986).

7.3 Refugee camps in North-West Frontier Province of Pakistan.
The map shows the approximate location of refugee camps as of 1986, many of the dots representing clusters of camps. According to Pakistani refugee authorities the number of official camps was 247 in mid-1986. To this shall be added an unknown number of unofficial refugee settlements. The majority of Afghan refugees in Pakistan are found in the North-West Frontier Province but many are also located around Quetta in Baluchistan. Zala Khān Khēl are settled in camps mainly in the districts of Peshawar, Mardan, and Abbottabad.

During the first years in exile many of the Zala Khān Khēl who were well-off in Afghanistan had economic resources to manage completely on their own as they had been able to flee with at least part of their property converted into cash, jewellery, or other easily transportable valuables. Their starting point in exile was thus different from the position of total dependence in which some of their relatives found themselves after crossing the frontier. They did not rely on refugee aid, they could set up their own camps, and they could even

7,5 Schools for the refugee children are too few and poorly equipped. Lacking proper educational facilities and being furthermore deprived of the normal cultural setting of an Afghan community it is to be feared that the refugee children will become a "lost generation" (G.P., Peshawar, Nov. 1986).

choose to avoid the hot season by moving to the mountains in Dir or Swat, north and north-east of Peshawar. These were the favourite places, but as transport is relatively expensive, some chose the shorter road to Landi Kotal close to the Afghan border. As resources dried up, many households had to moderate their lifestyle and give in, at least partly, to requirements and regulations of the refugee authorities. They no longer manage to move to the highlands in summer, but some of them still choose their form of encampment relatively freely.

Nine households are in this situation in the large Akkora Khattak Camp with about 40,000 registered inhabitants east of Peshawar. In all, thirty-one Zala Khān Khēl households live and receive their refugee rations here, but nine of these households live on rented land immediately outside the border of the camp. Though recognised as inhabitants of Akkora Khattak Camp and therefore receivers of refugee aid,

7,6 Afghan children at school in a refugee camp (G.P., Peshawar, Nov. 1986).

these households are more free as regards camping arrangement. The layout of the camp and the furnishing of the individual tents resemble completely the traditional nomad camps - though the rental for land has caused the households not to spread their dwellings over so large an area as they did in former days. Eight of the households live in ordinary refugee tents, which they have purchased, while one household has bought a particularly large tent of Pakistani manufacture. It was more expensive, but will last longer - and it is watertight, which many of the refugee tents unfortunately are not. Many tents stand so close together that there is only room for the guy-ropes between them. Space does, however, permit each household to have a large cleared and levelled area in front of it - edged by a low embankment and floored with gravel. Inside the floor is also covered with gravel, and belongings are piled up at the far end in chests and bundles rolled in cloth and rugs.

7,7 Young men and boys of the Regi camp gathered in front of the guest tent (G.P., Peshawar, Nov. 1986).

To supplement the refugee rations these households engage in a modest amount of trading. They have little to invest, and reap but small profits. They trade in anything they can lay their hands on, but mostly buy up small stocks of agricultural produce in the countryside which they sell in the bazaars of Nowshera or Peshawar. A few of the younger men tell that from time to time they join *mujāhedin*-groups in the fighting inside Afghanistan.

Some Zala Khān Khēl, in particular the former lorry-owning households from Qala-i Niazbeg, brought so much of wealth with them into exile that they could invest in commerce and the local property market. In the bazaar in Peshawar, for example, a number of business premises have

7,8 From the settled life of suburban Kabul to a refugee tent arranged in agreement with good nomad standards - the former lifestyle has not been forgotten (G.P., Akkora Khattak, Dec. 1986).

been rented and thereafter sub-let. It is difficult to estimate the range of these activities, but the profits are great enough to permit the buying of cars - both pick-ups for business and private cars. The incomes of the households are supplemented by salaries from young men working as migrant labourers in the Gulf. Such work is not for the ordinary poor, as it requires capital to achieve working permits and other necessary papers.

Greater economic freedom puts the prosperous Zala Khān Khēl in a different position as refugees. Although registered as refugees and assigned an official camp where they must live to get part of the official distributions, the fifteen former lorry-owning households from Qala-i

7,9-11 Zala Khān Khēl on the outskirts of the Akkora Khattak camp. The relative comfort of their refugee life is on borrowed time as they have no regular sources of income to sustain their livelihood; they now depend on refugee aid (G.P., Akkora Khattak, Dec. 1986).

Niazbeg disregard these options. Upon arrival in Pakistan they have established themselves on private premises - one household in a rented house in an industrial suburb west of Peshawar, and the others in a tented camp alternating between summer and winter sites.

The winter camp is situated in Regi, five to six kilometres northwest of Peshawar near to an asphalt road. Here fourteen households from Zala Khān Khēl live together with sixteen from Nur Khān Khēl. The land is rented from a local Pakistani landowner for about five winter months. The dwellings are all canvas tents of the type distributed to refugees, bought from other refugees. Most households have a single tent, some have put several tents together to form one large dwelling. There are no black goat's hair tents. Most households have not owned such a tent for many years. However, the physical arrangement of the camp and the furnishing of the individual tents resemble completely the traditional nomad camps with the modifications described above. In between the tents there are small huts and shelters for storage and for the livestock - some hens and a cow or two, locally bought to provide fresh dairy produce. The camp has a large guest-tent inside a fenced area. There are no walls around the dwelling tents or the camp as a whole, but towards a path used by the local villagers hang some large pieces of sacking to ensure a certain minimum of privacy. For here there is no open plain around giving early warning of the coming of strangers.

From this camp the men carry on their business affairs without difficulty. Peshawar is close by, and they can drive by car almost to the very door. Seven of the younger men have spent three years in Saudi Arabia as migrant workers. Some of them are "home on leave" and will soon leave again. They earn good money, they say, and their contribution to the economy is regarded as important. Some households say that the activities in Pakistan give no great profit. They live on the resources they brought with them and will depend in the long run on the incomes of the migrant workers, they claim.

7,12 In the refugee camps nomads often live in their own sections characterised by the lack of boundary-walls which are usually erected around the tents and huts of the village-refugees (G.P., Mardan, Nov. 1986).

7,13 Mir Ahmad Khān in front of his tent in a refugee camp near Peshawar (G.P., Dec. 1986).

7,14 A camp of newly arrived nomad refugees (G.P., Kurram, Dec. 1986).

7,15 "I am an old man, and I may never see Afghanistan again. But it is my sincere hope that all my poor relatives may one day return to a proper nomadism in Afghanistan." Mir Ahmad Khān in exile (G.P., Peshawar, Dec. 1986).

THE REVIVAL OF NOMADISM?

Considerable anxiety is expressed concerning the prospects for cultural development among Pashtuns in exile. Standards are broken down, and deep-rooted practices of self-support and cultural continuity can no longer be followed. Economic and political dependency on outsiders violates fundamental tenets of Pashtun culture. The consequences are rootlessness, social conflict, and the prospect of a new generation of Afghans with, seen through Pashtun eyes, an identity which does not match well with traditional norms and values. Many Zala

7,16 Old Zala Khān Khēl nomad in exile (G.P., Peshawar, Dec. 1986).

Khān Khēl already face these problems, and more are likely to do so in the future.[3]

Some changes can, however, be seen in a different light. This is the case, for instance, when the nomadic way of life becomes partly reestablished. Before their flight the lorry-owning households in Qala-i Niazbeg enjoyed a settled life for about fourteen years. The grown-ups, however, continued to maintain that "we are first and foremost *kūchey*." Due to their relative economic independence in exile these households have the freedom of choice in organising their way of life. They have decided to live in tented camps under their own management and maintain two annual migrations.

Will pastoral nomadism have new opportunities in Afghanistan? In Iran some former nomadic peoples utilised the political uncertainty after the fall of the Shah in 1979 to revive the nomadic way of life which they had been forced to abandon by the Shah's reform programmes. This was supported by a call from the new Islamic regime for an increase of the national meat production (see for example Beck 1980a, 1980b, and 1984; and Safizadeh 1984). Whether something similar is going to happen in Afghanistan will not depend on organisational and pastoral skills, nor be a question of willingness from the potential nomads. Skills are certainly there, and among the nomads, including the poor sections of Zala Khān Khēl who for years have suffered the set-

7,17 Refugee nomads who have brought animals to Pakistan are facing many difficulties trying to continue stock-breeding. Lack of pasture, especially during the hot summers, has caused most nomads to part with their animals. Only a few keep on, seeking fodder for their small flocks along railway tracks and as here in the streets of towns (G.P., Peshawar, Dec. 1988).

7,18 While most nomads have had to part with sheep and goats, camels have often been kept for use in local transport business (G.P., Kurram, Dec. 1986).

tled life in crowded refugee camps in Pakistan, there is a marked wish to return to pastoral nomadism in Afghanistan. The main problem will be whether grazing grounds are available to the nomads.

In the course of war the Hazara people of the central Afghan highland are reported to have gained considerable strength and to have declared their country liberated and independent of the central power of Kabul. Will the Hazara acknowledge the old *farmān*s of the Iron Amir and accept the nomads' claim of ownership to the highland summer pastures? During the first years of the war, air raids and land-mines put an end to much of the movement of the nomads, in particular to the longer migrations of the East Afghan Pashtun nomads. A few nomad groups who did venture their way to Hazarajat in the early 1980s were met by Hazara armed forces who demanded tax on the animals to let them pass on to the summer pastures. The Zala Khān Khēl ask themselves whether this will also be the situation when nomads wish to return to Hazarajat in larger numbers?

7,19 Refugees have started returning to "safe areas" in Afghanistan. This load of furniture is taken across the border from Pakistan into Khost (G.P., Khost, June 1992).

7,20 Returned to Afghanistan, repatriated refugees unload the lorry which carried them and their household belongings home (G.P., Khost, June 1992).

It is likely that in many places where the nomads, and for that matter also other Afghans, may try to revive pre-war subsistence patterns, they will face a socio-political set-up different from the one they left behind when they fled. Former ownership may not be reckoned and pre-war rights based on holding the upper hand in a local power structure may be waved as a consequence of a new power balance created through years of local resistance fighting.

The winter grazing grounds in Pakistan will hardly be reopened to Afghan nomads after the war, but it is possible that the destructions caused by the war ironically enough may give increased room for nomadism for some years within Afghanistan. Afghan agriculture has suffered severely under the ravages. The vital irrigation systems have been destroyed in many places by bombardment or have fallen into disrepair. This devastation of agricultural land may take years - even generations according to some assessments - to overcome. Tragic as this situation is in general, it may mean that the only people who can utilise the ruined areas are the pastoralists - and among them quite naturally those Zala Khān Khēl who since the 1970s have regarded themselves as being nomads on the waiting list.

NOTES

1 A short presentation of the experiences gained in the field-visit to Pakistan in November-December 1986 can be found in Pedersen 1990. A summary, in Danish, of the history of Zala Khān Khēl - from Afghanistan to exile in Pakistan - will be found in Pedersen 1987/88.

2 Again, the following presentation, based on data gathered in 1986, is written in "ethnographic present tense". At the time of printing the repatriation of Afghan refugees to certain "safe" areas has been going on for some time, but it is unknown whether any of the Zala Khān Khēl households have as yet left their exile and returned to Afghanistan.

3 These problems are thoroughly discussed for Pashtun refugees in general in Inger W. Boesen 1979 etc.

7,21 War time has enabled a revival of caravaneering in the borderland of Afghanistan. This string of camels is running supply to the *mujāhedin* inside Afghanistan (G.P., Kurram, Dec. 1986).

A REFLECTION

When nomads are forced by circumstances to leave their pastoral trade most of them face settlement and a livelihood as unskilled labourers with little prospect of prosperity. One such settled nomad household has found a way to supplement the earnings of the men: they have set up their tent next to a historical monument in Herat and put themselves on display as "nomads" for the bypassing Western tourist. They have, as it is, turned themselves and their old trade into a museum object. Admittedly, during my work and travels in Afghanistan I often felt myself to be in a situation not much different from that of the American lady, dressed in nomad fashion (in the mid-right of the photo), who gets a feeling of authenticity by visiting the "tourist nomads" (G.P., Herat, Oct. 1975)

BIBLIOGRAPHY

Ahmed, A. S. 1981 — Nomadism as Ideological Expression: The Case of the Gomal Nomads. *Nomadic Peoples*, 9: 3-15.

1982 — A Taste for Freedom: The Case of the Gomal Nomads. *Asian Affairs*, 13, 2: 172-83 (republication of 1981).

Ali, M. 1946 — *Commercial Afghanistan.* (Frontier Exchange Press) Delhi.

Anderson, E. W., and Dupree, N. H. (eds.) 1990 — *The Cultural Basis of Afghan Nationalism.* (Pinter Publishers) London.

Andrews, P. A. (ed.) (forthcoming) — *Tent Types of the Middle East.* Beihefte zum Tübinger Atlas des Vorderen Orients (TAVO), B, 74. (Dr. Ludwig Reichert Verlag) Wiesbaden.

Bacon, E. E. 1954 — Types of Pastoral Nomadism in Central and Southwest Asia. *Southwestern Journal of Anthropology*, 10: 44-57.

Balikci, A. 1981 — Pastoralism and Class Differentiation among the Lakenkhel. *Journal of Asian and African Studies*, XVI, 1-2: 150-7.

s. a. — *Sons of Haji Omar: A study guide.* (PCR: Films and Video in the Behavioral Sciences, Audio Visual Services. The Pennsylvania State University) Pennsylvania.

Balland, D. 1982 — Constraintes écologiques et fluctuations historiques dans l'organisation territoriale des nomades d'Afghanistan. *Production pastorale et société: Bulletin de l'équipe écologie et anthropologie des sociétés pastorales*, 11: 55-67.

1985 — Afghanistan: Political History. *Encyclopædia Iranica*, I: 547-58.

1988a — Nomadic Pastoralists and Sedentary Hosts in the Central and Western Hindukush Mountains, Afghanistan. *Human Impact on Mountains.* N. J. R. Allan et al. (eds.): 265-76. (Rowman and Littlefield) Totowa, N.J.

1988b — Le déclin contemporain du nomadisme pastoral en Afghanistan. *Neue Beiträge zur Afghanistanforschung.* E. Grötzbach (ed.). Schriftenreihe der Stiftung Biblioteca Afghanica, 6: 175-88. Liestal.

1989 — *Wanderweidewirtschaft. Beispiele: 12.7 Afghanistan. Nomadismus und Halbnomadismus.* Tübinger Atlas des Vorderen Orients (TAVO), A X 12. (Dr. Ludwig Reichert Verlag) Wiesbaden.

1991 — Nomadism and Politics: The Case of Afghan Nomads in the Indian Subcontinent. *Studies in History*, 7, 2, NS: 205-29.

Balland, D., and Kieffer, C. M. 1979 — Nomadisme et sécheresse en Afghanistan: l'exemple des nomades Pastun du Dast-e Nāwor. *Pastoral production and society/ Production pastorale et societé*. Equipe écologie et anthropologie des sociétés pastorales (eds.): 75-90. (Cambridge University Press and Editions de la Maison des Sciences de l'Homme) Cambridge and Paris.

Barfield, T. J. 1978 — The Impact of Pashtun Immigration on Pastoralism in Northeast Afghanistan. *Ethnic Processes and Intergroup Relations in Contemporary Afghanistan*. J. Anderson and E. Strand (eds.). Occasional Paper No. 15 of the Afghanistan Council of the Asia Society.

1979 — The Impact of Colonial Disputes on Isolated Populations in the Upper Oxus: The Case of Central Asian Arabs. *Journal of Asian and Middle Eastern Studies*, III, 2.

1981 — *The Central Asia Arabs of Afghanistan: Pastoral Nomadism in Transition.* (University of Texas Press) Austin.

Barth, F. 1959a — Segmentary Opposition and the Theory of Games: A Study of Pathan Organization. *Journal of the Royal Anthropological Institute*, 89, 1: 5-21.

1959b — *Political Leadership among Swat Pathans.* London School of Economics. Monographs on Social Anthropology, 19. (Athlone Press) London.

1960 — The Land Use Pattern of Migratory Tribes of South Persia. *Norsk Geografisk Tidsskrift*, XVII, 1-4: 1-11.

1961 — *Nomads of South Persia. The Basseri Tribe of the Khamseh Confederation.* (Universitetsforlaget) Oslo.

1962 — Nomadism in the Mountain and Plateau Areas of South West Asia. *Arid Zone Research: The Problems of the Arid Zone, II: Nomadism in Relation to Grazing Resources*: 341-55. Proceedings of the Paris symposium. (UNESCO) Paris.

1964 — Capital, Investment and the Social Structure of a Pastoral Nomad Group in South Persia. *Capital, Saving and Credit in Peasant Societies.* R. Firth and B. S. Yamey (eds.): 69-81. (George Allen and Unwin) London.

1968 — Forasien. *Verdens folkeslag i vor tid.* J. Nicolaisen et al. (eds.): 220-40. (Politikens Forlag) Copenhagen.

1969 — Pathan Identity and Its Maintenance. *Ethnic Groups and Boundaries: The Social Organization of Culture Difference.* F. Barth (ed.): 117-34. (Universitetsforlaget and George Allen & Unwin) Oslo and London.

1973 — A General Perspective on Nomad-Sedentary Relations in the Middle East. *The Desert and the Sown: Nomads in the Wider Society.* C. Nelson (ed.): 11-21. Research Series, 21. (Institute of International Studies. University of California) Berkeley.

Beck, L. 1980a — Revolutionary Iran and Its Tribal Peoples. *Merip Reports*, 87: 14-20.

1980b — The Tribe and State in Revolutionary Iran: The Return of the Qashqa'i Khans. *Iranian Studies*, 13, 1-4: 215-55.

1984 — The Qashqa'i of Iran. *Cultural Survival Quarterly*, 8, 1: 19-22.

Behnstedt, P., and Kieffer, C. M. 1984 — *Afghanistan: Sprachen und Dialekte.* Tübinger Atlas des Vorderen Orients (TAVO), A VIII 11. (Dr. Ludwig Reichert Verlag) Wiesbaden.

Benoist, A. de 1980 *Approche du monde nomade afghan*. INED, Synthèse des récessements africains. Documents d'information, 24. Paris.

1981 *Nomadic Survey of Afghanistan by Province (July 1978)*, 1- 3. (United Nations Publication) Kabul.

Boesen, I. W. 1979 Pashtun-kvinder i Østafghanistan. *Stofskifte*, 4.

1980 Women, Honour, and Love: Some Aspects of Pashtun Woman's Life in Eastern Afghanistan. *Folk*, 21-22: 229-39 (republished in *Afghanistan Journal*, 7, 2: 50-59).

1983 Conflicts of Solidarity in Pakhtun Women's Life. *Women in Islamic Societies*. B. Utas (ed.): 24-47. London.

1985a From Autonomy to Dependency: Aspects of the "Dependency Syndrome" among Afghan Refugees. *Migration Today*, XIII, 5: 17-21.

1985b "Vi er alle afghanere, og vi kæmper alle den samme kamp." *Jordens folk*, 20, 3: 110-19.

1986 Honour in Exile: Continuity and Change among Afghan Refugees. *FOLK*, 28: 109-24 (republished in *The Tragedy of Afghanistan*. B. Huldt and E. Jansson (eds.) 1988: 219-39, and in *The Cultural Basis of Afghan Nationalism*. E. W. Anderson and N. H. Dupree (eds.) 1990: 160-74).

1987 Fem millioner på flugt. *Kontakt*, 39, 6: 38-41.

1988 Ten years of war and civil war in Afghanistan - an educational catastrophy for an entire generation. *WUFA Quarterly Journal*, 3, 3: 32-44.

Bourgeois, J. and D. 1972 *Les seigneurs d'Aryana: Nomades contrabandiers d'Afghanistan*. (Flammarion) Paris.

Briggs, L. C. 1960 *Tribes of Sahara*. (Harvard University Press) Cambridge, Massachusetts.

Broadfoot, J. S. 1885 Reports on Parts of the Ghilzai Country, and on Some of the Tribes in the Neighbourhood of Ghazni. *The Royal Geographical Society Supplementary Papers*, 1, 3.

Bruce, C. E. 1929 *Notes on the Ghilzai and Powindah Tribes*. Peshawar.

Burnes, A. 1973 (1834) *Travels into Bokhara: Being the Account of a Journey from India to Cabool, Tartary, and Persia*. (Oxford in Asia Historical Reprint) Karachi, London, New York, Delhi.

Caroe, O. 1958 *The Pathan*. (Macmillan) London.

Casimir, M. J., Winter, R. P., and Glatzer, B. 1980 Nomadism and remote sensing: Animal husbandry and the sagebrush community in a nomad winter area in western Afghanistan. *Journal of Arid Environments*, 3: 231-54.

Census of India 1931 1933 XV: *North-West Frontier Province*. Peshawar.

Census of the North-West Frontier Province 1911 *Report on the Census of the North-West Frontier Province*. Peshawar.

Centlivres-Demont, M. 1976 *Popular Art in Afghanistan: Paintings on Trucks, Mosques and Tea-Houses*. (Akademische Druck- u. Verlagsanstalt) Graz.

Christensen, A. 1980 The Pashtuns of Kunar: Tribe, Class and Community Organization. *Afghanistan Journal*, 7, 3: 79-92.

1981 Stammesamfund og statsmagt: Pashtunerne i Afghanistan. *Jordens folk*, 16, 3: 310-16.

1982 Agnates, Affines and Allies: Patterns of Marriage among Pakhtun in Kunar, North-East Afghanistan. *FOLK*, 24: 29-63.

1983 Afghanistan - ikke kontrarevolution, men befrielseskamp. *Jordens folk*, 18, 1: 3-12.

1984a "Udvikling" ovenfra - modstand nedefra: Socialisme og stammefolk i Afghanistan. *Stofskifte*, 10: 63-91.

1984b Afghanistan: Socialism and Tribesmen. *Cultural Survival Quarterly*, 8, 1: 70-3.

1988 When Muslim Identity Has Different Meanings: Religion and Politics in Contemporary Afghanistan. *The Tragedy of Afghanistan*. B. Huldt and E. Jansson (eds.): 3-19. (Croom Helm) London.

Dor, R. 1975 *Contributions à l'étude des Kirghiz du Pamir afghan*. Paris.

Dor, R., and Naumann, C. M. 1978 *Die Kirghisen des Afghanischen Pamir*. (Akademische Druck- u. Verlagsanstalt) Graz.

Dupree, L. 1978 Language and Politics in Afghanistan. *Contribution to Asian Studies*, XI. Leiden.

1980 *Afghanistan*. 2nd edn. (Princeton University Press) Princeton

1985 Afghanistan: Ethnography. *Encyclopædia Iranica*, I: 495-501.

Dupree, L., and Albert, L. (eds.) 1974 *Afghanistan in the 1970s*. (Praeger Publishers) New York.

Edelberg, L. 1950 Afghanistan, nomadernes land. *Ledetråd ved Folkelig Universitetsundervisning*, 263. (Folkeuniversitetsudvalget) Copenhagen.

1952 Afghanistan som arbejdsområde for fremtidige etnografiske undersøgelser. *Naturens Verden*, 36, 3-4: 97-128.

1958 ARSELAN: Et udblik over dansk forskning i Centralasien. *Naturens Verden*, 41: 257-89. (In collaboration with Klaus Ferdinand).

Elphinstone, M. 1972 (1815) *An Account of the Kingdom of Caubul*, I-II. (Oxford in Asia Historical Reprint) Karachi, London, New York.

Encyclopædia Iranica 1985 (Routledge and Kegan Paul) London.

Enriquez, C. M. 1910 *The Pathan Borderland*. Calcutta and Simla.

Faegre, T. 1979 *Tents: Architecture of the Nomads*. (John Murray) London.

Feilberg, C. G. 1944 *La tente noire: Contribution ethnographique à l'histoire culturelle des nomades*. Nationalmuseets Skrifter, Etnografisk Rk., II. Copenhagen.

Ferdinand, K. 1956a På ekspedition til uudforskede stammer i Afghanistan. *Ledetråd ved Folkelig Universitetsundervisning*, 330. (Folkeuniversitetsudvalget) Copenhagen.

1956b Afghanistans nomader: Henning Haslund-Christensens Minde-Ekspedition 1953-55. *Fra Nationalmuseets Arbejdsmark 1956*: 61-70. (The National Museum) Copenhagen.

1957 Nomadestudier i Afghanistan. *Menneskets Mangfoldighed.* K. Birket-Smith (ed.): 126-41. (E. Wangels Forlag) Copenhagen.

1959a The Baluchistan Barrel-Vaulted Tent And Its Affinities. *FOLK,* 1: 27-50.

1959b Les nomades afghans, in J. Humlum *La géographie de l'Afghanistan*: 277-89. (Gyldendal) Copenhagen.

1959c Preliminary Notes on Hazāra Culture. (The Danish Scientific Mission to Afghanistan 1953-55). *Historisk Filosofiske Meddelelser,* 37, 5. (Det Kongelige Danske Videnskabernes Selskab) Copenhagen.

1960 The Baluchistan Barrel-Vaulted Tent: Supplementary Material from Iranian Baluchistan and Sistan. *FOLK,* 2: 33-50.

1962 Nomad Expansion and Commerce in Central Afghânistân: A Sketch of some Modern Trends. *FOLK,* 4: 123-59.

1964a Nomadisme: Nogle økologiske betragtninger med eksempler fra Arabien og Afghanistan. *KUML, Årbog for Jysk Arkæologisk Selskab 1963*: 108-47.

1964b Ethnographical Notes on Chahar Aimâq, Hazâra and Moghôl. *Acta Orientalia,* 28: 175-203.

1968a Afghanistan og Vestpakistan. *Verdens folkeslag i vor tid.* J. Nicolaisen et al. (eds.): 241-50. (Politikens Forlag) Copenhagen.

1968b Centralasien. *Verdens folkeslag i vor tid.* J. Nicolaisen et al. (eds.): 121-49. (Politikens Forlag) Copenhagen.

1969a Nomadism in Afghanistan: With an Appendix on Milk Products. *Viehwirtschaft und Hirtenkultur.* L. Földes (ed.): 127-60. (Akadémia Kiadó) Budapest.

1969b Ost-Afghanischer Nomadismus - ein Beitrag zur Anpassungsfähigkeit der Nomaden. *Nomadismus als Entwicklungsproblem.* W. Kraus (ed.): 107-30. (Bertelsmann Universitätsverlag) Bochum.

1970 Aspects of the Relationship Between Nomads and Settled Population in Afghanistan. *VII Congrès International des Sciences Anthropologiques et Ethnologiques,* X: 125-33. Moscow.

1974 Some Considerations on the Yurt with References to Afghanistan and Mongolia. *Role of the Nomadic Peoples in the Civilization of Central Asia.* S. Bira and A. Luvsandendev (eds.): 285-8. Ulan Bator.

1975 Afghanistan. *Jordens folk,* 11, 4: 147-8.

1978a (Sh 1356/57) Marriage Amongst Pakhtun Nomads of the Kabul-Laghman Area and Matrimonial Songs: With an Analysis of Case-Material Concerning Marriage Ties. *Pasto Quarterly,* 1, 2-3: 183-90. (International Centre for Pashto Studies) Kabul.

1978b Nomadebazarer i Central-Afghanistan: Et rids af deres opståen, udvikling og bortvisnen. *Venner af Prins Peter.* M. M. Hansen (ed.): 133-53. (Finansbanken) Copenhagen.

1979 Nomader som stammefolk: Pashtunerne i Østafghanistan. *Jordens folk,* 14, 1: 207-17.

1981 Pashtun-nomaderne i Østafghanistan og deres forhold til de omliggende statsdannelser i 1800- og 1900-årene. *Jordens folk,* 16, 4: 339-49.

1982 Marriage among Pakhtun Nomads of East Afghanistan. *FOLK*, 24: 65-87.

1990 The bedouin of the Gulf states facing a museum future. *Årsskrift for Etnografi 1989*: 24-32. (Department of Ethnography and Social Anthropology, Aarhus University) Aarhus.

1993 *Bedouins of Qatar*. (Rhodos and Thames and Hudson) Copenhagen and London.

(forthcoming, a) *Caravaneering and Nomad Bazaars in East and Central Afghanistan*. (Rhodos and Thames and Hudson) Copenhagen and London.

(forthcoming, b) The Nomad Tent of East Afghanistan. *Tent Types of the Middle East*. P. A. Andrews (ed.). Beihefte zum Tübinger Atlas des Vorderen Orients (TAVO), B, 74. (Dr. Ludwig Reichert Verlag) Wiesbaden.

Fischer, D. 1970 *Waldverbreitung, bäuerliche Waldwirtschaft und kommerzielle Waldnutzung im östlichen Afghanistan*. Afghanische Studien, 2. (Verlag Anton Hain) Meisenheim am Glan.

Frederiksen, B. 1978 *Handelens betydning for ændringer af de socio-økonomiske strukturer i et pastoralt nomadesamfund: Et case-study af Hazarbuz (Mohmand) Østafghanistan*. Danish Scientific Mission to Afghanistan 1975-76, 2. (Moesgaard) Aarhus.

1988 Når nomader bliver købmænd. *Jordens folk*, 23, 3-4: 154-9.

(forthcoming) *Nomads and bazaar merchants: The Hazarbuz of Afghanistan*. (Rhodos and Thames and Hudson) Copenhagen and London.

Frederiksen, B., and Pedersen, G. 1978 Fra nomade til...? *Jordens folk*, 13, 3: 115-30.

Galaty, J. G., Aronson, D., Salzman, P. C., and Chouinard, A. (eds.) 1981 *The Future of Pastoral People*. (International Development Centre) Ottawa.

Galaty, J. G., and Salzman, P. C. (eds.) 1981 Change and Development in Nomadic and Pastoral Societies. *Journal of Asian and African Studies*, XVI, 1-2.

Gattinara, G. C. C. 1967 *L'Islam dei nomadi afghani: Note di viaggio*. Studio di Sociologia della Religione, I. (Centro Internazionale di Studii Umanistici) Rome.

1970 *I nomadi kuci dell'Afghanistan*. (Edizioni Abete) Roma.

Gilberg, R. (forthcoming, a) *Mongol Shamans and their Costumes*. (Rhodos and Thames and Hudson) Copenhagen and London.

(forthcoming, b) *Mongol Nomads*. (Rhodos and Thames and Hudson) Copenhagen and London.

Glatzer, B. 1977 *Nomaden von Gharjistan*. Beiträge zur Südasien-Forschung, 22. (Franz Steiner Verlag) Wiesbaden.

1982 Processes of Nomadization in West Afghanistan. *Studies in Third World Societies*, 18. Contemporary Nomadic and Pastoral People: Asia and the North. P. C. Salzman (ed.): 61-86. Williamsburg.

1983 Political Organization of Pashtun Nomads and the State. *The Conflict of Tribe and State in Iran and Afghanistan*. R. Tapper (ed.): 212-32. (Croom Helm) London.

1988 Afghan Nomads Trapped in Pakistan. *The Tragedy of Afghanistan.* B. Huldt and E. Jansson (eds.): 240-7. (Croom Helm) London.

Glatzer, B., and Casimir, M. J. 1983 Herds and Households among Pashtun Pastoral Nomads: Limits of Growth. *Ethnology*, XXII, 4: 307-27.

Grötzbach, E. 1972 *Kulturgeographischer Wandel in Nordost-Afghanistan seit dem 19. Jahrhundert.* Afghanische Studien, 4. (Verlag Anton Hain) Meisenheim am Glan.

Huldt, B., and Jansson, E. (eds.) 1988 *The Tragedy of Afghanistan.* (Croom Helm) London.

India Office Records 1922-32 *Afghanistan: Trade agents at Quetta, Peshawar and Parachinar.* File 1597/1922. L/P+S/10/1060. London.

1939-? *Measures for dealing with Afghan Powindahs when entering British Territory.* R/12/1/42 379, Part II. London.

Janata, A. 1972 *Nomadismus.* Grundlagen und Empfehlungen für eine Perspektivplanung zum Regionalen Entwicklungsvorhaben Paktia/Afghanistan, 7: Sozialökonomie, V. (Institut für Ausländische Landwirtschaft der TU Berlin) Berlin-Dahlem.

1975 Beitrag zur Völkerkunde Afghanistans. *Archiv für Vökerkunde*, 29. Vienna.

Jentsch, C. 1967 Erste Ergebnisse geographischer Forschungen in Afghanistan, Herbst 1965. *Geographische Zeitschrift*, 55: 52-61.

1973 *Das Nomadentum in Afghanistan.* (Verlag Anton Hain) Meisenheim am Glan.

Kakar, M. H. 1971 *Afghanistan: A Study of Internal Political Development, 1880-1896.* Kabul.

1979 *Government and Society in Afghanistan: The Reign of Amir 'Abd al-Rahman.* Austin.

Krader, L. 1959 The Ecology of Nomadic Pastoralism. *International Social Science Journal*, XI, 4: 499-510.

Kraus, W. (ed.) 1969 *Nomadismus als Entwicklungsproblem.* (Bertelsmann Universitätsverlag) Bielefeld.

Lefebvre, A. 1984 En overset folkekunst: Malerier og dekorationer af lastbiler i Pakistan. *Jordens folk*, 19, 1: 3-11.

1985 Den dekorerede lastbil som tegnsprog. *Louisiana Revy*, 25, 3: 59-62.

Lerch, O. 1986 The 'monde du voyage': French Carnival Nomads' View of Peripatetic Society. *Nomadic Peoples*, 21/22: 71-7.

Masson, C. 1975 (1842) *Narratives of Various Journeys in Balochistan, Afghanistan, and the Panjab.* (Akademische Druck- und Verlagsanstalt) Graz.

Mohammad, F. 1915 (AHQ 1333) *Saraj ul-Tawarikh* III. ("The Lantern of History" - selections privately translated from Persian by Ashraf Ghani). Kabul.

Naderi, N. A. 1971 *The Settlement of Nomads and its Social and Economic Implications.* (Institute for Social Studies and Research, Teheran University) Teheran. Documentary Unit No. 20 370/E1. FAO. Rome.

Nemeth, D. 1986 Service Nomads: Interime Masters of Imperfect Markets. *Nomadic Peoples*, 21/22: 135-51.

Olesen, A. 1977 *Fra kaste til pjalteproletariat.* Danish Scientific Mission to Afghanistan 1975-76, Report No. 1. (Moesgaard) Aarhus.

1981 Musalli - Østafghanistans kornrensere. *Jordens folk*, 16, 3: 317-24.

1982 The Musallis - the Graincleaners of East Afghanistan. *Afghanistan Journal*, 9, 1: 13-19.

1985 The Sheikh Mohammadi - A Marginal Trading Community in East Afghanistan. *FOLK*, 27: 115-46.

1987 Peddling in East Afghanistan: Adaptive strategies of the peripatetic Sheikh Mohammadi. *The Other Nomads. Peripatetics in Cross-Cultural Perspective.* A. Rao (ed.): 35-63. (Böhlau Verlag) Cologne.

1988 En anden slags nomader. *Jordens folk*, 23, 3: 160-6.

1994 *Afghan Craftsmen: The Cultures of Three Itinerant Communities.* (Rhodos and Thames and Hudson) Copenhagen and London.

Orywal, E. 1983 *Afghanistan*: Ethnische Gruppen. Tübinger Atlas des Vorderen Orients (TAVO). A VIII 16. (Dr. Ludwig Reichert Verlag) Wiesbaden.

1986 (ed.) *Die ethnischen Gruppen Afghanistans: Fallstudien zu Gruppenidentität und Intergruppenbeziehungen.* Beihefte zum Tübinger Atlas des Vorderen Orients (TAVO) B, 70. (Dr. Ludwig Reichert Verlag) Wiesbaden.

Ovesen, J. 1978 Ethnographic Field Research among the Pashai People of Darra-i Nur. *Anthropological Quarterly*, 32, 1: 87-98.

1981 The Continuity of Pashai Society. *Folk*, 23: 221-34.

1982a Marriage and Social Groupings among the Pashai. *Folk*, 24: 143-56.

1982b A Note on the Relation Between Language and Culture: The Pashai Case. *Monumentum Georg Morgenstierne*, Hommages et Opera Minora, VII: 131-40. Leiden

1983a The Construction of Ethnic Identities: The Nuristani and the Pashai, Eastern Afghanistan. *Identity - Personal and Socio-Cultural. A Symposium.* A. Jacobson-Widding (ed.): 321-33. Stockholm.

1983b Environment and History in Pashai World-View. *Folk*, 25: 167-84.

1984 On the Cultural Heritage of the Pashai. *Anthropos*, 79: 397-404.

Patai, R. 1951 Nomadism: Middle Eastern and Central Asian. *Southwestern Journal of Anthropology*, 7: 401-14.

Pedersen, G. 1978 *Zala Khan Khel: En undersøgelse af den socio-økonomiske udvikling hos en gruppe tidligere handelsnomader i Østafghanistan.* Danish Scientific Mission to Afghanistan 1975-76, 3. (Moesgaard) Aarhus.

1981 Socio-Economic Change among a Group of East Afghan Nomads. *Afghanistan Journal*, 8, 4: 115-22.

1984 Om feltarbejdsproblemer i Afghanistan. *Antropologisk feltarbejde - oprindelse, metode og anvendelse.* M. Gravers (ed.): 139-54. (Marxistisk Antropologis Bogserie, 3. Moesgaard) Aarhus.

1985a *Nomadisme og bosætningsanalyser.* (Moesgaard) Aarhus. (Unpublished thesis).

1985b Nomadisk kulturel identitet belyst ud fra iransk og afghansk materiale. *Årsskrift for Etnografi 1984/85*: 260-83. (Moesgaard) Aarhus.

1987 Liv og levned i Afghanistan. *Kontakt*, 39, 6: 6-9.

1987/88 Det er bedst at være rig! Ændringsprocesser, kontinuitet og identitet blandt afghanske nomader. *Stofskifte*, 16: 45-53.

1988a Afghan Nomads in Exile - Patterns of Organization and Re-Organization in Pakistan. *The Afghanistan Studies Journal*, 1, 1: 18-28.

1988b Nomadismens sammensatte økonomi. *Jordens folk*, 23, 3-4: 148-53.

1988c Is there a future for the nomads of Afghanistan? Notes towards a clarification of the situation of Afghan nomads. *WUFA Quarterly Journal*, 3, 4: 72-85.

1990 (reprint of 1988a) Afghan nomads in exile: patterns of organization and reorganization in Pakistan. *The Cultural Basis of Afghan Nationalism*. E. W. Anderson and N. H. Dupree (eds.): 154-9. (Pinter Publishers) London.

1991 Har nomadismen en fremtid i Afghanistan ? *Klaus Khān Bābā: En etnografisk kalejdoskop tilegnet Klaus Ferdinand den 19. april 1991*. S. Dybbroe et al. (eds.): 29-44. (Aarhus Universitetsforlag) Aarhus.

Peter, Prince of Greece and Denmark 1954 The Abul Camp in Central Afghanistan. *Royal Central Asian Journal*, XLI, 1: 44-53.

Poullada, L. B. 1962 Problems of Development in Afghanistan. *Journal of the Royal Central Asian Society*, XLIX: 33-9.

1973 *Reform and Rebellion in Afghanistan, 1919-1929: King Amanullah's Failure to Modernize a Tribal Society*. (Cornell University Press) Ithaca.

Rai, J. 1922 *Rough Notes on the Nasar, Kharot and other Afghan Pawindahs*. Quetta.

Rao, A. 1982a Non-food-producing Nomads and the Problem of Their Classification: the Case of the Ghorbat of Afghanistan. *The Eastern Anthropologist*, 35, 2: 115-34.

1982b *Les Gorbat d'Afghanistan: Aspects économiques d'un groupe itinérant "Jāt"*. Institut Français d'Iranologie de Téhéran. Bibliothèque Iranienne, 27. (Éditions Recherche sur les civilisations) Paris.

1987 (ed.) *The Other Nomads: Peripatetic Minorities in Cross-Cultural Perspective*. (Böhlau Verlag) Cologne.

Rathjens, C. 1962 Karawanenwege und Pässe im Kulturlandschaftswandel Afghanistans seit dem 19. Jahrhundert. *Festschrift für Hermann v. Wissmann*: 209-22. Tübingen.

Rhein, E., and Ghaussy, G. 1966 *Die wirtschaftliche Entwicklung Afghanistans 1880-1965*. (Leske Verlag) Opladen.

Robinson, J. A. 1935 *Notes on the Nomad Tribes of Eastern Afghanistan*. (Government of India) New Delhi.

Rosman, A., and Rubel, P. G. 1976 Nomad-Sedentary Interethnic Relations in Iran and Afghanistan. *International Journal of Middle Eastern Studies*, 7.

Rowton, M. B. 1973a Autonomy and Nomadism in Western Asia. *Orientalia*. NS 42: 247-58.

1973b Urban Autonomy in a Nomadic Environment. *Journal of Near Eastern Studies*, 32: 201-15.

1974 Enclosed Nomadism. *Journal of the Economic and Social History of the Orient*, XVII, I: 1-30.

1976a Dimorphic Structure and the Tribal Elite. *Studia Instituti Anthropos*, 28: 219-57.

1976b Dimorphic Structure and Topology. *Oriens Antiquus*, XV, fasc. 1: 2-31. Rome.

Safizadeh, F. 1984 Shahsavan in the Grip of Development. *Cultural Survival Quarterly*, 8, 1.

Salzman, P. C. 1971 Movement and Resource Extraction Among Pastoral Nomads: The Case of the Shah Nawazi Baluch. *Anthropological Quarterly*, 44, 3: 185-97.

1972 Multi-Resource Nomadism in Iranian Baluchistan. *Perspectives on Nomadism*. W. Irons and N. Dyson-Hudson (eds.): 60-8. (Brill) Leiden.

1974 Political Organization Among Nomadic People. *Man in Adaptation: The Cultural Present*. 2.edn. Y. A. Cohen (ed.). (Aldine Publication) Chicago. (Reprint from Proceedings of the American Philosophical Society, III, 2, 1967).

1980 (ed.) *When Nomads Settle: Processes of Sedentarization As Adaptation and Response*. (Praeger Publishers) New York.

1982 (ed.) Contemporary Nomadic and Pastoral People: Asia and the North. *Studies in Third World Societies*, 18. Williamsburg.

1983 The Psycology of Nomads. *Nomadic Peoples*, 12: 48-55.

Shahrani, M. N. M. 1976 Kirghiz Pastoral Nomads of the Afghan Pamir: An Ecological and Ethnographic Overview. *FOLK*, 18: 129-43.

1978 The Retention of Pastoralism among the Kirghiz of the Afghan Pamir. *Himalayan Anthropology*. J. F. Fisher (ed.): 233-50. World Anthropology. (Mouton) The Hague.

1979 *The Kirghiz and Wakhi of Afghanistan: Adaptation to Closed Frontiers*. (University of Washington Press) Seattle.

1984 Afghanistan's Kirghiz in Turkey. *Cultural Survival Quarterly*, 8, 1: 31-4.

Siiger, H. 1951 Statuer af træ hos kalash-kafirerne i Chitral: Materiale fra Den 3. danske centralasiatiske Ekspedition. *Fra Nationalmuseets Arbejdsmark* 1951: 29-38.

1956 *Ethnological Field Research in Chitral, Sikkim, and Assam: Preliminary Report. From the Third Danish Expedition to Central Asia*. Historisk Filosofiske Meddelelser, 36, 2. (Det Kongelige Danske Videnskabernes Selskab) Copenhagen.

1967a-b *The Lepchas: Culture and Religion of a Himalayan People*, I: Results of Anthropological Field Work in Sikkim, Kalimpong and Git.
II: Lepcha Ritual Texts and Commentary by Halfdan Siiger. Phonetic Transcriptions of Lepcha Ritual Texts with Introduction by Jørgen Rischel. *Nationalmuseets Skrifter, Etnografisk Rk.*, XI, I-II. Copenhagen.

1976 Two Indigenous Peoples of the Hindukush-Himalayan Regions. *Temenos*, 12: 93-9.

1978 "The Abominable Snowman": Himalayan Religion and Folklore from the Lepchas of Sikkim. *Himalayan Anthropology: The Indo-Tibetan Interface*. J. F. Fisher (ed.): 421-30.

1981 The Lepcha Semi-divine Beings of Agricultural Fertility - from the Lepchas of Sikkim. *Folk*, 23: 197-204.

Siiger, H., Castenfeldt, S., and Fentz, M. 1991 Small Functional Items and Regeneration of Society: Dough Figurines from the Kalash People of Chitral, Northern Pakistan. *Folk*, 33: 37-66.

(forthcoming) *The Old Kalash Society: A Field Research in the Hindukush in 1948.*

Sopher, D. E. 1965 *The Sea Nomads: A Study based on the Literature of the Maritime Boat People of Southeast Asia.* Memoirs of the National Museum, 5. Singapore.

Stucki, A. 1978 Horses and Women: Some Thoughts on the Life Cycle of Ersari Turkmen Women. *Afghanistan Journal*, 5, 4: 140-9.

Sweetser, A. 1984 Afghan Nomad Refugees in Pakistan. *Cultural Survival Quarterly*, 8, 1: 26-30.

Tapper, N. 1973 The Advent of Pashtun Maldars in North-Western Afghanistan. *Bulletin of the School of Oriental and African Studies*, XXXVI, I: 55-79.

1977 Pashtun Nomad Women in Afghanistan. *Asian Affairs*, 8, 2: 163-70.

1983 Abd Al-Rahman's North-West Frontier: The Pashtun Colonisation of Afghan Turkestan. *The Conflict of Tribe and State in Iran and Afghanistan*. R. Tapper (ed.): 233-61. (Croom Helm) London.

1991 *Bartered Brides: Politics, Gender and Marriage in an Afghan Tribal Society.* (Cambridge University Press) Cambridge.

Tapper, N., and Tapper, R. 1982 Marriage Preferences and Ethnic Relations among Duranni Pashtuns in Afghan Turkestan. *FOLK*, 23: 157-77.

1988 Concepts of Personal, Moral and Social Disorder among Duranni Pashtuns in Northern Afghanistan. *The Tragedy of Afghanistan*. B. Huldt and E. Jansson (eds.): 38-54. (Croom Helm) London.

Tapper, R. 1974 Nomadism in Modern Afghanistan: Asset or Anachronism? *Afghanistan in the 1970s*. L. Dupree and L. Albert (eds.). (Praeger Publishers) New York.

1983 (ed.) *The Conflict of Tribe and State in Iran and Afghanistan.* (Croom Helm) London.

Tavakolian, B. 1979 Sheikhanzai Pastoral Nomads of Northwest Afghanistan. *Newsletter of the Commission on Nomadic Peoples*, 4: 9-16.

1984a Women and Socioeconomic Change among Sheikhanzai Nomads of Western Afghanistan. *Middle East Journal*, 38, 3: 431-53.

1984b Sheikhanzai Nomads and the Afghan State: A Study of Indigenous Authority and Foreign Rule. *Revolutions and Rebellions in Afghanistan*. M. N. Shahrani and R. L. Canfield (eds.): 249-65. (Institute of International Studies) Berkeley.

1984c Religiosity, Values and Economic Change among Sheikhanzai. *Islam in Tribal Societies: From the Atlas to the Indus*. A. S. Ahmed and D. M. Hart (eds.). (Routledge) London.

UNESCO 1962 *Arid Zone Research. The Problems of the Arid Zone, II: Nomadism in Relation to Grazing Resources.* Proceedings of the Paris symposium. (UNESCO) Paris.

Wald, H.-J. 1969 *Landnutzung und Siedlung der Paschtunen im Becken von Khost.* Schriften des Deutschen Orient-Instituts, Materialien und Dokumente. Opladen.

INDEX

A

Abbottabad 227, 228, 229
Abdur Rahman Khān, Amir (1880-1901) 59, 103, 129
Abul 27, 28, 29, 31, 32, 36, 102, 120, 145
Afghan Nomad Survey (1978) 41, 80, 86
Afghanistan, buffer-state 59
Afghanistan, consolidation of state 59
Afghanistan, frontiers fixed 59
Afghanistan, history 57ff.
Afghanistan, the people 68
agriculture and nomadism 7, 9, 54, 69, 133, 171, 174, 176, 177, 178, 220, 244
Agriculture in Dahana-i Ghori 96, 148, 173ff.
Ahmad Shah Durrani, Amir (1747-1772) 58, 69
Ahmadzai 12, 27, 39, 43, 78, 98, 99,100, 125, 126, 127, 150, 193, 203, 216, 219
Aimaq 12, 24, 25, 29, 31, 32, 35, 36, 47, 68, 81, 133
Akkora Khattak 228, 230, 233, 235
'allafi 17, 182, 184, 185, 191, 201, 204
Alexander the Great 57
Almara 120, 136, 228
Amanullah Khān, King (1919-29) 60
Amu Darya 29, 38, 45, 80
Anglo-Afghan Trade Convention of 1921 136
Anglo-Afghan War 59, 60
Arab 7, 45, 69, 80, 81, 86, 211

B

Baghlan 45, 101, 120, 147, 148, 162, 172, 174, 175, 176, 177
Bajaur 228
Balkh 102, 103
Baluch 54, 69, 81, 82
Balluchistan 228,
Bamiyan 32, 47, 61, 76, 107, 117, 120
Bangladesh 19, 129
Bannu 120, 137, 228
Basawal 203
Basseri 147, 214
Bazaar-i Omaid 88, 89, 103, 129, 178, 206, 207, 208, 209, 210, 211, 226
Behsud 38, 120
Bengal 36
biswā 17, 160
Bokhara 9, 29, 38, 126
Bombay 129
Brahui 69
British colonial administration 27, 129
British colonial expansion 59ff.
British India 19, 27, 30, 36, 42, 46, 59, 89, 106, 135, 137, 138, 140
British witdrawal from India 1947 60ff.
Buddhism 57

C

Calcutta 129
Caravaneering 19, 21, 27, 29, 31, 34, 35, 36, 38, 45, 57, 93, 125, 125, 244
Central Asia 7, 8, 10, 24, 25, 26, 29, 46, 47, 57, 59
Chaghcharan 32, 33, 34, 35, 36, 40, 42, 45, 70, 71, 76, 120, 122, 124, 142, 144, 145, 179, 182, 185, 187, 189
Chaman 138
Charas 120, 171, 179
Charikar 120
Chendawul 159
China 24, 57
Chinghiz Khān 57
Chitral 10, 46, 47
cloth-stalls 178, 194, 201

D

Dahan-i Ghori 90, 96, 103, 120, 147, 148, 151, 161, 162, 163, 167, 168, 171, 173, 174, 175, 176, 178, 179, 194, 201, 203, 207, 213, 214, 217, 220, 221, 223, 224
Danish Expedition to Central Asia 24, 25, 26, 46
Danish Scientific Mission to Afghanistan 1953-55 24, 26
Danish Scientific Mission to Afghanistan 1975-76 21, 31
Daoud Khān 61, 62
Daulatzai 149
Day Zangi 35
dihqan 17, 177
Dera Ismael Khan 120, 129, 137, 228
detribalisation 220
Dir 230
drought (of 1971-72) 35, 145
Durand, Sir Mortimer 59
Durand Line 59, 61, 137, 138
Durrani 45, 58, 59, 69, 79, 98

E

ecological basis of nomadism 106
economy 11, 13, 30, 36, 39, 69, 76, 105, 111, 121, 124, 125, 133, 141, 145, 149, 162, 179, 189, 212, 214, 218, 236
Elphinstone, Mountstuart 77, 126, 216
ethnic groups 65, 68, 69, 81, 82, 167
European imperialism 59ff.
exile 15, 63, 68, 86, 97, 103, 178, 213, 223, 226, 227, 229, 232, 238, 239, 244

F

farmān 129, 130, 131, 178, 179, 194
flock 30, 116, 117, 121
frontier 29, 59, 93, 129, 137, 144, 145, 148, 149, 174, 179, 193, 214, 229

G

Gardez 87, 99, 100, 102, 103, 120
genealogy 55, 79, 87, 88, 89, 90, 91, 92, 98, 100, 127
General Transport 17, 150, 151, 154, 157
Ghamai Transport 151, 156
Ghazni 31, 120, 126
Ghilzai 45, 78, 79, 98, 99, 100, 140
Ghor 32, 109, 145
Ghorband valley 103, 120
Ghorghori 35, 96, 103, 120, 131, 132, 133, 135, 148, 178, 179, 182, 189, 194, 220
Gomal 31, 36
Gomao 27, 145
grazing grounds 17, 78, 93, 97, 105, 107, 108, 109, 111, 117, 126, 127, 128, 131, 132, 133, 138, 147, 148, 179, 211, 212, 218, 221, 241, 244
Great Game 59, 137

H

Hajigak 32
hamsāya 17, 18, 30
Haslund-Christensen, Henning 24, 25, 29, 47
Hazara 24, 25, 27, 36, 47, 58, 59, 68, 69, 81, 96, 129, 130, 133, 134, 135, 141, 189, 241
Hazarajat 17, 27, 29, 31, 32, 35, 36, 38, 39, 43, 47, 59, 102, 129, 130, 132, 133, 134, 137, 148, 149, 187, 189, 201, 212, 241
Hazarbuz 12, 38, 39, 125, 132
Henning Haslund-Christensen Memorial Mission 24
Herat 19, 34, 76, 79, 83, 86, 145, 154
Hindu 19, 129, 137, 226
Hindukush 45, 57, 96, 126, 138, 148, 162, 176, 178

I

Imam Sahib 80
India 19, 27, 29, 30, 36, 42, 46, 47, 58, 59, 60, 78, 89, 105, 106, 129, 135, 136, 137, 138, 140, 172
India Office Library 27
Indus 57, 61, 120, 121, 126, 129
industry 69, 175
infrastructural development 138
Iran 8, 13, 14, 24, 54, 57, 63, 147, 151, 211, 214, 223, 240
Ishaqzai 45
Islam 57, 63, 93

J

Jalalabad 44, 76, 82, 93, 103, 120, 179, 182, 183, 185, 189, 190, 191, 192, 193, 194, 197, 198, 200, 201, 202, 204, 205, 209, 213, 215, 218, 221, 226, 228
jarīb 17, 18, 147, 175, 178
jihād 18
jirgah 18, 219

K

Kabul 10, 15, 19, 24, 27, 29, 32, 34, 35, 38, 39, 43, 47, 59, 63, 76, 78, 84, 86, 87, 88, 89, 90, 96, 97, 103, 116, 120, 129, 134, 137, 138, 145, 149, 150, 151, 152, 154, 155, 159, 160, 162, 171, 172, 173, 176, 178, 179, 183, 184, 185, 187, 189, 191, 192, 193, 201, 203, 206, 207, 208, 209, 210, 211, 215, 223, 224, 226, 233, 241
Kandahar 19, 34, 47, 58, 76, 86, 120, 138, 145, 154, 160, 185
Karezemir 184
Kashmir 10
Kassi 145
Kerman 32, 36, 132
Khalq 19
khān (defined) 18
Khēl (defined) 18, 98
Khwaja Khān 102, 103
Khost 39, 45, 67, 93, 120, 126, 136, 148, 179, 185, 205, 213
Khwazak 33, 42, 122, 142, 145
Khyber 31, 38, 120, 193
kin-group 19, 39, 99, 127, 128
Kirghiz 8, 9, 45
Kohat 120, 228
Kote Sangi 88, 152, 154, 156, 159, 160, 161
kūchey 18, 49, 54, 97, 219, 220, 221, 239
Kurram 31, 39, 120, 136, 237, 241, 244
Kuz Baru 38

L

labour 111, 116, 117, 125, 127, 135, 171, 177, 189, 215, 216, 221, 226, 227

Lahore 78, 120, 129, 149, 210
Lal 32, 187
lalmi 108
land measure 17, 18 147, 175, 178
land prices 148
land purchase 146
land reform 206, 223, 225
Landi Kotal 230
language 10, 69, 86, 93, 105
leadership 93, 100, 111, 128, 133, 219
lineage 18, 39, 87, 98, 100, 102, 106, 127, 128, 216, 217, 219, 220
livestock 7, 36, 40, 116, 121, 128, 133, 135, 138, 147, 148, 178, 179, 183, 185, 187, 189, 191, 192, 194, 211, 214, 215, 235
livestock market 36, 40, 183, 187, 189
Logar 43, 113, 118, 120, 126, 146, 147, 148, 189, 191, 219
lorry 18, 32, 34, 87, 88, 89, 91, 96, 97, 103, 138, 144, 145, 149, 150, 151, 152, 154, 155, 156, 157, 159, 160, 161, 162, 166, 171, 176, 178, 179, 185, 189, 191, 201, 203, 208, 209, 210, 211, 213, 215, 216, 219, 220, 226, 232, 233, 239

M

malik 18, 93, 128, 216, 218
Mardan 227, 229, 236
Markuh 152, 203
marriage 217, 218
Mashriqi 31
Matani 122, 201
Maydan 120, 151, 189
Maydan Transport 151
Mazar-i Sharif 76, 177
mechanisation 177
migration 27, 29, 36, 38, 41, 49, 54, 78, 79, 103, 118, 120, 124, 126, 127, 132, 136, 140, 178, 179, 182, 189, 205, 211
military coup 62, 103
Miranshah 120, 228
Moghul Empire 58
Mohmand 12, 27, 38, 117, 125
moneylenders 129, 137
Mongol 9, 10, 13, 58
Mongolia 9, 10, 14, 24
mosque 167, 190, 193, 197, 200, 201
mujāhedin 18, 223, 224, 226, 232, 244
mullah 18, 19, 171, 195, 203
Musa Khēl 27, 43, 113, 146, 152, 185, 203, 219
Mustaf Khēl 43, 137, 147, 173, 177, 193

N

Nangarhar 27, 29, 31, 38, 93, 96, 103, 120, 126, 148, 152, 179
Naochak 57
National Archives of India 78
Niazi 35, 137
nomad, the term 49ff.
nomad-agriculturalist relation 106ff.
nomad bazaar 12, 21, 29, 31, 32, 33, 34, 36, 38, 43, 45, 133, 171
nomad camp 79, 86
nomad economy 105ff.
nomad expansion 79
nomad statistics 79ff.
nomad trade 27, 29, 33, 35, 36, 38, 39, 49, 55, 87, 93, 96, 102, 133, 144, 145, 147, 149, 150, 161, 171 178, 179, 182, 191, 213, 214, 215, 216, 219
nomad typology 8, 54
North-West Frontier Province 129, 136, 227, 228, 229
Nur Khān Khēl 100, 127, 185, 235
Nuristan 11, 24, 26, 47
Nurzai 45

O

Organisation 127
Omaid Market (see Bazaar-i Omaid)

P

Pakistan 13, 15, 19, 21, 29, 30, 42, 43, 46, 55, 57, 59, 60, 61, 63, 69, 78, 87, 92, 93, 96, 97, 98, 103, 106, 120, 137, 138, 144, 147, 148, 149, 151, 172, 174, 179, 205, 206, 211, 213, 214, 215, 217, 223, 225, 226, 227, 228, 229, 235, 236, 240, 241, 244
Paktika 31
Paktya 31, 41, 47, 93, 126, 148, 179
Pamir 24, 45
Panjab 132
Parachinar 120, 136, 137, 228
Parcham 19
Pashtun 8, 12, 17, 18, 21, 24, 26, 27, 28, 29, 30, 31, 36, 38, 39, 41, 42, 43, 45, 46, 47, 49, 55, 59, 67, 68, 69, 70, 71, 77, 79, 81, 82, 86, 87, 93, 97, 98, 100, 103, 106, 116, 125, 126, 127, 133, 140, 142, 149, 171, 198, 202, 211, 214, 217, 218, 219, 238, 241, 244
Pashtun lineage system 98ff.
Pashtun tribal organisation 98ff.
Pashtunistan 59, 61, 69, 93, 137, 205
Pashtunwali 127
People's Democratic Party of Afghanistan (PDPA) 19, 59, 62, 63, 223
Persia 9, 58, 126
Peshawar 27, 38, 45, 77, 78, 120, 129, 136, 138, 205, 227, 228, 229, 230, 232, 235, 236, 237, 238, 239, 240
political 11, 13
political changes 28, 29, 129
powindah 19
Pul-i Khomri 120, 162, 163, 166, 176, 224
Punjab 36, 59, 129
purdah 19, 160, 162

Q

Qais 93, 98
qal'a 166, 167, 168, 171, 201
Qala-i Niazbeg 88, 97, 149, 151, 154, 156, 159, 160, 161, 162, 166, 169, 194, 219, 221, 226, 232, 233, 239
Quetta 136, 138, 229
qurūt 19, 171, 195, 203

R

Rawalpindi 228
refugee 223, 226, 227, 228, 229, 230, 231, 232, 233, 235, 236, 237, 241
Regi 228, 229, 232, 235
regional analysis 105
Robinson, J. A. 36, 79, 87, 100, 121, 126, 127, 128, 129, 137, 138, 140, 216
Russia Tsarist expansion 58ff.

S

Safavid Empire 58
Salang 96, 120, 172, 176, 178, 220
Saudi Arabia 236
Saur revolution 62, 97, 223
segmentary lineage system 98
sēr 19, 150, 183, 184
serāy 19, 88, 89, 154, 155, 156, 157, 159
serāydār 19, 154, 156
Seray Herati 152
settlement 31, 106, 146, 147, 149, 151, 213, 214, 215
Shaharak 35
Shawali Transport 151, 156
Shia-islam 134
Sikh businessmen 226
Silk route 57

slaughter 111, 116, 121, 187
Sohak 200, 209
Soviet Central Asia 29
Soviet invasion of Afghanistan (1979) 62
Soviet Union 57, 59, 62, 63, 223
Soviet withdrawal from Afghanistan (1989) 63
Spin Nasar 140
Stanizai 116
subsistence production 111, 211
Sulaiman mountains 129, 135
Sunni-islam 93, 134
Swat 230
Syed Khān Transport 151

T

Taghar 39, 43, 87, 97, 100, 103, 133, 137, 146, 147, 151, 152, 172, 173, 193, 216, 219
Taghar Transport 97, 151
Tajik 68, 73
tālib 19, 195, 197, 200
Tara Khēl 27, 78, 84, 218
Taywara 35
tea trade 38
tenant farmer 148, 163, 173, 174, 177,
Thal 39, 93, 120, 126, 128, 129, 132, 136, 137, 149, 210, 228
Torkham 193
transport 13, 17, 28, 29, 35, 38, 45, 83, 89, 93, 97, 119, 125, 126, 127, 128, 138, 140, 144, 145, 149, 150, 151, 152, 154, 156, 157, 159, 160, 161, 162, 171, 183, 185, 189, 191, 204, 211, 212, 213, 220, 226, 230, 241
tribal confederations 98
Tsarist Russia 89
Turkestan 9, 102, 168, 176, 178
Turkey 151
Turkoman 69, 81

U

Uruzgan 101, 102
Uzbak 69, 72, 81

W

Wardak 108, 202
weaving 113, 133, 202

Y

Yakawlang 32

Z

Zahir Shah, King Mohammad (1933-1973) 223
zai 18, 19, 98
zamīn-dārī 19, 177

INDEX OF AUTHORS

Albert, L. 86
Ali, M. 211
Andrews, P. A. 86
Bacon, E. E. 47, 54
Balicki, A. 45
Balland, A. 41, 42, 80, 86
Barfield, T. J. 86, 211
Barth, F. 31, 46, 105, 106, 140, 147, 214
Beck, L. 240
Behnstedt, P. 65
Benoist, A. de 41, 42
Boesen, I. W. 21, 46, 244
Bourgeois, J and D. 31, 42, 43
Briggs, L. C. 49
Broadfoot, J. S. 126
Burnes, A. 78
Caroe, O. 93
Casimir, M. J. 45
Castenfeldt, S. 46
Centlivres-Demont, M. 150
Christensen, A. 9, 10, 12, 21, 24, 25, 29, 46, 47, 140
Dor, R. 45
Dupree, L. 86
Edelberg, L. 9, 10, 11, 12, 24, 25, 26, 46, 47
Elphinstone, M. 77, 126, 216
Enriquez, C. M. 126, 135, 136
Faegre, T. 86
Feilberg, C. G. 8, 9, 11, 24, 27, 86
Fentz, M. 46
Ferdinand, K. 9, 11, 12, 13, 14, 15, 21, 24, 25, 26, 27, 29, 30, 31, 34, 35, 36, 38, 39, 43, 44, 46, 47, 49, 86, 87, 130, 132, 133, 135, 137, 141, 145, 218
Fischer, D. 45
Frederiksen, B. 12, 21, 32, 34, 35, 38, 39, 46, 47, 125, 132, 154
Galaty, J. G. 46
Gattinara, G. C. C. 43
Ghaussy, G. 138
Gilberg, R. 14
Glatzer, B. 30, 31, 45, 80, 227
Grötzbach, E. 43
Janata, A. 31, 41, 81
Jentsch, C. 31, 43, 77, 81
Kakar, M. H. 36, 86, 106, 130, 134
Kieffer, C. M. 41, 65
Kraus, W. 46
Lefebvre, A. 150
Lerch, O. 49
Masson, C. 78
Mohammad, F. 36, 47, 93, 98, 130, 131, 134, 198, 201, 218, 219, 223
Naderi, N. A. 46
Naumann, C. M. 45
Nemeth, D. 49
Olesen, A. 12, 15, 21, 32, 34, 35, 47, 49
Orywal, E. 65, 86

Ovesen, J. 21, 46
Patai, R. 54
Peter, Prince of Greece and Denmark 9, 21, 46
Poullada, L. B. 106
Rai, J. 54, 126
Rao, A. 21, 49
Rathjens, C. 45
Rhein, E. 138
Robinson, J. A. 36, 79, 87, 100, 121, 126, 127, 128, 129, 137, 138, 140, 216
Rowton, M. B. 147
Safizadeh, F. 240
Salzman, P. C. 46, 49, 54
Shahrani, M. N. M. 45
Siiger, H. 24, 46, 47
Sopher, D. E. 49
Stucki, A. 45
Sweetser, A. 227
Tapper, N. 45, 86, 106
Tapper, R. 31, 45
Tavakolian, B. 45
Wald, H. -J 45

PHOTO CREDITS

K.F. = Klaus Ferdinand
B.F. = Birthe Frederiksen
M.K. = Mogen Køie
G.P. = Gorm Pedersen
P.F = Polfoto
P.F.J.S. = Polfoto / Jan Stage

Maps by Gorm Pedersen